Food Values in Europe

Also available from Bloomsbury:

Food and Museums, edited by Nina Levent and Irina D. Mihalache
Making Taste Public, edited by Carole Counihan & Susanne Hojlund
Representing Italy Through Food, edited by Peter Naccarato,
Zachary Nowak, Elgin K. Eckert

Food Values in Europe

Edited by
Valeria Siniscalchi and Krista Harper

BLOOMSBURY ACADEMIC
LONDON • NEW YORK • OXFORD • NEW DELHI • SYDNEY

BLOOMSBURY ACADEMIC
Bloomsbury Publishing Plc
50 Bedford Square, London, WC1B 3DP, UK
29 Earlsfort Terrace, Dublin 2, Ireland

BLOOMSBURY, BLOOMSBURY ACADEMIC and the Diana logo
are trademarks of Bloomsbury Publishing Plc

First published in Great Britain 2019
This paperback edition published in 2021

Cover design: Tjaša Krivec
Cover image © Franco Zecchin

A catalogue record for this book is available from the British Library.
Library of Congress Cataloging-in-Publication Data

Names: Harper, Krista, editor. | Siniscalchi, Valeria, editor.
Title: Food values in Europe / Edited by Krista Harper and Valeria Siniscalchi.
Description: London; New York: Bloomsbury Academic, 2019. |
Includes bibliographical references and index.
Identifiers: LCCN 2019020645 (print) | LCCN 2019980208 (ebook) |
ISBN 9781350084773 (hardback) | ISBN 9781350084797 (epub) |
ISBN 9781350084780 (pdf)
Subjects: LCSH: Food habits–Europe–History. | Food habits–Social
aspects–Europe. | Cooking, European. | Europe–Social life and customs.
Classification: LCC GT2853.E8 S56 2019 (print) | LCC GT2853.E8 (ebook) |
DDC 394.1/2094–dc23
LC record available at https://lccn.loc.gov/2019020645
LC ebook record available at https://lccn.loc.gov/2019980208

ISBN: HB: 978-1-3500-8477-3
PB: 978-1-3502-4915-8
ePDF: 978-1-3500-8478-0
ePub: 978-1-3500-8479-7

Typeset by Deanta Global Publishing Services, Chennai, India

To find out more about our authors and books visit
www.bloomsbury.com and sign up for our newsletters.

Contents

Part Four: Consuming Values

Illustrations

Figures

Table

Acknowledgments

This book is the result of a collective reflection that started some years ago between scholars interested in food and in social movements. Some of the authors of this volume contributed to the edited book *Food Activism: Economy, Agency and Democracy* (published in 2014) which helped to outline the comparative framework to study different kinds of mobilizations around food production, distribution, and consumption. In 2013, we launched a discussion of food activism in Europe by organizing a round table at the American Anthropological Association meetings in Chicago on "Food activism in Europe: Changing paradigms, changing practices." In June 2014, Susana Narotzky and Valeria Siniscalchi organized a conference in Marseille at the École des Hautes Études en Sciences Sociales (EHESS) titled "Value and Values in Agro-Food Systems" that brought together scholars from the Centre Norbert Elias, the Groupement de recherche en économie quantitative d'Aix-Marseille (GREQAM), the Grupo de estudios sobre la Reciprocidad of the Universitat de Barcelona, and other universities.

In the years that followed, we organized a series of panels during the American Anthropological Association (AAA) annual meetings and the biannual European Association of Social Anthropologists (EASA) conference that brought together the scholars who contributed to this book. These panels included "Food Activism in Europe: Networks, alliances, strategies" (conveners Carole Counihan and Valeria Siniscalchi, Washington DC, 2014), "Food values in Europe: Sustainable Economies, Power and Activism" (conveners Krista Harper and Valeria Siniscalchi, Denver, 2015), "Food Value and Values in Europe: Economic Legacies and Alternative Futures in Production and Consumption" (conveners Krista Harper and Valeria Siniscalchi, Milan, 2016), and "Alternative Food Spaces and Economies in Europe" (conveners Dana Conzo, Krista Harper and Valeria Siniscalchi, Minneapolis, 2016).

A series of seminars organized alternately at our institutions, the EHESS (Centre Norbert Élias) in Marseille and the University of Massachusetts Amherst, allowed us to extend the discussion to graduate students from both our institutions and to draw the different lines connecting our fieldworks and the topics that are at the core of this book. The seminars were titled "*Anthropologie des formes de mobilisation*" (EHESS-UMass, Marseille, June 2015), "Mobilizing the visual/*Mobiliser la dimension visuelle*" (EHESS-UMass, Marseille, March 2016), "Ethnography of Europe: Junior Scholars' Research Forum" (Amherst, November 2016), and "Grassroots: economies, politics and communities" (EHESS-UMass, Marseille, May, 2017). These student workshops were partially funded by the Culture and Heritage in European Societies and Spaces program, an international research and training grant awarded by the National Science Foundation (IIA-1261172). We would like to thank all of the people who participated in these initiatives that nourished reflections around food values. We thank our institutions—the University of Massachusetts Amherst and EHESS—for funding some of these meetings and supporting this project.

Many colleagues gave us encouragement, feedback, and helpful exchanges around food values, resistance, and resilience as we worked on this book. A few who deserve special appreciation for discussing versions of this work with us are Laura Centemeri, Yuson Jung, Boone Shear, and Jacqueline Urla.

We would like to thank the editors at Bloomsbury, Miriam Cantwell and Lucy Carroll, for encouraging this project and supporting us throughout the process. Three anonymous reviewers offered us helpful suggestions that allowed us to improve our project. We are grateful to Dana Conzo for her editorial assistance in the last steps of this work.

The cover image, by photographer Franco Zecchin, Valeria's husband, was taken in Marseille, during a vegetable distribution. We thank Christian Nador and his son, Clément, members of the Saint Giniez farm "basket" group, who are represented in the picture. We express special gratitude to Noé Guiraud for preparing the map of contributors' field sites that appears in our introduction.

Finally, we thank our families for hosting this multiyear collaboration: Franco and Adriano Zecchin in Marseille and Michael, Zeke, and Rafi Ash in Massachusetts.

Foreword

Food Values in Europe offers an important contribution to the growing literature on food activism with its thirteen chapters examining how Europeans negotiate values through alternative food practices in diverse settings. Its particular significance is twofold. First, it considers simultaneously two forms of value—on the one hand, economic or market value measured by price and, on the other, moral, political, and social values established by human actions and beliefs. Examining how these two kinds of value are interconnected enhances the understanding of both and of food activism more broadly. Second, the book is significant because it presents rich ethnographic studies of food activism from across the European Union, which applies the same agrofood policies and regulations to diverse countries and regions. Looking at food projects is one way to examine a key EU challenge of maintaining unity within diversity.

The book builds on the fact that food is multidimensional: a key human need, a commodity, a gift, an environmental product, a relational glue, and an embodiment of beliefs. Through their contestatory and alternative initiatives, practitioners of food activism put their values into the forefront of their actions as they clarify their economic, cultural, and political objectives. Harper and Siniscalchi have gathered diverse case studies from Western, Southern, and Eastern Europe to assess "whether and how food projects can be transformative of larger institutions and society."

The book explores a wide range of alternative food initiatives—including urban gardens, small-scale farming and pastoralism, consumer cooperatives, basket systems, and counter-hegemonic consumption practices—and highlights their common goals. First and foremost they share a resistance to market penetration of food provisioning and human relationships. They reflect the "double movement" observed by economic anthropologist Karl Polanyi: as the market increasingly penetrates, people increasingly push back and emphasize social over economic relationships, particularly by connecting consumers and producers and eliminating middlepersons. Food activists experiment with new kinds of networks and alliances such as those forged between urban consumers and rural farmers in the AMAP basket system in Marseille, France (Siniscalchi). They share a search for high-quality local food, contrast it with insipid industrial food, and use it to attract consumers. The food projects feature new forms of production, exchange, and consumption, which the book organizes into four main categories—prosuming, contesting, connecting, and consuming.

"Prosuming" is producing for one's own consumption. It involves non-market values such as self-sufficiency, gift-giving, and barter. Many of the chapters show that self-provisioning and informal distribution networks are important in feeding people, but economic statistics largely ignore their contribution and dismiss them as unproductive leisure pastimes. Kosnik's chapter on subsistence farmers in Austria reveals their significant impact in providing food for their families, and their broader reach through the exchange of produce and seeds via informal networks and local markets. Lisbon urban gardeners (Harper and Afonso) make valuable contributions to food-provisioning and develop civic cooperation by managing the gardens, administering common land, and resolving conflicts. Through gardening, they enact values of *sabor* (flavor), *saber* (knowledge), *vizinhança* (neighborliness), and sharing. In the different context of the Czech Republic, urban gardeners practice what Speck calls "conspicuous food production" to ensure safe and adequate food, connect with longstanding food traditions, and proclaim political beliefs.

"Contesting" includes cases where producer-activists explicitly weigh the market price of their product with its broader value in terms of environmental impact, food quality, maintenance of cultural heritage, and quality of life for producers. Case studies of dairy farmers in Galicia, Spain (Martinez), shepherds in Sardinia, Italy (Zerilli and Pitzalis), and small farmers organizing for food sovereignty through the European Farmers Coordination (Thivet) uncover serious tensions over values that underlie the very survival of small producers in Europe. The market price for small farmers' products does not do justice to their broader contribution to environmental and cultural sustainability, animal welfare, heritage practices, and food quality, which small farmers and pastoralists bring to the forefront in their food activist mobilizations.

"Connecting" emphasizes short-chains between producers and consumers through cooperatives in Greece and Spain and basket systems in France. According to Rakopoulos, labor is a key factor in establishing and assessing value in Greek food cooperatives—a claim that can be applied to all food activist initiatives where labor is often ignored, undervalued, underpaid, or volunteer. In the French vegetable basket system or AMAP (Siniscalchi), consumers' volunteer labor enhances the value of farmers' work while emphasizing social connections over market relations and achieving shorter food miles, quality products, transparent production, and traceable sourcing. Food cooperatives in Catalonia, Spain (Homs and Narotzky), promote these same aims while enhancing the labor value of small organic producers and relying on volunteer labor to practice collective governance through assemblies. These chapters raise questions about how far consumer-producer solidarity can go to assure a living wage for small farmers who face serious challenges of surviving in a broader market economy favoring large producers and far-flung distribution.

"Consuming" explores the much debated role of consumers in shaping food values and transforming the food system. Participating in Fair Trade distribution networks is an important way consumers in the global north have enacted values of solidarity with farmers in the global south. But Fair Trade in post-socialist Latvia (Aistara) is complex and problematic because it promotes consumers' solidarity with far-away producers at the expense of their commitment to local farmers. Cash's research in Moldova shows how food consumption projects can resist poverty; subsistence food production and informal sharing within and between households enable people to overcome their lack of monetary resources. For immigrants, consuming traditional foods has always been a way to sustain community and culture in the face of oppression and exclusion. Conzo's chapter explores how food spaces established by Afro-Caribbean immigrants in the United Kingdom are welcoming sites where they find acceptance, practice food traditions freely, and resist exclusion and racism. Fischer examines social conflict in Denmark through a case study of halal food, whose consumption is a form of daily religious practice for Muslims. New Danish laws about halal slaughter have ignited debates about the moral, ethical, and cultural values expressed in religious food consumption, which has a significant economic impact.

While the food projects studied in this book never circumvent the market completely, they offer novel models of exchange between producers and consumers and express myriad values in addition to price—solidarity with small farmers, quality food, self-sufficiency, respect for diversity, and food justice. Although most food projects are small and localized, they introduce innovations in food production, distribution, and consumption that are more just, that appreciate labor and skill more fully, and that develop new relationships between consumers, producers, and public institutions. Food projects are not just economic, political, or cultural but always a complex intertwining of all three. The chapters reveal the merit of ethnographic research in uncovering this intertwining in diverse European contexts and encourage readers to ponder the influence of economic versus cultural values in transforming food systems.

Carole Counihan

Value and Values in Food Projects in Europe

Krista Harper and Valeria Siniscalchi

Food projects in comparative perspective

In Prague and Lisbon, residents cultivate vegetables in vacant lots, changing urban spaces through new kinds of sociability created by growing food together. At the same time, farmers in Galicia and shepherds in Sardinia launch protests to demand a better and more "just" price for their milk, one that not only recognizes the value of milk, but also the value of small and medium producers' work as a form of ecological stewardship. In Catalonia and in the south of France, people forge direct links with local vegetable producers through cooperatives and community-supported agriculture "basket systems," not only to have access to organic, fresh, and seasonal products but also to establish "solidarity" links with farmers. In Thessaloniki, activists debate the value of their own labor as volunteers in solidarity food-distribution groups. Meanwhile, consumers in the post-socialist Baltics express frustration at the higher cost of Fair Trade chocolate, coffee, and bananas—prized foods that were expensive and hard to find in shops before 1989. Across these instances, people in Europe are debating, acting on, and experimenting with the multiple values of food inside new social and economic spaces created through efforts to change the way the food is produced, distributed, and consumed. We approach food "values" in the plural sense, referring to political, economic, and moral orders, socially and culturally defined.

As new practices converge around the goal of changing the food system, creating "sustainable" economies, or building solidarity, food offers a powerful catalyst for emergent economic imaginations and new interpretations of the notion of value. Europe provides a strategic site for comparative analysis of food projects, as an internally diverse political, economic, and geographic entity with a common food regulation system and a common economic policy.

In Europe, people confront the food system in different national, social, and cultural settings, responding to a range of issues related to crisis, austerity, immigration, changing agricultural livelihoods, and post-socialist transformations. In the interstices of the dominant system, people have developed systems of production, distribution, and exchange, conceived as "alternatives" to or innovations in the mass-market food system. In this collection, we seek to understand the intersecting cultural, economic, and political objectives that producers and consumers pursue through their engagement with the food system. What kind of values do they express through their protests or through their forms of production, distribution, and consumption?

Bringing together ethnographic case studies from across Europe, this edited volume aims to compare how food values are expressed in daily life and livelihoods, and policy debates; how diverse actors are transforming food production, distribution, consumption in practice and rethinking the economic system through experiments in everyday routines. Narotzky, writing about the post-2008 economic crisis in southern Europe, calls for ethnographers to place economic value and moral values in the context of real people's "life projects" (2012). Anthropologists, with their commitment to understanding embedded practices and meaning-making, take us beyond formal economic concepts of value—"models [that] are at pains to include much of what sustains actual human behavior: meaning, moral value, ambiguity, contradiction, affect, emotion, expectations and responsibilities" (Narotzky 2012: 630).

Our perspective here is to apply, extend, and challenge anthropological insights on cultural and economic value in people's "life projects" to the realm of "food projects," paying attention to the way in which people create space of action through food. We borrow the term "food project" from Bartlett's examination of one specific kind of program, university campus food projects (Bartlett 2011). Like Bartlett, we are interested in investigating whether and how food projects can be transformative of larger institutions and society. Just as "life projects" provide a useful entry point for studying value and values in contemporary society, "food projects" too are strategic points where value and values are enacted and contested in the individual and collective action.

Food projects bridge different dimensions of the concept of value and stimulate alternative economic imaginaries that are often also political imaginaries (Wilk 2006; Pratt and Luetchford 2014; Counihan and Siniscalchi 2014, Siniscalchi 2015, 2019). We consider these food projects as examples of food activism, which may include "efforts by people to change the food system across the globe by modifying the way they produce, distribute, and/or consume food," as well as food movements and protests taking place at scales of action ranging from the local to the national or transnational (Counihan and Siniscalchi 2014: 6). Schlosberg and Coles characterize food activism as part of a new wave of movements operating within a "sustainable materialist" framework with a "focus on collective practices and institutions of provision of the basic needs of everyday life" (2016: 166). The "sustainable materialist" framework brings together issues of social justice and sustainability with strategies of "counter- and alter-circulation" (Schlosberg and Coles 2016: 171). With the notion of "food projects," we place the accent on the transformative capacity of material practices around food, which may create new kinds of economic spaces and relationships through the "coexistence of monetary and non-monetary values" (Pratt 2007: 288).

Theorizing value and values

The notion of value, from Marx and Polanyi to contemporary authors such as Graeber and Gibson-Graham, has a complex intellectual history covering very diverse semantic fields "from morality to finance, from philosophy to mathematics, from music to painting and linguistics" (Heinich 2017: 133). The aim of these pages is not to discuss all the different debates on the concept of value—already reviewed by other authors (see, among others, Graeber 2001; Werner and Bell 2004; Wilk and Cligett 2007 or, more recently, Narotzky and Besnier 2014)—but to address the theories of value and values as a framework for comparing the stakes of food projects in the different ethnographic contexts across Europe today. The principles underlying the evaluation and the value in the sense not only of importance but also of intrinsic quality of things—two of the main significations of the notion of value that Heinich (2017) points out—push us to pay attention to the evaluation criteria mobilized by the social actors that we observe in our various cases of studies, and the qualities they attribute to things and actions they valuate: ethnography shows clearly that these are indissociable dimensions of (e)valuation. Moreover, our challenge here is to use the ethnographic lens to focus attention on the way people put these values into practice.

Economic anthropologists have studied how value is socially produced, looking through the lenses of Marx and Mauss. Marx's theories of exploitation were built upon classical economist Ricardo's labor theory of value, which acknowledged that the value of any good encompasses the value of the labor required to produce it. Marx stresses that all production is social, rooted in norms and expectations of how labor is compensated and goods exchanged. Market exchange abstracts and obscures the social production relations embedded in goods through the process that Marx calls "commodity fetishism." As societies grew and trade became global, the distance between producers and consumers also grew making disembedded market exchange the main social relationship for negotiating value.

Richard Wilk and Lisa Cliggett note how Mauss, like Marx, sought to understand the transformation of Western societies and how both "believed capitalism was ruining the social world" (2007: 160) at the end of the nineteenth century. Mauss compared "gift economies" in different parts of the world with concepts of value that seemed radically different from the capitalistic system and offered alternatives that "emphasized communality, morality, and social aspects of production and exchange" (ibid.). The existence of these "other" economies allowed Mauss and the economic anthropologists who followed him to pay attention to other kinds of value than those that are at the core of a commodities economy and exchange.

While both Marx and Mauss treat value as socially produced, their two perspectives have given rise to a sort of rigid separation between two kinds of exchange and two types of objects (gift versus commodity, Gregory 1982). We see a similar dichotomy in the two interpretations of the notion of value associated with each: value in the singular (market value that we can evaluate eventually through a price) and values in the plural (as moral, political, and social values), referring to other dimensions that cannot be evaluated by money. The tension between values and value—with values not always commensurable or corresponding to alienable objects—has been at the core of several anthropological debates (see Narotzky and Besnier 2014: 8–10). In a similar vein, Pratt and Luetchford (2014) underscore the tensions existing between "monetary" value and the "search for other kinds of value in the production or consumption of food" (2014: 7, see also Gudeman 2008). In *The Social Life of Things*, Appadurai pointed the way out of this impasse, showing how objects may change values when they change contexts (Appadurai 1986, see also Wilk and Cliggett 2007: 164–65). The ethnographic case studies analyzed in this volume show not only that the value of a same object changes in different *regimes of value* but also that new values and criteria of evaluation (for food and for food production and/or consumption) emerge in concrete settings and actions.

All this brings us closer to Graeber's perspective when, drawing from the work of Nancy Munn, he states that value can be understood as "the way in which actions become meaningful to the actor by being incorporated in some larger, social totality—even if in many cases the totality in question exists primarily in the actor's imagination" (Graeber 2001: xii). Discussions of value in economic anthropology often center around high-prestige durables seen as "unique and permanent" (Graeber 2001: 44), such as sacred jewelry exchanged in the *kula* ring or family heirlooms assembled for dowries and inheritance (Werner and Bell 2004). Food, in contrast, is mostly "perishable and generic" (Graeber 2001: 44), making it the least valuable kind of object. The exchange of food in social life, however, often produces value that transcends its ordinariness. Munn writes of food sharing and hospitality as a core action that produces and maintains value (1992). She conceptualizes value as "the importance of actions": the act of giving food creates alliances and obligations between hosts and guests that exceed the perishable, generic ingredients that make up a meal. Munn's formulation can be extended beyond ritual feasting to our varied daily exchanges of food, as a rich literature on "commensality" shows us (see Douglas 1979; Mintz and Du Bois 2002; Counihan 2004; Kerner et al. 2015; Counihan and Højlund 2018, among others).

A new generation of scholars and activists takes inspiration from Gibson-Graham's concept of "community economies" or "solidarity economies," which bring feminist perspectives on reproduction to Marx's production and Polanyi's embedded market (Gibson-Graham 2006, 2008). Gibson-Graham's analysis situates the market economy within the broader context of submerged labor and activities upon which it depends, including unpaid housework and care-work, maintenance of commons, and self-provisioning. Their work focuses on the collective effect of people's attempts to make "life projects" in which labor, production, and reproduction are organized in a more humane and solidaristic way. "Community economies" scholars take great interest in "community food economies" as sites where diverse actors come together to enact and reimagine different ways of organizing the economy (Cameron et al. 2014). Similarly, the "human economy" perspective, developed in the social sciences and adopted by certain movements in a back-and-forth exchange among research and political action, aims at reinserting the social and human dimension at the center of the economy (Hart et al. 2010).

The ethnographic cases in this book present a variety of "food projects" where food value and values are forged between food producers and consumers. In economic spaces often conceived as "alternative," we observe a resurgence of interest in forms of exchange and reciprocity that were the subject of important classical works of economic anthropology (Bohannan and Bohannan 1968; Sahlins 1972). Sometimes, reciprocity economies are imagined as existing or having existed in a "pure" form as opposed to the market economy; in other studies, reciprocity and solidarity are used to counterbalance the utilitarianism and dislocations of neoliberalism. Many draw upon Karl Polanyi's concept of the "double movement" (2001): that as market relationships expand, commodifying ever more dimensions of social life and livelihood, society itself pushes back and demands protection from the excesses of so-called laissez-faire marketization. In this counter-movement, different social groups demand reforms to re-embed the economy in social norms and relationships. Marc Edelman notes that cultural historians and anthropologists have expanded upon Polanyi's concept of the "moral economy" (Edelman 2005). E. P. Thompson popularized this term in his essay, "The Moral Economy of the Crowd in Eighteenth Century England" (1971), which analyzed urban food riots as a spontaneous site of social critique. Urban consumers raged against the high food prices set by producers and middlemen, and they also complained about the poor quality and adulteration of basic staples like bread and flour. James C. Scott transposed the moral economy concept to peasant protests for a "just price" that would meet basic subsistence needs (1976), and small producers continue to demand a "just price" and "Fair Trade" across Europe and the rest of the world today (Borras, et al. 2008, Li 2014). Food, with its dual valance as commodity and basic human sustenance, is central to these contests and struggles where value and values are redefined. Whether seen from the point of view of producers or consumers, the moral economy concept captures a wide range of struggles to re-embed markets in society, even if the dichotomous opposition of self-interest and morality is partially artificial and in concrete situations, markets and morals coexist (Gudeman 2001, see also Narotzky and Homs, Rakopoulos, and Siniscalchi, in this volume).

The historical background of food projects in Europe

Since values are forged in specific social contexts, it is important to take into consideration the historical dimension of these processes. As in many other parts of the world (Friedmann 2005; Mintz 2006), Europe's food system has transformed rapidly in the past centuries (Scholliers 2001). Pratt sketches the overall pattern of food production and consumption in Europe (2007). The first big shift was industrialization, which arrived at different points in different regions of Europe. Jack Goody and Sidney Mintz, both writing about England, show how industrialization created a class of consumers who needed to purchase processed foods because they were leaving the land and working in factories (Goody 1982; Mintz 1986). Shifting from agricultural production to industrial production had major cultural effects on food habits, from meal times to the diet itself. With modernization, agriculture has produced more food with less labor, using chemical inputs and mechanized processes. Since the Second World War we have seen a second great shift in which Europe's cities have grown with many rural areas gradually becoming depopulated and with fewer and fewer people engaged in agriculture. Buying most of their food through a few large supermarket chains, city dwellers seem ever further removed from agricultural production. In reality, agriculture never disappeared. In some regions, it has been more and more industrialized, while in other geographical areas, agriculture has been maintained with funds from the European Common Agricultural Policy (CAP), and in other regions, it continues to be practiced as an activity intended mostly for consumption. In light of these transformations, in the late twentieth and early twenty-first century, we observe the emergence of different cases of food activism, from "back-to-the-land" experiences to urban consumer cooperatives or urban gardens. These movements have generated a critique of the industrialized food system that calls for reconnecting producers with consumers through personalized or embedded economic relations rather than market exchange and through calls for higher-quality food that is local and "authentic" rather than industrialized and adulterated (Pratt 2007: 287; Friedmann 2005). These shifts are broadly applicable across Europe, but different regional histories also shade the kinds of food projects and food values that are emerging. We do not want to (re)create here typologies and territorializations that have already been criticized. Nevertheless, some common elements emerge in the different regions of Europe that help us to understand what we observe today in terms of food projects.

In northern and central Europe, food values relate closely to historical concepts of wholesomeness, institutions ensuring food quality, and the rise of supermarkets as a feature of the affluent postwar society. In broad terms, Germany, the UK, and the Scandinavian countries have a shared food history, linked by climate and trade between maritime cities (Notaker 2009). As nineteenth-century industrial powers, Germany and the UK saw the rapid growth of cities and urban food systems, where consumers' concerns about food adulteration led to the establishment of institutions to monitor food quality (Atkins et al. 2007; Scholliers 2008). Even today, northern European concepts of food quality center on hygiene, health, and ecology (Barjolle and Sylvander 2000). After emerging from hunger and rationing during and immediately following the Second World War, producers developed mass food production and distribution networks, and urban consumers quickly took up supermarket provisioning (Atkins et al. 2007).

In the south of Europe, local provenance and producer's savoir-faire have long been central to food values (Heller 2013; West 2013). Winemakers in Portugal and France developed systems certifying "controlled" products with official *appellations* and *dénominations* for wine and cheese producers, based on the notion of terroir that attributes unique qualities to local ecological conditions and "traditional" techniques (Hermitte 2001; Trubek 2008; Ulin 1996; Unwin 1991). The early decades of the twentieth century were a time of food scarcity for most of the population across the region because of poverty and wartime shortages (Domingos et al. 2014; Helstosky 2006). Industrialization reached the food system late, relatively speaking, in many parts of southern Europe, and so the region's consumers have tended to place their trust in regional producers and local retailers when assessing food quality and safety (Sassatelli and Scott 2001; Stanziani 2005). More recently, small-scale producers have struggled to compete in the new European CAP. The 2008 economic crisis affected food producers and consumers across southern Europe, provoking novel responses such as the growth of cooperatives, farmers' markets, and urban gardens.

Food projects in Eastern European countries reflect that region's history of state socialism and post-socialist marketization and privatization. All of these processes have profoundly affected food access and perceptions of food quality. The agricultural structure emerged from feudalism later than other regions in Europe, with the Habsburg Empire abolishing serfdom in 1848 and Russia in 1861. Since the sixteenth century, with the emergence and the consolidation of the core of a capitalistic economy in Western Europe, Eastern European countries occupied a peripheral position and attempted export-driven modernization that relied on selling agricultural products and natural resources to the industrial core (Wallerstein 1976). This strategy collapsed in the early twentieth century as prices for wheat, cattle, and other agricultural products collapsed across the globe (Berend 2001). Food systems and agricultural production were dramatically reorganized under the Soviet Union and state socialist governments of Eastern Europe. Throughout the region, communist party states collectivized farms and centralized food distribution and prices, policies that was often met with significant resistance from peasant producers and resulted in shortages of consumer goods (Verdery 1996). By the 1960s and 1970s, many Eastern Europeans produced and exchanged food in the informal "second economy" (Lampland 1991). Despite many problems, broad measures of food intake and nutrition improved throughout the region from the 1960s through the 1980s and declined after 1989 with the dismantling of welfare state institutions (Cornia 1994). This history continues to shape perceptions of food access, quality, and social trust in the food system well into the post-socialist period (Caldwell 2009; Jung et al. 2014). Given this history, the region's small producers and consumers perceive themselves as disadvantaged in European Union agricultural and food policy (Gille 2016; Harper 2004).

Food habits have become ever more diverse all across Europe with the growth of immigrant enclaves with international food shops and restaurants, transforming local cuisines through the popularity of immigrant-derived foods (Highmore 2009; Çaglar 1999; Beriss and Sutton 2007; Hassoun 2014). Supranational institutions influence food practices and national politics on food provisioning across these contexts, and Europe is especially interesting in this respect because there is a single market with common policies and regulations covering a wide variety of regions and countries. Most food producers have been directly affected by standards instituted by the European Union and its Common Agricultural Policy (CAP) (Welch-Devine and Murray 2011). Agriculture and food production in Europe has been and still is largely determined by the CAP and its funding system, supporting large and industrial exploitations more than small and medium ones. Smaller and medium producers have responded and interacted with the regulation and certification system, asking for PDO (protected denomination of origin, or *denomination d'origine protegée*, DOP) recognized by the European Commission or establishing links with other kinds of private organizations and brands promoting the singularization and visibility of artisanal products (as Slow Food *Presidia*, Siniscalchi 2013), or again improving organic practices of production and consumption. Through their "food projects," consumers and producers interact with global food markets, such as the market for halal- and kosher-certified products (Lever and Fischer 2018), as well as the Fair Trade and organic certification systems and standards.

Crosscutting dimensions of food values in Europe

Rooted in these diverse histories of food values across Europe, our contributors' case studies offer an ethnographic lens on contemporary food projects. We have chosen to group the chapters to highlight four broad types of social action within food projects: prosuming, contesting, connecting, and consuming.

Part One of our collection consists of ethnographic investigations of people *prosuming*, or growing and processing food for their own consumption, as gardeners and do-it-yourselfers (Kosnik 2018), exploring how they make sense of their own food production. In many cases, gardeners reckon economic value in terms of their ability to reduce *buying* food in markets, while they also attribute an array of positive cultural values to their homemade produce. Harper and Afonso study a group of urban gardeners in Lisbon who refer to *sabor* (flavor), *saber* (knowledge and skill), in addition to more calculated forms of market value as they plan and grow their garden plots. The garden's food project of "communing" the urban food system reveals tensions between these competing values as gardeners negotiate rules for food production in this shared space. Turning to Central Europe, Speck compares several different kinds of food-provisioning projects in Prague, from state-socialist-era *kolonia* and cottage gardens to post-socialist civic gardening initiatives. Czech urban gardeners are motivated to grow food in the city for multiple, sometimes contradictory reasons: as a family-oriented "productive leisure" pastime, as an expression of social solidarity with neighbors, and as a mode of "green gentrification" (Checker 2011). Kosnik's chapter looks at

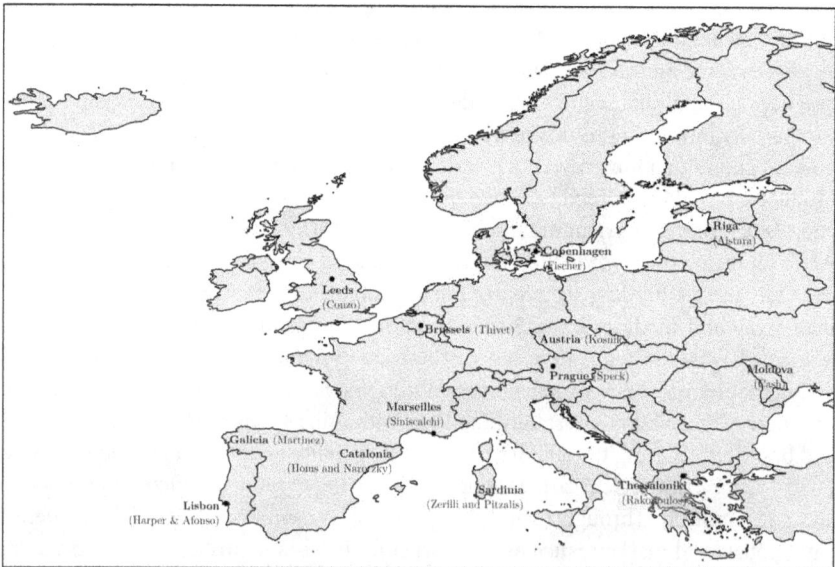

Figure 1.1 Fieldwork localization (Author: Noé Guiraud, 2019—Source: Eurostat, 2016).

"prosumer" farmers in rural Austria and how they understand their food production work in relation to market and non-market values. Kosnik draws our attention to the ways in which self-provisioning practices reframe prosumers' experience of time and natural processes. Across these case studies, we see that while the market is never completely removed from the picture, self-provisioning has the potential to open up spaces for putting different kinds of exchange and values into practice. Moreover, these cases studies show consumers becoming producers in specific (urban or rural) places for a time and for some kinds of food. Producing one's own food seems to transform food, its flavors, its taste, changing the relationship that people have with food and with provisioning.

In Part Two contributors examine cases where small producers articulate the *calculating* values of market price versus "just price." The dairy industry has been strongly affected by European policy shifts, from the 1984 establishment of milk quotas to prevent oversupply to the 2015 "Milk Package" replacing the quota system. Small producers, especially those in peripheral and mountainous regions, have struggled over the years to keep their place in the European common market. Our collection includes two case studies of such struggles in Spain and Italy. Martínez reports on dairy family farmers in Galicia, where small producers organized *tractorada* protests. Parading through city centers on their farm equipment, farmers made their food system work visible and directly appealed to city dwellers on moral terms to support their call for a "just price" for their product. The chapter by Zerilli and Pitzalis opens with the shocking story of the "great sheep massacre" when a Sardinian shepherd slaughtered his entire flock when his sheep's milk was rejected by the local producers' cooperative. The ethnographers examine small producers' response to this act of despair, which came to symbolize the high stakes of dairy policy for small producers. Following the *Movimento pastori sardi* (MPS), a social movement of Sardinian shepherds, they show how activists respond to globalization and neoliberal restructuring of sheep's milk and *pecorino* markets with appeals to the non-monetary value they generate by providing ecological services that maintain a heritage landscape and by keeping Sardinian cheesemaking alive as a traditional craft. Scoping out into the realm of transnational organizing, Thivet's chapter traces the European branch of *Via Campesina* to its origins in 1980s peasants' groups organizing transnationally for the first time in response to the CAP. As small farmers worked on gaining support from consumer and environmental groups and building linkages with producers around the world, their goal coalesced into a wider effort to promote "food sovereignty."

The ethnographers in Part Three draw focus on a specific kind of objective in food projects that has often been overlooked: *connecting* producers and consumers through short-chain food systems, cooperatives and other nascent distribution networks in the "solidarity economy." In these cases, consumers do not produce, but establish direct links with producers, involving themselves in production issues and/or in distribution and coordination activities. Siniscalchi's chapter analyzes how participants in a French community-supported agriculture network (or "organic vegetable baskets") weigh competing values of solidarity and calculation as they engage in a self-conscious alternative to market exchange. Different kinds of calculation cross paths in these economic spaces, and market logics come back inside through the window. Homs and Narotzky provide an ethnographic lens on how consumers and workers understand the exchanges that take place in organic food cooperatives, linking producers and consumers in Catalonia. While these alternative food networks attempt to reshape power relationships between consumer and producer by "cutting out the middleman," ultimately we find that distribution is its own kind of work. As Rakopoulos vividly describes in his chapter on cooperatives in Greece during the crisis, solidarity economies such as cooperatives often depend on a mix of paid and volunteer labor that result in contradictions as such initiatives scale up and solidify into organizations.

Part Four of the collection delves into *consuming*, specifically, the role of consumers in negotiating food values across a wide range of contexts. While we may be tempted to see consumers as individuals expressing desires for commodities, food consumption also reveals social tensions in everyday life around sharing, community, affordability, and dignity. Values are not just created as an individual relationship with a product but embedded in shared histories, relationships, and expectations. Aistara examines how Latvian consumers connect Fair Trade food products to local histories of food shortages and politicized access to special foods during the state socialist period. During that time, commodities like bananas, chocolate, and coffee were rare luxuries for most consumers, and so Latvian consumers view today's efforts to promote higher-priced Fair Trade versions of these products with a certain skepticism. Cash provides another lens on food values in a post-socialist society outside of the Schengen zone, examining the disjuncture between official calculations of the poverty line and the pride that rural Moldovans take in food provisioning and feasts. In both of these post-socialist settings, past and present food consumption serves as a marker of socioeconomic class distinctions and connections. Moving the discussion of consumption to Western Europe, we see how food values are negotiated in increasingly multicultural societies, where food consumption acts as a different kind of marker for difference. Conzo presents the role of food and meals in creating supportive spaces for Afro-Caribbean immigrants in a British city. Immigrants meet and discuss food traditions as well as their experiences of racism in the UK when they meet at community center lunches and neighborhood restaurants. Fischer writes about consumers' perspectives on halal foods in Denmark, showing wide variation in food values and practices within immigrant communities. Muslims gave each other feedback about eating halal and consuming alcohol in Denmark, with increasing adherence as halal food became more widely available. Fischer observes that the precise boundaries of halal observance vary and are negotiated within families and in relation to certification systems and food availability in Denmark over time.

Conclusion

Across these "food projects," food takes center stage as the embodiment of social and economic values, created by groups of people in relation to specific social relationships, histories, and memories. But food is also a powerful tool to (re)think consumption, distribution, and production, and links between them. Food unites multiple forms of value and values—quality, economic value, social value, and moral values—and recombines them in different recipes that we explore in these pages. Growing food in cities has the potential to transform the value of urban space for residents through commoning. Self-provisioning and prosuming enable people to experience new relationships to time and nature—which are hypercommodified under neoliberal capitalism—and to (re)engage in food sharing with family, friends, and neighbors. Channeling the spirit of Polanyi, small producers around Europe have responded to changes in the CAP with creative protests that retool the concept of "just price" in relation to contemporary values of sustainability, cultural heritage, and transnational peasant solidarity. New distribution practices, from community-supported agriculture to cooperative enterprises, attempt to bypass or short-circuit the mass market through more local and direct forms of circulation of goods. Organic production by small farmers is increasing, within a global trend of farm consolidation.

Although these may appear to be small and localized experiments, they allow people to imagine and experience different ways of organizing exchange and consumption. Moreover, the case studies analyzed here show people constructing networks and alliances between individuals, between groups, and between these and political and economic institutions. These alliances may be short-term instrumental or long-term institutional ones, micro-level personal alliances or broad formal partnerships between groups or institutions, or even coalitions with economic, political, ideological or moral aims and effects. These networks and relationships that each chapter analyzes in a specific context produce changes in the forms of activism and in food projects, connecting them with other local, national, or global experiments or forms of resistance. Social relations, solidarity exchanges, autonomy, direct links, just prices, become the key words articulating values in food projects, conceived as political and economic experimentations across Europe.

References

Appadurai, A., ed. (1986). *The Social Life of Things: Commodities in Cultural Perspective.* Cambridge: Cambridge University Press.

Atkins, P. J., P. Lummel, and D. J. Oddy, eds. (2007). *Food and the City in Europe since 1800.* Aldershot: Ashgate.

Barjolle, D., and B. Sylvander (2000). *Protected Designations of Origin and Protected Geographical Indications in Europe: Regulation or Policy? Recommendations.* European Commission, Fair CT 95-306: PDO and PGI Products.

Barlett, P. F. (2011). "Campus Sustainable Food Projects: Critique and Engagement." *American Anthropologist,* 113 (1): 101–15.

Berend, T. I. (2001). *Decades of Crisis: Central and Eastern Europe before World War II.* Berkeley: University of California Press.

Beriss D., and D. Sutton, eds. (2007). *The Restaurants Book: Ethnographies of Where We Eat.* Oxford and New York: Berg.

Bohannan, P., and L. Bohannan (1968). *Tiv Economy.* Harlow: Longmans.

Borras, Jr. S., M. Edelman, and K. Cristóbal, eds. (2008). *Transnational Agrarian Movements Confronting Globalization*. Chichester: Wiley Blackwell.

Çaglar, A. (1999). "Mc Kebap: Döner Kebap and the Social Positioning Struggle of German Turks." In Carola Lentz (ed.), *Changing Food Habits: Case Studies from Africa, South America and Europe*, no. 2, 263–80. New York: Taylor & Francis.

Caldwell, M. L., ed. (2009). *Food & Everyday Life in the Postsocialist World*. Bloomington: Indiana University Press.

Cameron, J., K. Gibson, and A. Hill (2014). "Cultivating Hybrid Collectives: Research Methods for Enacting Community Food Economies in Australia and the Philippines." *Local Environment*, 19 (1): 118–32.

Checker, M. (2011). "Wiped Out by the 'Greenwave': Environmental Gentrification and the Paradoxical Politics of Urban Sustainability." *City & Society*, 23 (2): 210–29.

Cornia, G. A. (1994). "Poverty, Food Consumption, and Nutrition during the Transition to the Market Economy in Eastern Europe." *The American Economic Review*, 84 (2): 297–302.

Counihan, C. (2004). *Around the Tuscan Table: Food, Family and Gender in Twentieth-Century Florence*. New York and London: Routledge.

Counihan, C., and V. Siniscalchi, eds. (2014). *Food Activism: Agency, Democracy and Economy*. London: Bloomsbury.

Counihan, C., and S. Højlund, eds. (2018). *Making Taste Public: Ethnographies of Food and the Senses*. London: Bloomsbury.

Domingos, N., J. M. Sobral, and H. G. West, eds. (2014). *Food between the Country and the City: Ethnographies of a Changing Global Foodscape*. London: Bloomsbury.

Douglas, M. (1979). *Implicit Meanings*. London: Routledge and Kegan Paul.

Edelman, M. (2005). "Bringing the Moral Economy Back in to the Study of 21st-Century Transnational Peasant Movements." *American Anthropologist*, 107 (3): 331–45.

Friedmann, H. (2005). "From Colonialism to Green Capitalism: Social Movements and the Emergence of Food Regimes." *New Directions in the Sociology of Global Development Research in Rural Sociology and Development*, 11: 227–64.

Gibson-Graham, J. K. (2006). *A Postcapitalist Politics*. Minneapolis: University of Minnesota Press.

Gibson-Graham, J. K. (2008). "Diverse Economies: Performative Practices for 'Other Worlds'." *Progress in Human Geography*, 32 (5): 613–32.

Gille, Z. (2016). *Paprika, Foie Gras, and Red Mud: The Politics of Materiality in the European Union*. Bloomington: Indiana University Press.

Goody, J. (1982). *Cooking, Cuisine, and Class: A Study in Comparative Sociology*. Cambridge: Cambridge University Press.

Graeber, D. (2001). *Toward an Anthropological Theory of Value: The False Coin of Our Own Dreams*. New York: Palgrave.

Gregory, C. A. (1982). *Gifts and Commodities*. London: Academic Press.

Gudeman, S. (2001). *The Anthropology of Economy: Community, Market, and Culture*. Malden, MA and Oxford: Blackwell.

Gudeman, S. (2008). *Economy's Tension: The Dialectics of Community and Market*. Oxford: Berghahn.

Harper, K. (2004). "The Genius of a Nation versus the Gene-Tech of a Nation: Science, Identity, and Genetically Modified Food in Hungary." *Science as Culture*, 13 (4): 471–92.

Hart, K., J. L. Laville, and A. D. Cattani, eds. (2010). *The Human Economy: A Citizen's Guide*. Cambridge: Polity.

Hassoun, J. (2014). "Restaurants dans la ville-monde: Douceurs et amertumes." *Ethnologie française*, 44 (1): 5–10.

Heinich, N. (2017). *Des valeurs: Une approche sociologique*. Paris: Gallimard.

Heller, C. (2013). *Food, Farms & Solidarity: French Farmers Challenge Industrial Agriculture and Genetically Modified Crops*. Durham, NC: Duke University Press.

Helstosky, C. (2006). *Garlic and Oil: Politics and Food in Italy*. Oxford and New York: Berg.

Hermitte, M. A. (2001). "Les appellations d'origine dans la genèse des droits de propriété intellectuelle." *Etudes et recherches sur les systèmes agraires et le développement*, 32: 195–207.

Highmore, B. (2009). "The Taj Mahal in the High Street: The Indian Restaurant as Diasporic Popular Culture in Britain." *Food, Culture & Society*, 12 (2): 173–90.

Jung, Y., J. Klein, and M. L. Caldwell, eds. (2014). *Ethical Eating in the Postsocialist and Socialist World*. Berkeley: University of California Press.

Kerner, S., C. Chou, and M. Warmind, eds. (2015). *Commensality: From Everyday Food to Feast*. London: Bloomsbury.

Kosnik, E. (2018). "Production for Consumption: Prosumer, Citizen-Consumer, and Ethical Consumption in a Postgrowth Context." *Economic Anthropology*, 5 (1): 123–34.

Lampland, M. (1991). "Pigs, Party Secretaries, and Private Lives in Hungary." *American Ethnologist*, 18 (3): 459–79.

Lever, J., and J. Fischer (2018). *Religion, Regulation, Consumption: Globalising Kosher and Halal Markets*. Manchester: Manchester University Press.

Li, T. M. (2014). "What Is Land? Assembling a Resource for Global Investment." *Transactions of the Institute of British Geographers*, 39(4): 589–602.

Mintz, S. W. (1986). *Sweetness and Power: The Place of Sugar in Modern History*. New York: Penguin.

Mintz, S. W. (2006). "Food at Moderate Speed." In R. Wilk (ed.), *Fast Food/Slow Food: The Cultural Economy of the Global Food System*, 3–11, Lanham, MD: Altamira Press.

Mintz, S. W., and C. M. Du Bois (2002). "The Anthropology of Food and Eating." *Annual Review of Anthropology*, 31: 99–119.

Munn, N. D. (1992). *The Fame of Gawa: A Symbolic Study of Value Transformation in a Massim (Papua New Guinea) Society*. Durham, NC: Duke University Press.

Narotzky, S. (2012). "Europe in Crisis: Grassroots Economies and the Anthropological Turn." *Etnográfica*, 16 (3): 627–38.

Narotzky, S., and N. Besnier (2014). "Crisis, Value, and Hope: Rethinking the Economy." *Current Anthropology*, 55 (S9): 4–16.

Notaker, H. (2009). *Food Culture in Scandinavia*. Westport, CT: Greenwood.

Polanyi, K. (2001). *The Great Transformation: The Political and Economic Origins of Our Time* (2nd ed.). Boston, MA: Beacon.

Pratt, J. (2007). "Food Values: The Local and the Authentic." *Critique of Anthropology*, 27(3): 285–300.

Pratt, J., and P. Luetchford (2014). *Food for Change: The Politics and Values of Social Movements*. London: Pluto Press.

Sahlins, M. D. (1972). *Stone Age Economics*. New Brunswick, NJ: Transaction.

Sassatelli, R., and A. Scott (2001). "Novel Food, New Markets and Trust Regimes: Responses to the Erosion of Consumers' Confidence in Austria, Italy and the UK." *European Societies*, 3 (2): 213–44.

Schlosberg, D., and R. Coles (2016). "The New Environmentalism of Everyday Life: Sustainability, Material Flows and Movements." *Contemporary Political Theory*, 15 (2): 160–81.

Scholliers, P., ed. (2001). *Food, Drink and Identity: Cooking, Eating and Drinking in Europe Since the Middle Ages*. Oxford and New York: Berg.

Scholliers, P. (2008). "Defining Food Risks and Food Anxieties throughout History." *Appetite*, 51 (1): 3–6.

Scott, J. C. (1976). *The Moral Economy of the Peasant: Rebellion and Subsistence in Southeast Asia*. New Haven, CT: Yale University Press.

Siniscalchi, V. (2013). "Environment, Regulation and the Moral Economy of Food in the Slow Food Movement." *Journal of Political Ecology*, 20 (1): 295–305.

Siniscalchi, V. (2015). "'Food Activism' en Europe: changer de pratiques, changer de paradigms." *Anthropology of Food* [Online], S11, http://journals.openedition.org/aof/7920 (accessed November 20, 2018).

Siniscalchi, V. (2019). "Mobilisation, Activism and Economic Alternatives." In J. Carrier (ed.), *A Research Agenda for Economic Anthropology*, 105–18. Cheltenham: Edward Elgar Publishing.

Stanziani, A. (2005). *Histoire de la qualité alimentaire. XIXe-XXe siècle*. Paris: Seuil.

Thompson, E. P. (1971). "The Moral Economy of the English Crowd in the Eighteenth Century." *Past & Present*, 50: 76–136.

Trubek, Amy B. 2008. *Taste of Place: A Cultural Journey into Terroir*. Berkeley: University of California Press.

Ulin, R. (1996). *Vintages and Traditions: An Ethnohistory of Southwest France Wine. Cooperatives*. Washington, DC and London: Smithsonian Institution Press.

Unwin, P. T. H. (1991). *Wine and the Vine: An Historical Geography of Viticulture and the Wine Trade*. London and New York: Routledge.

Verdery, K. (1996). *What Was Socialism, and What Comes Next?* Princeton, NJ: Princeton University Press.

Wallerstein, I. M. (1976). *Capitalist Agriculture and the Origins of the European World-Economy in the Sixteenth Century: With a New Prologue*. Berkeley: University of California Press.

Welch-Devine, M., and S. Murray (2011). "'We're European Farmers Now': Transitions and Transformations in Basque Agricultural Practices." *Anthropological Journal of European Cultures*, 20 (1). https://doi.org/10.3167/ajec.2011.200105.

Werner, C. A., and D. Bell, eds. (2004). *Values and Valuables: From the Sacred to the Symbolic*. Walnut Creek, CA: Altamira Press.

West, H. G. (2013). "Appelations and Indications of Origin, Terroir, and the Social Construction and Contestation of Place-Named Foods." In A. Murcott, W. Belasco, and P. Jackson (eds.), *The Handbook of Food Research*, 209–28. London: Bloomsbury.

Wilk, R., ed. (2006). *Fast Food/Slow Food: The Cultural Economy of the Global Food System*. Lanham, MD: Altamira Press.

Wilk, R., and L. Cliggett (2007). *Economies and Cultures: Foundations of Economic Anthropology* (2nd ed.). Boulder, CO: Westview.

Part One

Prosuming Values

2

Food Values in a Lisbon Urban Garden: Between *Sabor, Saber,* and the Market

Krista Harper and Ana Isabel Afonso

Introduction

Leaning on a hoe in the deep shade of a fruit tree, Maurício said, "It's for me, and I share everything. I give away almost everything. I've never sold it. I started selling green beans—€1.50 a pound, they said it was too expensive." We puzzled over his words, but in the context of the urban garden in Lisbon where retirees like Maurício tend rows of vegetables every day, it made perfect sense. His beans were valuable—homegrown and of a high quality that is hard to find in the market—but also not viable for sale. Maurício started out producing for his own household consumption, but through sweat and skill, he cultivates bumper crops to share for free with friends and neighbors. Urban gardeners work hard to grow crops and maintain a pleasant, shared public space, and they attribute multiple, at times contradictory values to the food they produce.

Horticulture and agriculture are fundamental forms of economic production around the world, but the rise of urban gardening presents new questions about the value of gardens as sites of food production and activism. Portugal has a history of rural radicalism around agricultural land reform, but *urban* food movements have only recently emerged. In other parts of Europe, people have responded to the rise of the industrialized food system by organizing "alternative food movements" that focus on relocalization and food quality (Goodman et al. 2012). These initiatives strive to reconnect producers and consumers along the length of the food chain: through personalized or embedded economic relations like cooperatives and community-supported agriculture (CSA) schemes rather than market exchange, and through calls for higher-quality food that is "local" and "authentic" rather than industrialized and adulterated (Pratt 2007: 287).

In Portugal, alternative food networks are less widespread. The changes that transformed the food system in other parts of Western Europe came much more recently in Portugal but have had profound effects that are visible in the contemporary food system. Under António Salazar's mid-twentieth-century *Estado Novo* dictatorship,

Portuguese agronomists ostentatiously pursued national food independence through the modernization of livestock and plant breeds (Saraiva 2016). On the ground, however, food production was in decline, and many people suffered from poor diet (Samara and Henriques 2013). The first supermarket only appeared in the Lisbon metropolitan area in the early 1970s, and large national and international supermarket chains did not take off until the 1980s. Organic farming accounted for less than 0.2 percent of the Portuguese market in 2011 (Willer and Schaak 2015: 209). On the shelves of organic grocery chains like Brio, many of the items—even "Mediterranean" products—are prohibitively expensive imports from Germany, so that "organic" and "local" are not paired ideas.

Relatively few people in Portugal consciously identify as activists in an "alternative food movement," but urban gardeners produce food informally in pockets of municipal land all across Lisbon. In these informal "food projects" (see Bartlett 2011 and the Introduction to this book), participants describe gardening as a hobby or pastime (*passatempo*) that is also productive, resonating with Acton's research on English allotment gardening as a "hobby, with benefits" (Acton 2011). Gardens produce food and serve as repositories of memory and knowledge, therapeutic havens, and sites for socializing (Bendt et al. 2013; Nadel-Klein 2010).

Atkinson proposes that we take seriously "do-it-yourself" (DIY) hobbies like gardening where non-professionals make and maintain objects. DIY represents "a more democratic design process of self-driven, self-directed amateur design and production activity carried out more closely to the end user of the goods created" (Atkinson 2006: 1). Similarly, Gibson-Graham (2006) posit that urban gardens create space for cultivating non-market subjectivities. Gardeners engage in diverse non-monetized economic practices such as self-provisioning and gift exchange that are "submerged" when social scientists focus attention on formal economic activities (Gibson-Graham 2006: 70). Urban gardeners carry out their hobby on public land, a process of "commoning" (Gibson-Graham 2006; Susser 2016). In the process of organizing a shared place to grow tomatoes and lettuce, they enact a new form of democratic planning and participation centered around food.

In the case of our research in Lisbon, we see a range of food values at work. Urban gardeners contrast the value of their own "do-it-yourself" produce with those foods available in supermarkets and the industrial food system. We explore the paired emic concepts *sabor* (flavor) and *saber* (knowledge) as values urban gardeners attach to their produce. We examine how gardeners talk about the value of their own labor in the garden, relating it to self-provisioning, leisure, gift exchange, and the market, with *vizinhança*, or neighborliness, as a key concept. At two specific moments, urban gardeners' diverse values came into conflict: the discussion of the garden's regulations on seeds and the heated "rototiller debate" about market relationships in the garden. These two incidents provoked intense arguments about the underlying meaning of urban gardening for its practitioners. In the process, urban gardeners articulated food values linked to their common space, whether or not they saw themselves as creating an "alternative food system" through DIY food cultivation.

The research setting

Since 2011, we have followed a gardening project under way in Alta de Lisboa, a neighborhood at the northern edge of the city. Urban gardens have always been an important feature of this landscape—local residents planted informal gardens on vacant municipal lands (Luiz and Jorge 2012). A century ago, Alta de Lisboa was farmland in the *zona saloia*, the peri-urban belt that once supplied the capital city with fresh produce, dairy products, and meat (Baptista 1999). Before the 1950s, the land where Alta de Lisboa today stands consisted of farm estates like the Quinta da Musgeira, crisscrossed by *azinhagas*, or small stone-walled cart paths marking the boundaries between *quintas*. To this day, many streets in the neighborhood still bear the name "*azinhaga*," and fragments of olive orchards persist in the vacant lots between the high-rise apartment buildings and modern streets.

As the nation moved from an agricultural and colonial economy to a light-industrial economy during the mid-twentieth-century Salazar dictatorship, the neighborhood changed. In the 1960s, migrants from rural Portugal built *bairros de lata* (or tin-shack shantytowns) on the lands of the old *quintas*. They were soon joined by working-class families displaced from the industrial Alcântara neighborhood when their homes were destroyed to make way for the construction of the massive new bridge across the Tejo. In the 1970s, immigrants from newly decolonized Lusophone countries of Africa began to settle in the neighborhood. In the process, the agricultural fringes of the city became the site of shantytowns, where residents planted informal urban gardens on unused public land to supplement their wages.

Since the end of the Salazar dictatorship in 1974 and Portugal's European Union accession in 1986, the neighborhood has been transformed by "new urbanist" planning, public-private partnerships, and the postindustrial service economy. In the 1980s, the city planned for the redevelopment of the shantytowns, and in 1998, it entered into a public-private partnership with international investors who formed an urban development corporation, the *Sociedade Gestora de Alta de Lisboa*. The old shantytowns were replaced with a "social mix" development of publicly subsidized social housing units alongside modern condominiums for middle-class residents. The neighborhood's vast Parque Oeste was created in 2005 by bulldozing residents' informal gardens. On most afternoons and weekends, the manicured paths of the park are empty. Residents complain that the neighborhood lacks vitality and cohesion across class and ethnic groups, counter to the planners' stated goals of creating a "social mix" (Cordeiro and Figueiredo 2012).

Against this backdrop, a neighborhood-level NGO called *Associação para a Valorização Ambiental da Alta de Lisboa* (AVAAL) has attempted to foster "civic ecology" through the construction of an urban garden park. AVAAL was co-founded by a local landscape architect and a neighborhood elder whose garden had been destroyed to make way for Parque Oeste. Their proposed Parque Agrícola would upgrade vacant, arable land and create an inclusive urban space where the neighborhood's "older gardeners" born in rural Portugal, Cape Verde, and Angola could share knowledge and skills with a younger generation of city-born residents seeking a more ecologically sustainable way of life. They consulted dozens of prospective gardeners using a participatory design process. In 2011, AVAAL secured an agreement from the municipality and the private development corporation to provide funds to landscape the park as a permanent, legally recognized plot of land for residents to cultivate. The Parque Agrícola garden would be run by AVAAL as a local civic organization representing the gardeners, rather than as a municipally administered allotment garden as is more common in Lisbon. Construction was delayed for several years during the economic crisis, but the Parque Agrícola finally opened in April 2015, after six years of community organizing. Today, over a hundred gardeners are cultivating food crops in the Parque Agrícola, and there is always a waiting list for a garden plot.

AVAAL's Parque Agrícola interests us because it is one of the largest and most socially diverse organizations concerned with urban gardens in Lisbon. Half of the gardeners live in public housing buildings near the park, while the other half live in market-rate buildings. There are older gardeners from rural Portugal and Africa, young urban professionals attracted to permaculture and sustainability, as well as gardeners with physical disabilities who grow food in AVAAL's *Horta Acessível* (Accessible Garden) at the entrance to the Parque Agrícola. Gardening is a "productive leisure" pastime for all of them, but for cash-poor pensioners and precariously employed gardeners, it is also a significant form of self-provisioning. Since initiating a participatory action research (PAR) partnership with the organization, we have conducted semi-structured individual interviews with over twenty people involved in Lisbon's urban gardening initiatives. We conducted informal interviews and participant observation at organizational meetings, at events, and in the Parque Agrícola. With the participation of two dozen AVAAL leaders and gardeners, we facilitated Photovoice focus groups and participatory evaluation exercises. We draw upon these data to explore how gardeners and organizers express and debate food values in relation to the Parque Agrícola.

Food values in an urban garden

Pratt observes that different food chains contrast "in the way they organize production and distribution, and in terms of the cultural values that run through them" (Pratt 2007: 285). But how are these values produced and expressed? In other words, how do the people engaged in food projects like urban gardening ascribe value to the foods they produce, exchange, and consume? We analyze these questions by looking at the Parque Agrícola from several different angles: its formal organization, the words of gardeners who took a break from their work to sit for an interview in the shade of their plot's toolshed, and moments in our fieldwork when we saw tension among competing values.

Geographer Luke Drake guides our attention to three key moments when organizers and participants articulate the meanings of community gardening in vivo, "expectations, encounters, and outcomes" (Drake 2014: 193). Garden regulations are a place where the values of organizers and gardeners coalesce in a formal document. To prepare their proposal for the Parque Agrícola in 2013, the leadership of AVAAL developed a draft list of goals and rules and assembled the membership, including prospective gardeners, to discuss and ratify the document. The organization's mission statement emphasizes values of sustainability—"to promote the practice of urban agriculture in an ecological way" and participation—"to ensure shared management by its users, AVAAL members" ("Proposal for Regulations for the Use of the PAAL," 2013). The founding document lists the rights of participating gardeners, which include the right to "use a plot of arable land at moderate cost, following the rules of ecological agriculture" and to "harvest and determine the destination of their production (own consumption, sale of surpluses or other)." The regulations also enumerate the obligations of participating gardeners, which include to "use environmentally friendly means of cultivation" and to "comply with the rules of good neighborliness [*vizinhança*], in particular by ensuring that their crops do not invade neighboring plots." Later, we would learn that gardeners had different understandings of organizational keywords like "ecological" and "*vizinhança*," as they applied the terms in different ways to problems that erupted in day-to-day life in the Parque Agrícola.

The regulations reflect the initial vision and priorities of the organization's founders, as well as negotiations with municipal officials and the gardeners themselves. Speaking with the co-founder of AVAAL just after the inauguration of the Parque Agrícola, Ana asked whether the organization would continue to play a role in running the garden, and he answered, "I hope so, because all the people here will share a common space—but maybe not yet common values." The garden itself would simply provide a new neighborhood "third space" (Oldenburg 1999) or "social infrastructure" (Klinenberg 2018), without any guarantees. The co-founder expected conflicts to arise within the garden but was hopeful that gardeners would negotiate these encounters in ways that would ultimately forge a stronger sense of community.

Drake's framework of "expectations, encounters, and outcomes" helps us see multiple ways of valuing food and gardens in practice since the 2015 launch of the Parque Agrícola. We explore different ways in which gardeners articulate the value of growing food in the city: *sabor* and *saber* as social and cultural values and the tension between market value and non-market values such as *vizinhança* as economic values. At times, conflicts arose when different values collided—key moments when gardeners made these values explicit and articulated their relative importance.

Valuing quality: *Sabor* and *Saber* as values

Fernando: You notice it in the vegetables.
Ana: Notice the flavor?
Anita: You can tell the flavor.
Ana: There's a difference?
Anita: Yeah.

Sabor or "flavor" is a value privileged by gardeners in the Parque Agrícola. A "good flavor," or simply the fact that flavor is present at all is synonymous with quality and authenticity. *Sabor* refers in part to the sensory value of garden produce and its quality relative to supermarket produce. Gardeners also used *sabor* to praise culturally appropriate varieties of produce and regional ingredients that were hard to find at most Portuguese low-cost supermarkets, which are fairly homogenous in offerings.

One hot afternoon under a fig tree we talked with a group of retired men who hold adjacent plots on the upper part of the hillside. The tree was originally planted by Senhor Ferreira, a wiry older man in a tweed cap who has cultivated his plot here long before the founding of the Parque Agrícola. AVAAL granted Senhor Ferreira a special dispensation for an extra-large plot so that he could maintain the fruit trees he had planted decades earlier. Doing fieldwork in the garden, we often walked up the steep hill to visit Senhor Ferreira because he spends more time in the garden than anyone else and is always ready to share some fresh morsel from his garden. When we asked about the quality of produce from the garden, Senhor Ferreira said, "Oh! These are much better. This is grown with a *flavor*, isn't it—not like in the greenhouse, no. Food from the greenhouse is not worth it." He shared a juicy strawberry from his patch, and he explained why it was better than store-bought. Supermarket produce is selected for looks, not flavor—"it tastes good to the eyes, but not to eat."

Down the hill, a novice gardener named Georgina talked about *sabor* as a defining feature of garden produce in contrast to mass production:

I think the taste of things is totally different. Because we go to the supermarket, we buy a lettuce, and it's water. And I go to the Alentejo, and my friend goes to the yard and picks a lettuce, and the lettuce has a *flavor*. So it's industrialization a little bit that got me thinking about having a garden.

Another gardener, Paulo, expressed wonder at the sensory impact of foods plucked from his garden in contrast with store-bought: "Very much so . . . even in *flavor*. It is very different. The first time I took home a cucumber—*sim, Senhor!*" Overwhelmingly, gardeners judged homegrown produce as superior to supermarket fruits and vegetables on the basis of flavor or *sabor*.

Curiously, in Portuguese language, a related word—*saber*—has multiple senses: knowledge, taste, and skill. *Saber* in the sense of traditional knowledge came up when gardeners also talked about growing herbs and crops associated with their region or even village of origin. Vicente, a retired municipal employee who was originally from Cape Verde, showed me a patch of *feijão mangalo* (*Lablab purpureus*) he was growing in his small plot, alongside six other Cape Verdean and Portuguese varieties of beans. As we tiptoed over beds to another corner of his plot, Vicente pointed at a small area where he cultivated Chinese medicinal herbs that he planned to prepare as infusions. Many other gardeners grow regional specialty crops that are rarely available in supermarkets, such as *poejos* (*mentha pulegium*), a wild mint used in dishes from the Alentejo. *Beldroega* (purslane or *portulaca oleracea*), a green used in traditional soups from southern Portugal, grows like a weed in the Parque Agrícola, but can only sometimes be found in grocery stores. These crops represent both *sabor* and *saber*, distinctive flavors and traditional ecological knowledge from many different places.

Saber also appears in the sense of discernment, social trust in relationships, and savoir-faire—the traditional knowledge of agricultural producers rooted in a specific place (Heller 2007). Older gardeners with rural backgrounds rely more on these forms of knowledge than younger and more formally educated gardeners who grew up in the city, and at times this leads to tensions within the organization around garden regulations. Many of the gardeners say they know their seeds are good quality because they have saved them from year to year, obtained them from rural friends and relatives, or purchased them from a trusted vendor.

People frequently used the term *saber* in a third sense, that of direct, empirical knowledge of food quality. Among the most common reasons gardeners gave for growing food were "knowing what's in my food" and "knowing there are no chemicals." They know their food is high quality because they have tended the crops from seedling to produce. Anita underscored *saber* as part of the subtle appeal of homegrown food: "When you know what you eat, it has a whole other palate, don't you think?" Gardeners described the sense of trust derived from growing food free of chemicals themselves—the shortest of all short food chains. Portugal has food regulations that comply with European standards that should offer protection against many food additives and chemicals; consumers "know" their food is safe and unadulterated because it has passed muster in the official transnational regulatory system. As in other parts of Europe, however, consumers in food systems operate according to diverse "trust regimes" that are predicated on forms of knowledge and social relationships that at times supersede official institutional assurances of quality (Sassatelli and Scott 2001). AVAAL's planners had strong ideas about chemicals and preferred "ecological" or organic techniques, values that are mostly shared with gardeners. But gardeners' understanding of "ecological cultivation" is based on their empirical knowledge of how they personally grow food in their plots, rather than strict adherence to certification standards.

Sabor and *saber* in conflict: Seeds of discontent

An early discussion of garden rules brought out the multiple ways of valuing food quality, *sabor*, and *saber*. AVAAL held a general assembly in a high school auditorium before the opening of the Parque Agrícola to hammer out the user regulations. Members of the AVAAL steering committee presented a draft of the garden rules, partially based on the rules for the municipal allotment gardens in keeping with AVAAL's agreement with the city. One of the most tense debates of the evening centered on the rules regarding seeds. Many gardeners wanted to explicitly ban GMO seeds and were surprised to meet opposition from gardeners who saved traditional seeds from year to year.

"Seed-savers" were gardeners with less formal education who maintained strong ties to their village of origin, whether in Portugal or in Africa. Senhor Ferreira told us about his seeds: "I save them from one year for the next. . . . I have beans, I have everything, potatoes. What else do I have? Tomato, just now I've been putting those oxheart tomatoes . . . out to dry." Paulo showed us a bushy *piri-piri* pepper plant he was growing in the *Horta Accessível* from seeds his relatives sent from São Tome because he preferred their intense heat and flavor. Most of these gardeners saved seeds out of thriftiness, nostalgic connection to their roots, and a preference for familiar flavors, rather than strict adherence to principles of agrobiodiversity conservation. As one retired couple told us: "We have some seeds, and we buy others."

"Anti-GMO" gardeners tended to have more formal education and were motivated to join the garden because of their commitment to environmentalism, permaculture, and organic production with non-GMO seeds. One man who also kept a beehive as hobby said, "It's important that each member knows where they can buy seeds—whether they are from a native seed bank or another supplier of seeds—and knows what are the origins of these seeds." Other stated their worries about how GMO pollen could cross-contaminate neighboring plots and affect bees and butterflies.

The gardeners at the assembly largely agreed on best practice: no gardeners stated support for using GMO seeds, and all of them supported saving non-GMO seeds. The question of enforcing this rule raised tensions, however. There is no way to visually distinguish non-GMO seeds in the garden aside from product packaging, which is not available for seeds saved from previous harvests. Seed-savers feared that a strict rule on non-GMO seeds could be interpreted to mean that gardeners must buy seeds from a certified commercial producer, and so they pushed back on the rule. One shouted out, "If I have to plant somebody else's seeds, I'm voting against it!" An elderly Guinean gardener complained, "I don't want anyone to tell me what seeds to plant!" because he brings his own seeds to grow foods from his home country. It was not until the group agreed that seed saving would be allowed that a consensus could be reached—meaning that the garden relies on an honors system to stay "GMO free." One of the "GMO-free" advocates proposed that the organization make space for organized trainings and discussions to build a shared understanding of the rules: "In this project where there are people who do not know anything about horticulture and there are people who know and have accumulated experience, it is important for people to talk to each other." The debate over the "no GMO seeds" rule revealed submerged conflicts between social trust of traditional *sabor/saber* and more abstract, technical forms of knowledge circulating in the form of purchased "GMO-free" seeds. Gardeners carry these understandings of *sabor* and *saber* into their assessment of the exchange value of their produce as something that might be sold on the market or shared as a gift.

Economic values: Market-price calculation versus sharing and *vizinhança*

The market value of produce grown in the garden is a puzzle, as when Maurício mused about his homegrown beans, which were too good to sell for the price offered and therefore could only be given away for free. Perhaps the most fundamental food value expressed in the Parque Agrícola is the right to grow small gardens in the city as an "insurance policy" against precarious employment—the moral economy of self-provisioning. Questions of what to grow is mainly determined by family food preferences rather than market or aesthetic value. The idea that the garden is a space for self-reliance wedded to solidarity and access to land is shared among both the middle-class and working-class gardeners. In this vision, the economic value of the garden appears in three dimensions: (1) selling produce in the market, (2) saving money by not buying produce or other goods and services, and (3) sharing produce in gift exchanges.

Selling produce for money is rare in the Parque Agrícola. AVAAL has a stall at the "Urban Market of Alta de Lisboa" held each month at the Quinta das Conchas park where members may sell produce and handicrafts. In theory, gardeners may sell some of their excess produce to offset the cost of seeds, tools, and garden membership fees. Typically, however, the market stall offers only a few bunches of greens or some seedlings and functions as an information booth for residents seeking to join the garden. Selling produce for money is not a priority, even for cash-poor gardeners.

Market calculation of value appears in gardeners' plans for what to plant, in that they consider the monetary value of "not buying" produce and other things. Maria José showed us a hand-sketched map of how she planned to plant her plot for the Parque Agrícola's first season (Figure 2.1). Much of the space was devoted to ordinary vegetables of the Portuguese kitchen garden—tomatoes, onions, lettuce, and pumpkin. Two sections, however, were given over to rows of strawberries. Maria José explained that strawberries were an expensive luxury, and if she grew them in the garden, her family would eat them without worrying about the cost. Maria José also hoped to raise a bumper crop and sell excess produce at the Urban Market stall to offset her garden fees. Calculation thus plays a part in gardeners' plans about what to grow, as inputs of space, labor, and water are considered in relation to the market price of the produce.

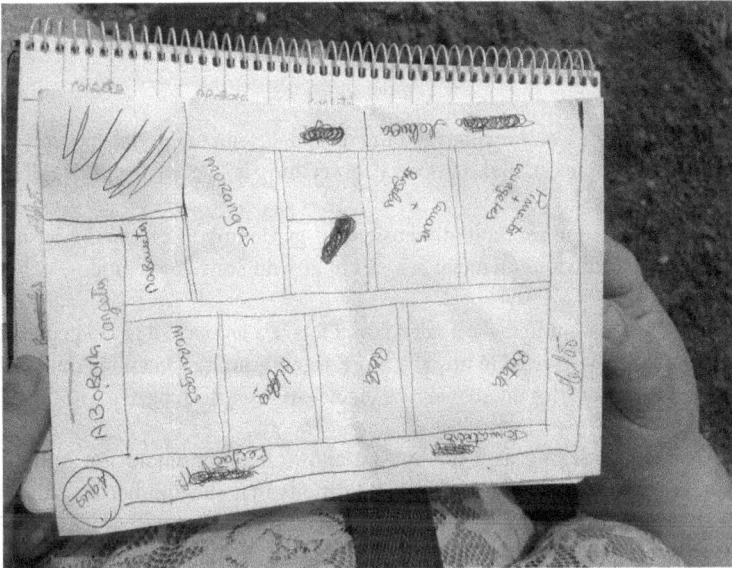

Figure 2.1 Gardener's hand-sketched map of crops (©Krista Harper).

Some gardeners told us that they do not bother planting potatoes because they are labor-intensive to grow and cheap to buy at a farmers' market. They preferred to grow items that were expensive to buy in stores, like strawberries and ripe tomatoes.

Gardeners also calculated the market value of "not buying" but nonetheless indulging in specialty produce. Most gardeners were budget-conscious in their household spending and expressed skepticism at the proposition of paying extra for certified organic produce imported from other countries. They often talked about the foods they produced in terms of the higher market value of organic produce, which they enjoyed for only the cost of their own time in the garden. Fernando and Anita repeatedly emphasized that the garden was a space for subsistence and self-sufficiency, NOT selling, but they appreciated knowing the high potential sales value of their produce as an elite "organic and local" commodity. They showed off the tiny yellow fruits on their Physalis plant, unsure of how they would prepare this novelty food. Nevertheless, they were proud of the fact that their fruits were similar in quality to those produced by Anita's sister in countryside, who sold her organic physalis berries for €9 a kilogram. Even if Anita and Fernando were skeptical of the use value of their strange golden berries, they delighted in the hypothetical market value the berries represented.

Gardeners tacked back and forth between the monetary and non-monetary value of gardening when talking about "not buying" or "saving money." Josefina tended a bountiful plot with her husband Vicente, the amateur botanist whose bean patch we had already encountered. She emphasized non-market values, speaking at length about gardening as exercise and as a hobby—a source of pure enjoyment:

> When you're retired you're alone at home, alone at home, alone at home, with health problems. So [gardening] occupies the time, you mess in the earth and get things moving. . . . Because I do not know how to read and write, I think it's good to pass the time with something like this.

When we asked if she was growing anything special, Josefina said, "I'd say everything— everything that people can make is special, everything is 'special' for us. It's all special. I love to make things."

Josefina stressed the multiple dimensions of gardening as *productive* leisure. She emphasized the health and financial benefits of growing one's own food:

> For example, if I want to make a salad now, I'll take a lettuce, I'll take a pepper, I'll take a tomato. I don't need to buy any more, right? And it's something that's good for your health that this doesn't take medicine—it takes nothing.

Josefina frames gardening as a hobby that allows her household not only to self-provision but also to "save money" on medications that she and her husband would need if they didn't get the exercise, fresh foods, and stress relief provided by their hobby. Otto and Fäber identify "everyday practices of saving" that contribute to urban greening and "low-budget urbanism" (2016). Such practices bring together two senses of the verb "save": "economizing" and "rescuing." Both senses of the term came up repeatedly in our interviews with retired men, who spoke how they saved money by gardening and also how gardening saved them from unhealthy habits. They favorably contrasted their healthy, productive hours in the garden with the time and money other pensioners wasted on drinking alcohol in cafés. Idleness is not only unproductive, from this perspective, it also carries health costs. In contrast, gardening promotes well-being in multifaceted ways, creating economic value "for nothing" as a byproduct of pleasure and leisure time.

Sharing and gift exchange are the most common forms of value enacted in the garden. Participants share common spaces, labor, knowledge, seeds, and tools with one another in the Parque Agrícola (Figure 2.2). Swapping gardening tips and an occasional helping hand are what makes the Parque Agrícola a site for building community and neighborliness—qualities they feel the new neighborhood lacks. A retired engineer told us, "It's gratifying to see people helping each other. I think this is the most important aspect—the exchange of experiences, and people just helping each other." The voluntary quality of sharing is important: Fernando and Anita acknowledged that offering help is a friendly gesture—but not to be expected. In the Parque Agrícola, they said, everyone should care of their own space to produce an aesthetically pleasing whole for all to enjoy. Their views echoed the regulation's stated norm of "being a good neighbor" or *vizinhança*. Gardeners who repeatedly take advantage of shared resources like cistern water or borrowed tools violate this informal reciprocity and attract their neighbors' resentment.

Sharing produce is a source of pride and respect in and out of the Parque Agrícola. Often, at the end of an interview, a gardener would press a lettuce or a bouquet of

Figure 2.2 Gardeners working alongside each other in the Parque Agrícola (©Krista Harper).

herbs into our hands. The economic value of gardening is externally validated when gardeners are able to give away fresh produce to friends, family, and even charitable institutions outside the garden. Cash-poor pensioners and precariously employed workers contribute items of tangible value and quality when they share the foods they grow in the garden. Emilio emigrated from Africa to work on construction sites, but as he gets older, finding jobs is more difficult. He relies on the local Catholic charity, but he told us that he donates his excess produce to the Santa Casa's kitchen. While talking with a group of gardeners at the top of the hill, Senhor Ferreira, widely recognized as the top "green thumb" of the Parque Agrícola, grinned and bragged, "I don't buy anything—I give!"

Market and non-market values in conflict: The great rototiller debate

The tensions between gardeners' concepts of market and non-market value came into vivid focus during a conflict centered around rototilling work. Breaking soil to start a garden in the spring is hard work. Many gardeners in the Parque Agrícola use shovels to double-dig their plots and add manure or compost, ensuring that the top half-meter of soil is loose and enriched with nutrients. Novice gardeners who skip this step of double-digging learn to their chagrin that plants cannot thrive when their roots are blocked by densely packed soil. The arduous task of manually double-digging can be bypassed by using a rototiller, a motorized tool with a small wheeled chassis, rotating blades, and a hopper for soil amendments. Rototillers are expensive items, and most gardeners do not possess one of their own.

One evening, Senhor Eduardo came in to the garden management committee meeting angrier than we had ever seen him. Senhor Eduardo, an elderly Cape Verdean gardener who co-founded AVAAL, recruited many people into the organization through his easygoing, quiet charisma and his volunteer work teaching children to garden in local public schools. Tonight, Senhor Eduardo was having difficulty holding back tears as he said that he had an "ugly" (*feio*) encounter in the park the previous day. As Senhor Eduardo entered the gate, he spotted a man rototilling the plot of a committee member, Maria José. While rototilling was permitted during the early part of the growing season, Senhor Eduardo was puzzled to see the work being performed by Manuel, a man who lived in the building across from the garden but had declined membership in the Parque Agrícola. Manuel was a chronically unemployed, middle-aged Portuguese man who had a complicated relationship with AVAAL—at times offering help, at other times yelling insults from his second-story window. When Senhor Eduardo approached Manuel in the garden, Manuel responded by hurling a racist epithet at him. Asking around, Senhor Eduardo learned that Maria José had paid Manuel €20 to prepare her plot, and Manuel was now approaching other gardeners to offer his paid services.

Manuel's verbal assault clearly violated the garden's norms of *vizinhança*, but many gardeners had had previous unpleasant encounters with Manuel that underscored his status as an unwelcome but unavoidable feature of the neighborhood. Senhor Eduardo came to the meeting incensed that Maria José had *paid* Manuel to work inside the park, and that Manuel was attempting to build a small rototilling business by charging an exploitative fee. Both Maria José and Manuel had violated garden regulations, but Maria José's gaffe was especially glaring because she was a committee member who should know better.

Maria José protested that she had not meant to break the rules, but she was simply overwhelmed as a new gardener breaking ground for the first time. Digging up her 40 square meter plot was more physically taxing than she had expected. As a cafeteria worker with children in the house, she had less time and experience than the retirees in the Parque Agrícola. She worried that she would not be able to recoup the cost of her plot if she didn't get her plants in the ground fast, and so she had hired Manuel.

Maria José shifted in her chair defensively, and Senhor Eduardo was visibly upset as the rest of the AVAAL committee members analyzed the incident. One member pointed out that another gardener had offered people the use of *his* rototiller for no fee, just the cost of gas, and was willing to show people how to use it. This practice of sharing tools and work echoes the traditional rural Portuguese system of labor exchange of the *torna-jeira* as well as Cape Verdean mutual-aid practices. Most of the committee members supported this kind of tool-sharing over Maria José's and Manuel's market arrangement. Mafalda said: "The problem is making a business. Because the issue is that PAAL was born from solidarity. If someone is willing to lend a machine, why pay another to do the job?"

Maria José protested that when the other man offered the rototiller, she had already made the deal with Manuel, so it was too late. Senhor Eduardo said, "You should have talked with AVAAL direction and mentioned that you had a problem—we would help. Because what that man is doing is exploitative. It's not allowed to do business or exchange money within *Parque Agrícola*." Maria José and Senhor Eduardo parted amicably, but everyone left the meeting feeling rattled and emotional as they made their way home.

The rototiller fight exposed the gardeners' ways of thinking about the economic relations within the garden. Maria José fretted that as an inexperienced gardener and harried working mother, her garden would not break even on costs, let alone fulfill dreams of saving money on supermarket purchases, as represented by her sketch map of family-pleasing crops. Other members of the committee stressed their preference for informally sharing tools and labor over replicating market values and wage labor in this alternative space. Interestingly, people objected to the wage labor for two opposing reasons. A few quietly criticized Maria José for hiring out work like a boss. Others thought Manuel was taking advantage of Maria José as a novice gardener by overcharging her for his rototilling work. Both criticisms reflect the idealized values that many gardeners attribute to self-provisioning as a practice that bypasses intermediate channels of labor exploitation. Gardeners often referred to their direct contact with the soil (*mexer na terra* or getting one's hands dirty), both literally and as a metaphor for the many ways they profited from growing food with their own hands. The transformation of urban gardening into a wage labor and Manuel's abusive treatment of Senhor Eduardo were both violations of the gardeners' largely shared social values of self-provisioning and *vizinhança*.

Analysis and conclusions

In the two conflicts in the Parque Agrícola, debates unfurled around different ways of valuing garden inputs for garden production—labor, tools, and seeds. Seeds are one of the most basic natural inputs in a garden, and in debating the kinds of seeds allowed in the Parque Agrícola, AVAAL members expressed the tension between formal regulations to promote food quality and informal practices of seed saving. The rototiller fight was about ways of valuing the labor of growing food in the garden, within the broader context of conflictual relationships in the neighborhood and the desire to create a new space ruled by *vizinhança*.

Despite having different views on how to regulate seeds and labor in the garden, the gardeners found common ground in their shared enjoyment of time spent in the garden and its output. Bypassing the supermarket by consuming and sharing food from the garden, gardeners enthuse about food quality, the health benefits they experience, and their sense of pride in making and giving something of value to people in their social networks and even to local charities. They sometimes "translate" these benefits into the language of market prices, but more often, they refer to non-market values of *sabor, saber, vizinhança*, and sharing.

Pratt (2007) observes that alternative food movements often work by reconnecting producers with consumers through personalized or embedded economic relations like cooperatives and CSAs rather than market exchange. In our view, only a small minority of Parque Agrícola gardeners recognize themselves as being part of an "alternative food movement." However, embedded economic values are widely shared by many of the gardeners—the social values of subsistence, sharing, and neighborliness over market exchange. The perceived market value of food grown in the Parque Agrícola is not irrelevant—it shapes gardeners' decisions about what to plant and adds value to the produce they share with friends and family as gifts. In the garden, the value of the local and the authentic emerge in the ways people refer to *sabor* and *saber*—in terms of flavor, traditional varieties, "knowing what's in your food," and the gardeners' skills and knowledge incorporated into the produce. These qualities are seen as "what is lacking" in market produce that can be created through gardening. Most of Lisbon's urban gardeners do not self-consciously see themselves as part of an alternative food "movement." Nevertheless, as "prosumers" (Kosnik 2018), they hold up quality, authenticity, and place as food values, and many gardeners envision the garden as a shared urban commons where non-market values of *vizinhança* can be played out with neighbors and strangers.

All these tie in to the larger whole of what is being created: a shared urban public space where these social relationships can be performed, even if it is not always a beautiful day in the garden. This dimension of the Parque Agrícola as a food project— of "commoning" (Susser 2016; Gibson-Graham et al. 2016), of building social infrastructure (Klinenberg 2018) that supports the goals of ecological sustainability, individual health and well-being, and *vizinhança*—is fragile and cannot be maintained without resources for mediating disputes. As Gibson-Graham state, "The community that commons is not pre-given, rather, communities are constituted through the process of commoning" (2016: 196). The Parque Agrícola's seed debate and the rototiller dispute illustrate some of the different ways of valuing food, time, and labor at play in the garden, as well as the work required to hold together the food project despite these differences.

The Parque Agrícola is not a self-conscious "alternative food movement" for most of its participants. A few of the gardeners referred to the "right to the city" or ecological sustainability in describing their interest in gardening, but many more talked about the garden as a space for self-reliantly growing one's own food, staying physically active, getting out of the house, socializing, or clearing the mind through meditative tasks like weeding. The Parque Agrícola is a shared project where the task of producing food in a common space continually generates encounters between actors with these diverse motives for gardening. Unlike Lisbon's municipal allotment gardens, the Parque Agrícola's organizational structure requires gardeners to resolve conflicts through a volunteer management committee and the general assembly. As Susser writes: "Commons and commoning contribute to social transformation as alternate ways of relating and forms of horizontalism become real if momentary experiences" (2016: 195). These debates are rarely pretty, but they are encounters when participants forge a shared ethical understanding of the garden and how it will be maintained as a common space for producing high-quality food for all involved.

References

Acton, L. (2011). "Allotment Gardens: A Reflection of History, Heritage, Community and Self." *Papers from the Institute of Archaeology*, 21: 46.

Atkinson, P. (2006). "Do It Yourself: Democracy and Design." *Journal of Design History*, 19 (1): 1–10.

Baptista, L. V. (1999). *Cidade e habitação social: O Estado Novo e o programa das casas económicas em Lisboa*. Oeiras: Celta.

Barlett, P. F. (2011). "Campus Sustainable Food Projects: Critique and Engagement." *American Anthropologist*, 113 (1): 101–15.

Bendt, P., S. Barthel, and J. Colding (2013). "Civic Greening and Environmental Learning in Public-access Community Gardens in Berlin." *Landscape and Urban Planning*, 109 (1): 18–30.

Cordeiro, G., and T. Figueiredo (2012). "Intersecções de Um Bairro Online. Reflexões Partilhadas Em Torno Do Blogue Viver Lisboa." In M. M. Mendes, C. H. Ferreira, T. Sá, and J. L. Crespo (eds.), *A Cidade Entre Bairros*, 9–20, Lisbon: Caleidoscópio.

Drake, L. (2014). "Governmentality in Urban Food Production? Following 'Community' from Intentions to Outcomes." *Urban Geography*, 35 (2): 177–96.

Heller, C. (2007). "Techne versus Technoscience: Divergent (and Ambiguous) Notions of Food 'Quality' in the French Debate over GM Crops." *American Anthropologist*, 109 (4): 603–15.

Gibson, K., J. Cameron, and S. Healey 2016. "Commoning as a Postcapitalist Politics." In A. Amin and P. Howell (eds.), *Releasing the Commons: Rethinking the Futures of the Commons*, 192–212, New York: Routledge.

Gibson-Graham, J. K. (2006). *A Postcapitalist Politics*. Minneapolis: University of Minnesota Press.

Goodman, D., E. M. DuPuis, and M. K. Goodman (2012). *Alternative Food Networks: Knowledge, Practice, and Politics*. New York: Routledge.

Klinenberg, E. (2018). *Palaces for the People: How Social Infrastructure Can Help Fight Inequality, Polarization, and the Decline of Civic Life*. New York: Crown.

Kosnik, E. (2018). "Production for Consumption: Prosumer, Citizen-consumer, and Ethical Consumption in a Postgrowth Context." *Economic Anthropology*, 5 (1): 123–34. https://doi.org/10.1002/sea2.12107

Luiz, J. T., and S. Jorge (2012). "Hortas Urbanas cultivadas por populações caboverdiana na Area Metropolitana de Lisboa: entre a produção de alimentos e as sociabilidades no espaço urbano não legal." *Miradas En Movimiento*, 4: 142–58.

Nadel-Klein, J. (2010). "Gardening in Time." In P. Collins and A. Gallinat (eds.), *The Ethnographic Self as Resource: Writing Memory and Experience into Ethnography*, 165–81, New York: Berghahn Books.

Oldenburg, R. (1999). *The Great Good Place: Cafés, Coffee Shops, Bookstores, Bars, Hair Salons, and Other Hangouts at the Heart of a Community*. New York [Berkeley, CA]: Marlowe; Distributed by Publishers Group West.

Otto, B., and A. Fäber (2016). "Saving (in) a Common World: Studying Urban Assemblages through a Low-budget Urbanities Perspective." In A. Blok and I. Farías (eds.), *Urban Cosmopolitics: Agencements, Assemblies, Atmospheres*, 25–44, New York: Routledge.

Pratt, J. (2007). "Food Values: The Local and the Authentic." *Critique of Anthropology*, 27(3): 285–300.

Samara, M. A., and R. P. Henriques (2013). *Viver e resistir no tempo de Salazar: histórias reais contadas na 1a pessoa*. Lisboa: Verso da Kapa.

Saraiva, T. (2016). *Fascist Pigs: Technoscientific Organisms and the History of Fascism*. Cambridge, MA and London: The MIT Press.

Sassatelli, R., and A. Scott (2001). "Novel Food, New Markets and Trust Regimes: Responses to the Erosion of Consumers' Confidence in Austria, Italy and the UK." *European Societies* 3 (2): 213–44.

Susser, I. (2016). "Considering the Urban Commons: Anthropological Approaches to Social Movements." *Dialectical Anthropology*, 40 (3): 183–98.

Willer, H., and D. Schaack (2015). "Organic Farming and Market Development in Europe." In H. Willer and J. Lernoud (eds.), *The World of Organic Agriculture: Statistics and Emerging Trends 2015*, 174–214, Research Institute of Organic Agriculture (FiBL) and International Federation of Organic Agriculture Movements (IFOAM), Frick, Switzerland.

3

Growing Together: Conspicuous Production and Quality Produce in Czech Community Gardens

Cary Speck

A stone's throw from Prague, dwindling clusters of *kolonia*, or socialist-era allotment gardens, line the spiderweb of roads leading to the Czech Republic's capital city. Here, in modest orchards and vegetable plots fenced off behind barbed wire, a select few Czechs continue to tend gardens they've cultivated since before the Velvet Revolution of 1989. In the late socialist era, *kolonia* were common destinations for Czechs after work and on weekends. Both larder and refuge, the fresh fruit and vegetables grown in these gardens supplemented the limited assortment of produce available in state stores, while the privacy they afforded families offered a reprieve from the intrusion of socialist politics into everyday life. For the luckiest Czechs, bucolic cottage gardens in the Bohemian countryside served a similar role at an even further remove from the bustle of city life.

Despite the significance of these gardens for the twentieth-century Czech foodways, the end of state socialism left *kolonia* and cottage gardens under siege. As international grocery chains established footholds in the country and expanded year-round access to fresh produce, fewer and fewer Czechs grew cabbages, carrots, and plums that could just as easily be bought at the corner store. Encroached upon by highways, warehouses, and other urban redevelopment projects, hundreds of allotments and cottage gardens were simply swallowed up or abandoned in the late 1990s.

Today, a new form of horticulture has taken root in Prague's city center. Nestled among former railyards and factories, between brutalist panel houses and high-rise luxury flats, dozens of community gardens have sprouted up in neighborhoods once far removed from any sort of urban greenspace. Sponsored by a variety of NGOs and social enterprises, these community gardens have elicited the interest of politically active young professionals and pensioners who came of age at the height of the Cold War. In these eclectic enclaves, environmental and community values are converging with the Czechs' desire for high-quality produce, growing together in ways that conflate the cultivation of quality produce with the advancement of post-socialist civil society.

This contrasts with Smith and Jehlička's position that the Czechs' historically high rates of eco-friendly behavior compared to Western Europeans represents a sort of "quiet" sustainability, not an overt environmentalist agenda. Citing patterns of gardening and foraging throughout Central and Eastern Europe (CEE), Smith and Jehlička argue the sustainability of many Czech practices is "quiet"—more epiphenomenal than intentional—because these behaviors are rooted in local practitioners' attitudes toward food, family, and tradition rather than any overarching environmentalist ideology (Smith and Jehlička 2013). Nevertheless, many community gardens in Prague are grafting the globalized language of sustainability onto longstanding Czech gardening traditions. Consequently, these community gardens are emerging as cosmopolitan sites of environmental activism, intentional political engagement, and conspicuous food production. Counihan and Siniscalchi's concept of "food activism" perhaps best encapsulates the actors' overt and covert forms of engagement and resistance in these gardens, where the gardeners' goals range from the top-down transformation of urban food systems to solitary circumventions of suspect food quality standards (Counihan and Sinichalchi 2014).

Based upon ethnographic fieldwork conducted in Czech colony, cottage, and community gardens in the spring of 2015, I argue that the values Czechs attach to growing food in gardens are changing. While socialist-era gardeners saw private allotments as havens from political surveillance, community gardens are gaining ground in Prague precisely because they are seen as overtly environmental enterprises. Though Czechs still see gardening as a surefire way to secure quality food, an increasing number of politically active Czechs are joining community gardens as a way of manifesting their emergent environmental and cultural beliefs in horticultural practices. Such multifunctional food production elicits interest from local stakeholders while at the same time it legitimates the value of not-for-profit local food production to granting agencies and municipal councilors. Vitally, these community gardeners' converging ideologies about self-provisioning, environmentalism, and food quality are not just valuations, but justification for participating in a process that positions them relative to one another, Czech civil society, and Europe as a whole.

Drawing upon Veblen's notion of "conspicuous consumption" whereby elites jockey for and display status through the consumption of luxury goods, I also argue that food activism in Czech community gardens can be understood as a mode of "conspicuous production." By this, I mean gardeners' highly visible and not-for-profit production of fresh food in communal spaces facilitates their accumulation of cultural and political capital by circumventing strictly capitalist modes of consumption (Veblen 1899). By extolling the ecological, economic, and cultural virtues of growing their own food to their peers, individual gardeners demonstrate savoir-faire as post-socialist subjects and engage in status management vis-à-vis their friends and neighbors. Community gardens' sponsoring organizations, in turn, often leverage gardeners' conspicuous production activities as evidence of their organizations civic virtues, legitimating their various projects to municipal authorities, local stakeholders, and increasingly neoliberal funding agencies. This conspicuous production undergirds newfound interest of many Czechs in community gardens and is a key reason why more and more

Praguers have recently turned from traditional modes of horticulture to higher-profile community gardens.

The rest of this chapter is organized into four sections. The first of these traces Czech attitudes toward different food regimes since late socialism and the changing understandings of food "quality" relative to collectivized, commercialized, and subsistence agriculture. The second considers the changing usage of Czech cottage and colony gardens in the same time period, referencing ethnographic fieldwork conducted at two cottage gardens in the Krkonoše Mountains and at one Prague-adjacent *kolonia* garden. Sections three and four consist of two case studies of community gardens in Prague: Prazelenina in the centrally located Holešovice neighborhood, and Vidimova on the city's southern outskirts. In these sections, I pay particular attention to the food ideologies and conspicuous production practices of individual gardeners and community garden organizers.

Questions of quality

Contemporary food production in Czech gardens cannot be understood without reference to late socialist food values or to post-socialist consumerism in CEE. As Smith and Jehlička argue, preparing and consuming food in present-day CEE is still "one of the most tangible ways [people] have made sense of, and placed themselves . . . within the dramatic social, political and economic upheavals during and after the fall of the state socialist system" (Smith and Jehlička 2007: 397). Consuming self-provisioned produce from community gardens is part of this general process of identification and localization; vegetable plots, kitchens, and dinner tables endure as discursive spaces where Czechs can contest or affirm ongoing political, economic, and cultural transformations.

As many social theorists have shown, modes of food consumption are bounded by ideologies about proper and prestigious forms of eating, on the one hand, and molded by the modes and scales of food production, on the other (Bourdieu 1984; Douglas and Isherwood 1979). Consumption can be a hedonistic pleasure, a quotidian routine, or a practice to be undertaken with great care and ethical consideration. The decision by the Czechs to consume particular sorts of food in particular ways thus orders them as social subjects. As Pierre Bourdieu famously wrote in *Distinction*, taste not only classifies, "it classifies the classifier" (Bourdieu 1984: 6). To extrapolate from Bourdieu, patterned modes of production can also order social groups along any number of social axes. In other words, Czech gardeners produce more than just vegetables when they choose to grow their own food: they produce cultural notions regulating post-socialist subjects' idealized behavior and relationship to the material world.

In the case of the former Czechoslovakia, Haukanes and Pine have demonstrated that the end of state socialism prompted a profound shift in the locals' understanding of modernity, "particularly in relation to the family, local identity or belonging, and the nation" (Haukanes and Pine 2003: 103). In the arena of food, this shift extended to "changing understandings of what constitute traditional and modern aesthetics and practices," especially vis-à-vis local food values and regimes. With the opening of Czech markets to foreign capital in the 1990s, hypermarkets hawking produce from all over Europe rapidly displaced socialism's centralized food system and, to some extent, Czech traditions of subsistence agriculture in private gardens. Jiřina, a retired office worker and current member of the Vidimova community garden, summarized the change succinctly:

> Under socialism, most people grew vegetables since we just had a few options for food. Then we started to import goods . . . and developers started to buy up land allotments, so people couldn't grow. After socialism people stopped growing vegetables, fruits, and there were only ornamental gardens. . . . Today, the wealthy have pleasure gardens, simply because they believe what a man grows himself is good, whereas what is in the stores is poor.

As Haukanes and Pine note, the quality of food in the late socialist period was imagined as inversely correlated with its proximity to centralized state production. Food from factory canteens and state shops was "viewed as of inferior quality and sometimes even impure, in terms of overfertilization and poor quality control," Haukanes says, while food "produced on a family's own plot or smallholding, or obtained from village kin . . . was viewed as essentially good" (2003: 108). Though many Czechs warmed to commercially available groceries after the 1990s, most continued to praise homegrown vegetables and meat as healthier and of a higher quality, bar none. Significantly, Haukanes observes that the positive appraisals by the Czechs of homegrown foods shifted away in the early 2000s from the discourse of anti-statism to that of ecological purity; in this new rationale, self-provisioning was valorized not as evidence of self-reliance, but because it was the only way Czechs could guarantee their vegetables were chemical-free and genetically "unmodified" (121).

The ecological shift Haukanes describes in late post-socialist food values aligns with Jiřina's more recent assessment of Czech's positive attitudes toward pleasure gardens and subsistence agriculture. Jiřina's opinion that Czechs believe food "in the stores is poor" however, touches on a further food ideology isolated to former socialist states: that Western corporations are intentionally foisting off subpar goods on Central and Eastern Europeans, subjecting consumers to what Bulgarian prime minister Boyko Borrisov characterized as "food apartheid."[1] Far from new, Central and Eastern Europeans' experience of being treated as second-class consumers stretches back decades. Harper notes that Hungarian consumers felt Western European companies were taking advantage of former socialist republics as early as the 1990s. As one of her participants complained: "To this day one gets the impression from the West that they don't take us seriously as partners but are just palming stuff off on us, saying, 'This is good enough for the keletiek [Easterners], this is good enough for the Hungarians'" (Harper 2005: 230).

The Czechs enduring mistrust of the multinational and corporate food regimes has prompted them to adopt an array of practices to protect themselves from gastronomic fraud. For some of my participants, bio-certification—the European equivalent of "organic"—was considered a rough indicator of food quality that consumers could rely on, but many interviewees were leery of buying bio-certified groceries designated for Eastern European markets. As one interlocutor elaborated:

> Quality means food that doesn't contain chemicals and isn't cheap . . . the Germans have dual warehouses where they keep what goes to the west and what goes to the Eastern markets . . . when I find any product that is intended only for the Eastern market, with ingredients listed just in Slovakian or Hungarian or Czech . . . I don't buy it, because to me it's clear that it's simply poor in quality. But when a product is going to England or Italy, I'll buy it because I know . . . [the Germans] cannot afford to give Western Europeans such crap.

Other participants I interviewed went so far as to drive several hours across the border into Germany for their monthly shopping trips. Shopping in the same stores as Germans, they rationalized, was the only way to guarantee groceries wouldn't be of poor quality. In circumstances where groceries provenance couldn't be ascertained, its price often stood in as an emblem of its quality. As one Czech woman summed up, "Bio doesn't mean better, but we buy it anyway."

The Czechs' mistrust of industrial food systems has even colored their perception of relatively unmediated forms of producer-consumer interactions. Pervasive skepticism of vegetables sold in Prague's farmer's markets, in particular, was another theme that emerged in the course of my interviews with local gardeners. More than once I was told that the trucks that delivered vegetables to Prague's farmers' markets were the same ones that delivered food to Tesco, insinuating that the produce sold through these fruit and vegetable stands was not local, but rather interpolated into an industrial food system duplicitously branded as "local" by conniving merchants looking to swindle honest consumers. Growing one's own food, my participants reiterated, was thus one of the few ways to ensure the provenance of produce and guarantee its quality.

Despite consumers' association of "bio," "expensive," and "German" with high-quality food, virtually all the gardeners I interviewed still equated top-quality produce with local provenance, small-scale production, and a short supply chain. As Haukanes found in her earlier study, many Czechs still see homegrown vegetables as the be-all end-all of top-quality food. However, many of my participants, particularly young gardeners, felt such high-quality produce was too labor-intensive to self-provision in great quantities. For these young professionals, the prospect of substantially supplementing their diets with self-produced foodstuffs was framed as impractical both in terms of cost and time, the effort expended too great compared to the economic rewards of wage-labor. Still, they wanted to do *something*, they related, and so had turned to growing small amounts of vegetables, herbs, chilies, or of other flavorful produce in addition to consuming bio, local, and other categories of food that they felt represented "quality" produce.

As Klein, Jung and Caldwell argue, "Market socialist and postsocialist consumers are constantly making deliberate choices that reflect their understanding of whether the present food systems are good for their health, their families, their communities, their business and their nations" (Caldwell et al. 2014: 4). Accordingly, the navigation of complex and often conflicting indicators of food quality represents to the Czechs an assertion of social and economic agency rather than a passive acceptance of exogenous food values. Their localization of environmentalist and consumer ideologies regarding "quality" food also integrates local traditions with new forms of food production. In this context, these changing processes and emerging food values all contribute to many Czechs' motivation to grow their own food—in cottages, *kolonia*, and in urban community gardens.

Colony and cottage gardens

Since before the first Czechoslovak Republic, the *chata* or country cottage has proved a respite for families struggling to get away from the grind of urban life. These small buildings, constructed over generations from an array of stockpiled or "liberated" materials, became especially important during the uncertainty of late socialism. As Holy elaborates, the "internal emigration" to countryside cottages and gardens following the suppression of the Prague Spring in 1968 reflected the significance of these spaces as shelters from state influence and the monotonous diets of centralized food production (Holy 1996: 26). In contrast to the shopping queues, limited groceries, and omnipresent fears of surveillance that characterized public life after 1968, *chaty* were spaces where Czechs could cultivate both food and family intimacy. In the thirty years between the Prague Spring and the collapse of state socialism, the number of *chaty* in Czechoslovakia tripled. Today, cottage gardens are no longer strictly necessary as sites of supplementary production yet Czechs still boast "the highest per capita number of weekend houses in Europe" with one in seven owning their own cottage or cabin (Kenety 2005). How these spaces are used, however, varies widely, with intensive food production mostly undertaken by marginally employed Czechs with the time required to do so. In many cases, cottage gardeners are elderly and often retired. Continuity of food production practices among older Czechs contrasts with the cessation of intensive food production by their children and grandchildren, and, in my observations, the use of *chaty* and *chalupy* as primarily social spaces.

In my participant observation alongside cottage owners in the Krkonoše Mountains near the northern towns of Náchod and Červený Kostelec, stark generational divides emerged in patterns of contemporary cottage use. Grandparents were far and away the most likely demographic to use *chaty* for private, intensive food production, while their children and grandchildren preferred to use these spaces for socialization and tokenized production of a select amount of highly valued, high-quality food. One of my participants, Terka, related to me that her grandfather lived at his *chata* six months in the year, where he grew potatoes, tomatoes, turnips, carrots, and all manner of vegetables in a series of greenhouses and hothouses he had built himself. A one-room, unincorporated property lacking plumbing or electricity but surrounded by sprawling garden plots, raised beds, and bean-bedecked lattices, Terka's grandfather's cottage contrasted sharply with her parents' *chata*, which they had constructed in the late

1990s as a weekend home and space for Terka and her sisters to play. This second, two-story structure with central heating, plumbing, a playroom, guest rooms and a sauna—but no gardens—was financed largely by proceeds from her family's successful import/export business. Its construction, Terka confessed, was also a nontaxable investment her father used to protect company profits.

Though neither Terka nor her parents used this second cottage for growing anything more than a few berries, her father Libor started raising sheep in the surrounding pastures after his fortieth birthday. A successful entrepreneur, Libor became interested in raising livestock after his son Matěj was born and his older children took over most of the day-to-day responsibilities of running the business he had built with his brother. While Terka's family does process one or two sheep a year for meat, they are the only family in the area who raise livestock and the cost of pasture, veterinary care, and butchering far outweigh the money saved by not buying meat from grocery stores. As such, Libor's recent interest in animal husbandry seems to be less a coping strategy for compensating for food scarcity than mode of food production that allows him to produce high-quality food for his family while reconnecting with an imagined pastoral past in a very particular way. In a similar vein, Terka's mother told me she actually hates gardening, and at most keeps a couple of raspberry bushes at the cottage so she can make jam occasionally and so her young son can see "how things grow." Terka, for her part, told me she spent little time at these cottages since her teenage years, has never gardened at either, and now makes only occasional visits to her grandfather's cottage in the summer and her parents' cottage perhaps twice a year, usually to socialize with friends.

For families living nearer city centers, *kolonia* functioned as similar site of supplementary food production and familial intimacy. Originating under Austro-Hungarian rule, these allotment gardens were once key sites for Czech smallholding. Leased from the state for a nominal fee during the socialist period, many garden allotments featured rustic huts on their land in addition to a few small seedbeds and scattered fruit trees. Though these gardens were invaluable for their occupants in the late socialist period, in years since they have come to be seen as an impediment by developers: underperforming properties occupying highly valuable tracts of urban and suburb lands. In the rough years of the early 1990s, relatively open and unpoliced *kolonia* often served as refuges for Prague's burgeoning homeless population. Today, nearly half of Prague's *kolonia* have been demolished or redeveloped, while waiting lists for remaining allotments grow longer every year (Gibas et al. 2013). At present, Prague's remaining colony gardens are predominantly occupied by older cohorts of gardeners still invested in the "productive leisure" of producing, preserving, and storing as much food as possible, either due to having more time since their retirement or as a consequence of their marginal employment. For many of these pensioners, *kolonia* like the Starý Suchdol allotment garden I visited just north of Prague have become the only year-round housing they can afford. In part because of decreasing access to colony and cottage gardens and in part because of the heightened focus upon consuming ethical, healthy, and quality foods by the Czechs, community gardens have emerged as newly popular sites of supplementary food production in Prague.

Prazelenina: An urban pleasure garden

In Prazelenina, the first community garden where I conducted fieldwork, small-scale food production and peer socialization seemed more central for most gardeners than intensive food production or overt ecological activism. Despite this, organizers frame Prazelenina's goals and origins in ways that underscore its ecological virtues and connections to the global urban gardening movement, while the gardeners themselves participate in an array of not-for-profit food activism and production activities that signal their epicurean food values and class and national identities. Founded in 2012 in the former industrial district of Holešovice, Prazelenina received widespread attention in local English- and Czech-language media as one of Prague's first urban gardens. Surrounded on three sides by the Vlatava River, the abandoned brewery where Prazelenina now sits was inundated by extensive flooding in 2002. Before the floods, the neighborhood was, in the words of one founder, "quite gypsy, with filth and shit everywhere." This racist language tacitly frames Prazelenina's reclamation of the space as an improvement, part of a broader enwhitened push toward the revitalization of Holešovice as a whole. Yet the gardeners' practices in Prazelenina indicate the site is nearer to an insular family leisure garden than a change agent for far-reaching ecological activism or extensive urban re-greening. In the course of my interviews and participant observation, it became clear that the main motive of many gardeners in joining Prazelenina was in fact securing safe green spaces for their children to play, while their secondary objectives included the production of small amounts of chemical-free produce and socialization with likeminded young professionals.

Sitting behind the high walls of the old Holešovice brewery and overlooked by a colorful block of expensive new apartments, the Prazelenina garden stands in sharp relief to the old socialist-era panel-apartments looming just across the street. Started by a loose circle of young, white-collar professionals and their friends, Prazelenina has since become a collectively governed social enterprise including many Western European and American expatriates. From an informal association of some thirty bankers, architects, and artists Prazelenina has expanded to over one hundred gardeners as of 2015. The brainchild of green architect Matěj Petránek, Prazelenina's website says the garden's particular mode of horticulture is modeled on the UN's Food and Agriculture Organization's (FAO) micro-garden's initiative, using small, one-meter square canvas bags of soil to "help low-income households improve food and nutrition security by growing their own vegetables."[2] In my own interview with Matěj, he explained that he first heard of such micro-gardens from a Scandinavian colleague of his who told him of a similar urban gardening initiative in their hometown.

As one of the few community gardens in Prague funded solely through membership dues, Prazelenina organizers are free to operate without the entanglements of corporate sponsorship. Renting lots from individual landlords rather than the city, Prazelenina is less troubled by the political agendas of fickle city councilors than other gardens who rent municipal lots at a discount. The cost of this independence, however, comes in the form of a 700 Czk annual price tag for gardeners per cubic meter of soil, some six times more expensive than other community gardens I attended and prohibitively expensive for many long-term residents of Holešovice. From a cost/yield perspective, the expense of leasing space in the garden is also somewhat impractical for intensive subsistence agriculture on the scale of Czech cottage and colony gardens. Though gardeners like Antina, a thirty-something German transplant to Prague, can and do grow potatoes, carrots, and lettuce intensively in their small patches of soil, most, like Luke, an English teacher interested in starting his own hot sauce business, instead grow small quantities of chilies, coriander, and other herbs and spices that are otherwise hard to find in the Czech Republic. "You can't get good jerk sauce in Prague," Luke explained wistfully when I asked him about the scotch bonnet peppers he had chosen to plant, "you just can't." Many gardeners also grow their vegetables at a remove, choosing to travel throughout the growing season, planting only small numbers of vegetable, or arranging for an organizer to periodically water their plants while they are away. The gardeners' decision to engage in such tokenized, small-scale cultivation of flavorful produce to accentuate their broader diet clearly evokes Bourdieu's central argument in *Distinction* and stands as a form of conspicuous production that signals their epicurean affinities as part of Prague's young, cosmopolitan middle class (Bourdieu 1984).

As much a beer garden as a horticultural space, Prazelenina gardeners also present aspects of their collective and individual identities through activities indirectly tied to food production. Retiring after their weekly weeding and watering to picnic tables conscientiously provided by garden organizers, these young professionals and parents would unwind, commiserate about work frustrations, and swap tips for improving their gardens. Over open-faced *chlebíčky* sandwiches sold by Prazelenina organizers out of a small concession stand and half liters of Únětice lager special-bought, Luke told me, because it was a preferred brand of group organizers that the local pubs wouldn't stock, gardeners found refuge in commensality with their peers. Outside of this informal socialization, organizers would also regularly host cook-outs, concerts, and movie nights till well after dark, despite repeated noise complaints made by some neighbors to the city.

Presencing their national and local affinities, gardeners would also compete in personalizing their vegetable plots in highly visible, even outlandish ways. While young parents were more likely to help their children make paper flowers or colorful nameplates to customize their vegetable plots, a few Czech gardeners constructed elaborate lattices for their garden out of hockey sticks. One of the most popular sports in the Czech Republic and a source of national pride, these enthusiasts went so far as to drape scarves and flags from their favorite local teams around their plants.

Explicitly invoking the language of ecological purity and food justice, Prazelenina's webpage stands at something of a remove from these and other everyday practices I saw enacted by garden members. Describing the garden's objectives, the "About Us" section encourages interested parties to "reject passive criticism" of the status quo and "participate in events around us." Posing the rhetorical question "Why Urban Gardening?" Prazelenina's organizers offer four interlocking justifications for joining the gardens and participating in the global urban garden movement:

1) Protože plodiny, které si sami vypěstujeme, nám budou víc chutnat, a navíc nás nebude tížit svědomí, že je někdo za námi vezl stovky kilometrů z plantáží, kde pracují novodobí otroci.	1) Because the crops we grow ourselves will be more flavorful and we won't be overwhelmed knowing our food was grown by modern-day slaves working hundreds of miles away on plantations.
2) Protože se nebudeme muset bát škodlivých pesticidů, herbicidů nebo genetických modifikací. Protože pomůžeme rozšířit městskou zeleň a oživit místní kulturu.	2) Because we won't have to worry about harmful pesticides, herbicides or genetic modifications. Because we will expand urban greenery and revive local culture.
3) Protože dáme urbanistům jasně najevo, jak chceme ve městě žít. Protože ukážeme cestu dalším lidem.	3) Because we'll send a clear message to urban planners about how we want to live in the city. Because we'll show other people the way.
4) Protože nás to bude bavit.	4) Because we're going to have fun.

"About Prazelenina," http://prazelenina.cz/o-prazelenine/

The rationale of "showing other people the way" through growing of fruits and vegetables and sending "a clear message to urban planners about how we want to live in the city" seems to be clear evidence of the logic of conspicuous production at work. Indeed, such posturing may very well be an essential survival strategy given Prazelenina's lack of formal municipal patronage. Unlike other community gardens run by established NGOs that sign multiyear leases with Prague's municipal councils, Prazelenina's independent funding model has led to enduring problems regarding space from year to year. Subject to the whim of profit-motivated landlords, Prazelenina has had to move several times since its inception. Before signing a lease with the owners of the Holešovice brewery, the organizers were abruptly evicted from their last garden when the landlord decided he'd rather use the lot for metered parking just two weeks before their contract was scheduled to be renewed. The corrugated steel fence around this old garden, festooned with hand-painted anthropomorphic vegetable brandishing signs attesting gardeners' right to non-GMO food stands as a somewhat anachronistic sight.

In point of fact, Prazelenina's organizers themselves have described the purpose of the garden as the cultivation of intimate community spaces for (some) local residents rather than the neighborhood as a whole. In a 2014 interview with Radio Prague, Prazelenina founder Matěj Petránek related that "Prazelenina is not about cultivating plants but rather good relations" (Fraňková 2014). Another group organizer, Marcela Straková described the garden as follows:

> We are a community garden. Initially it was just a place to meet our friends. We loved the idea so we decided to join. . . . We pay for the soil and make the decisions together with our friends, so for us it is more about socializing rather than about

growing.... This is a community project designed for a local community of people. The place has become very popular so a lot of people want to visit.... But we still want to keep it on a community basis. It is not a public spot. It is open to public and everybody is welcome to join us, but we make sure that everybody knows what the project is about.... Sometimes growing vegetables is not the main activity which brings the people here, they just want to do something together. (Fraňková 2014)

In the course of my own interviews with Marcella, it also became clear that she and other organizers had decided that 2015 would be the last year Prazelenina expanded its membership. In a conversation with Milan, Prazelenina's then CFO, I learned that the organization's governing council had decided to cap the membership at 100 gardening bags from 2016 onward and were actively debating whether to raise membership fees so as to finance the purchase of additional gardening supplies, beehives, and other side projects current members had proposed.

In short, the gardeners seem more interested in signaling to their immediate peers rather than urban planners regarding their emergent food values as producers and consumers. Despite the activist overtones espoused on Prazelenina's website, the gardeners' insular focus upon "taste" and socialization with a select group of peers seems more central in explaining their motivation to grow vegetables in emblematic, low-intensity ways. By growing chilies or herbs that presence emerging middle-class attitudes toward "quality" food and proper post-socialist consumption these gardeners activities align less with the FAO's food justice–focused micro-gardens initiative and more with Jiřina's allusion to wealthy Czechs' "ornamental" gardens in the early post-socialist period. Nevertheless, in this community garden, Czechs and expats with substantial economic means have found common ground with each other through communal food production. For young parents, Prazelenina is a safe green space for their children to play, a facsimile of the cottage and colony gardens many of their parents took them to as children. While it might be seen as "a bit hipsterish" by outsiders compared to other, more overtly political agriculture projects in Prague, Prazelenina nevertheless endures as a site of conspicuous food production, small-scale food activism, and cosmopolitan civil society.

Vidimova: Emerging urban commons

In contrast with Prazelenina, the Vidimova community garden in Prague's southern outskirts operates as a site of more overt ecological activism and comingled foodways. On a breezy afternoon in April 2015, one of the first warm days of the year, a mix of community organizers, pensioners, and young families converged on Vidimova to celebrate the start of the growing season. Sponsored by Kokoza, a five-year-old NGO dedicated to the "cultivation of the urban food cycle ... and the development of civil society" Vidimova's opening was covered by local news media and carefully choreographed to be part mixer, part promotion.[3] Founded in 2010 by two Czech social workers, Kokoza was initially financed by Impact Hub Praha, the Czech branch of the international Impact Hub network which promotes grassroots entrepreneurship by hosting events and leasing office space to NGOs and startups. Despite this robust NGO support, the Vidimova community garden's first season was only a modest success. While the surrounding Jižní Město suburbs are home to over 70,000 Czechs, Vidimova opened late in the season and hosted just five gardeners its first year. Now, under of the watchful eye of a local television news crew, dozens of parents gaily bantered over carefully tended campfires in the center of the garden while children cycled through workshops hosted by Kokoza volunteers. By the end of the evening, even the youngest attendees had learned to sort recyclables, plant flowers, and make their own vermicomposters. As guests trickled out, children gleefully took fistfuls of stickers exhorting them to "Maintain the food cycle!" while adults were invited become members for a modest fee. By the time Vidimova's gates closed for the night, local interest and garden membership had increased dramatically.

Afterward, I asked one organizer why so many residents now seemed interested in Vidimova compared to its first year. "It seems to me that the recent trend, or the fashion" Daniel related, "is that people opt to pay more for food that is supposedly better quality. The demand for growing food in community gardens is part of the same trend. . . . People are interested because they're community-oriented, but also because of the food itself." Daniel's observation suggests food values and community politics are converging in Vidimova, drawing interest from Czechs interested in both the production of quality foods in common spaces and the cultivation of Czech civil society.

Operated in concert by Kokoza managers, local volunteers, and a few paid garden supervisors, Vidimova is steeped in politics and enmeshed in a delicate political equilibrium. As an NGO-sponsored project, Vidimova not only created a space for Czechs in the socialist-era local housing development to regain access to green commons but also played host to a variety of workshops for Slow Foods activists, Kokoza organizers, and social enterprises affiliated with Impact Hub Praha. Funded by a 100,000-czk T-Mobile grant in 2014, the Vidimova community garden also sits on a municipal lot rented for the symbolic cost of one crown per square meter per year, drastically cheaper than the multimillion crown expense of leasing Prazelenina's lot from the Holešovice brewery. Kokoza webpage describes the organization as a "social enterprise," dedicated to promoting composting and urban gardening initiatives like the Vidimova garden; it also valorizes these gardens and gardeners for their civic virtues and argues that they "directly encourage the sharing of experiences and the development of civil society."[4] In my time as a participant in Vidimova, this cross-pollination of food values and political ideologies bore fruit in the form of seedbomb workshops, fundraisers co-hosted by Kokoza and Prague's Slow Foods Youth Network, and additional educational and environmentalist workshops for children in the area. Like all of Kokoza's gardens, Vidimova also operates as part of an ongoing job training and rehabilitation program for mentally ill Czechs who helped construct and maintain the garden grounds and facilities.

Despite these myriad activisms and partnerships, the gardeners' own diverging interests could occasionally make coordinated political action difficult. Though described in the abstract as a nexus for a several social enterprises and activist groups, on the ground Vidimova often has to navigate the sometimes conflicting needs and desires of the communities it creates. In particular, semi-structured interviews revealed that organizers' overtly environmental aims occasionally clashed with gardeners' apolitical and food-centered motives. As Vidimova's manager Kateřina related to me one afternoon, the Kokoza organizers initially envisioned the new garden as more than "just a space where people could come to grow tomatoes." In practice, this proved difficult for her to realize. "My experience is that people are much more interested in just growing food than doing things together," Kateřina explained to me. "Unless [you're] sort of pushing people into these situations, they won't communicate that much. I think [community building] is a good thing, but I don't want to force anyone just to say we have a community."

Such gardens can also inadvertently advance selective definitions of community that place active stakeholders more centrally in imaginaries of emerging civil society. On the metro ride back from the garden one day, I asked Kokoza's director Lucie what made Kokoza's gardens and supporters different from others in Prague. "There are two types of gardens here," she told me, "ones like Kokoza—community gardens where it's about community—and gardens where it's more like a service. At Prazelenina it costs more because you are paying for a service." Taken aback by this unprompted comparison I asked Lucie where she thought colony gardens fell in this binary.

"Well actually colony gardens don't fit, don't fall into either model," she admitted.

And that is something we are working on now, but it's quite hard. It's at the top of the to-do list, but it seems to always be at the top of the to-do list. We're trying to find a way to reach them, but it's tough and we don't have time. It's hard to foster cooperation between us and them.

This allusion to the broadening gulf between community and colony gardeners evinces the difficulty of finding common ground for certain sorts of political projects in post-socialist Prague. In the case of Vidimova, colony gardeners remain difficult to engage precisely because of the political nature of Kokoza's work. In this context, the gardeners' intent disinterest in community building and their focus simply upon continuing to grow food might be seen as perhaps another form of food activism, which uses the logic of productive leisure and tradition to evade political recruitment.

Conclusion

While compensating for food scarcity is no longer a primary motivation for most gardeners in the Czech Republic, changing values regarding growing one's own food have led many Czechs to join community gardens to protect themselves from suspect food regimes, connect with national traditions, and to manifest their political beliefs. Regarded warily by city councilors and often reliant upon grant funding and corporate sponsorship, such organizations have to maintain not only a complex web of administrators, volunteers, and space but also a positive public image via conspicuous food activism. The generational divide between some gardeners' quiet sustainability and conspicuous food production also points to a broadening gulf between older cohorts of gardeners for whom gardening is rooted in apolitical nationalist food ways and a younger generation of politically active and epicurean Czechs concerned with sustainable consumption of high-quality produce.

For some community gardeners, growing one's own food is a way to presence particular class identities and political sensibilities; for others, it is a means of maintaining continuity with national and family tradition. Community gardening is thus entangled in an array of food activisms which cultivate civil society, accumulate cultural capital, and deploy conspicuous production to collective and individual ends. Ultimately, Prague's community gardens are nurseries for seeds and selective imaginaries of civil society, rooted in local traditions but fertilized by global political movements, new food values, and emergent modes of food production.

Notes

1 Boffey (2017), https://www.theguardian.com/inequality/2017/sep/15/europes-food-apartheid-are-brands-in-the-east-lower-quality-than-in-the-west (March 26, 2019).
2 "FAO Microgardens Approach," http://www.fao.org/ag/agp/greenercities/en/microgardens/index.html (March 26, 2019).
3 http://www.kokoza.cz/nase-mise/ (March 26, 2019).
4 http://www.kokoza.cz/nase-mise/ (March 26, 2019).

References

Bourdieu, P. (1984). *Distinction: A Social Critique of the Judgement of Taste*. Cambridge, MA: Harvard University Press.
Boffey, D. (2017). "Europe's Food Apartheid: Are Brands in the East Lower Quality than in the West?" *The Guardian*, September 15, 2017. https://www.theguardian.com/inequality/2017/sep/15/europes-food-apartheid-are-brands-in-the-east-lower-quality-than-in-the-west.
Caldwell, Melissa, Yuson Jung, and Jakob Klein, eds. (2014). *Ethical Eating in the Postsocialist and Socialist World*, 1–24. Berkeley: California.
Counihan, C., and V. Siniscalchi, eds. (2014). *Food Activism: Agency, Democracy and Economy*. London: Bloomsbury.
Douglas, M., and B. Isherwood (1996 [1979]). *The World of Goods. Towards and Anthropology of Consumption*. New York: Basic Books.
Fraňková, R. (2014). [Radio] "Urban Gardening Takes Root in Prague." *Radio Prague*, 9 June.
Gibas, P., L. Matějovská, A. Novák, E. Rolfová, V. Tvardková, I. Valešová, and M. Veselý (2013). *Zahrádkové Osady: Stíny Minulosti Nebo Záblesky Budoucnosti?* Praha: Egmont.

Harper, K. (2005). "'Wild Capitalism' and 'Ecocolonialism': A Tale of Two Rivers." *American Anthropologist*, 105 (2): 221–33.

Haukanes, H. (2003). "Ambivalent Traditions: Transforming Gender Symbols and Food Practices in the Czech Republic." *The Anthropology of East Europe Review*, 21 (1): 77–82.

Haukanes, H., and F. Pine (2003). "Ritual and Everyday Consumption Practices in the Czech and Polish Countryside: Conceiving Modernity through Changing Food Regimes." *Anthropological Journal on European Cultures*, 12: 103–30.

Holý, L. (1996). *The Little Czech and the Great Czech Nation: National Identity and the Post-Communist Transformation of Society*. Cambridge: Cambridge University Press.

Kenety, B. (2005). "Panorama Cottage Industry: Photographing the Dreamy, Maniacal History of the Czech 'chata'" *Radio Prague*, September 15, 2005. http://www.radio.cz/en/section/panorama/cottage-industry-photographing-the-dreamy-maniacal-history-of-the-czech-chata.

Smith, J., and P. Jehlička (2007). "Stories around Food, Politics and Change in Poland and the Czech Republic." *Transactions of the Institute of British Geographers*, 32 (3): 395–410.

Smith, J., and P. Jehlička (2013). "Quiet Sustainability: Fertile Lessons from Europe's Productive Gardeners." *Journal of Rural Studies*, 32: 148–57.

Veblen, T. (2017 [1899]). *The Theory of the Leisure Class: An Economic Study in the Origin of Institutions*. Project Gutenberg. www.gutenberg.org/files/833/833-h/833-h.html.

4

Subsistence Farming in Styria, Austria

Elisabeth Kosnik

Recently, well-known Austrian agricultural scientist Andrea Heistinger (2018) published her latest book, detailing how to succeed at subsistence farming in the twenty-first century. It is certainly not the only book of this kind—the shelves in bookstores and public libraries are lined with similar publications of recent years. But it surely is thorough—a large tome of almost 500 pages, and Heistinger uses the first paragraphs to dispel any romantic notions of country life a reader might have. Instead, she insists that subsistence farming is hard work and requires a lot of time and investment, commitment involving the entire family, and collaboration. The topic not only seems to fascinate readers. Heistinger's examples of contemporary subsistence farmers in Austria, Germany, and Switzerland demonstrate that many people already attempt to live a life of self-provisioning. In this ethnographic account, I explore the issue further by discussing the lifeworlds of subsistence farmers in the province of Styria in the southern part of Austria.

Activities of self-provisioning become increasingly visible in contemporary industrialized societies, in apparent contradiction to dominant perceptions of modernity and progress. From do-it-yourself to urban gardening—as activism, hobby and lifestyle—these practices receive much attention in media as well as academia (Baier 2017; Langreiter and Löffler 2017). However, production for consumption, as well as distribution along informal networks, remains largely unrecognized as economic activities that provide food for people and instead is sidelined as unproductive labor and leisure activity (Alber and Kohler 2008; Holloway 2000; Murton et al. 2016; Roelvink et al. 2015). Yet, as Stephen Gudeman and Chris Hann point out: "Despite accelerating globalization and neoliberal markets, it is still the case in the early twenty-first century that hundreds of millions of households produce with their own labor the greater part of staples consumed by household members" (2015: 6). Subsistence farming exists in advanced market economies, providing staple foods for household members, while the assumption prevails "that only wage work and the sale and production of commodities truly feed people" (Murton et al. 2016: 4).

While subsistence farming has historic roots in Styria, because of government intervention and market forces most farmers began to produce predominantly for the market by the twentieth century (Kaser and Stocker 1987). Nevertheless, there are small-scale family farms in Styria today that produce predominantly or exclusively for

Figure 4.1 Remains of rabbit, Styria (Austria), August 2017 (©Elisabeth Kosnik).

direct consumption. Their practices for self-provisioning include cultivation, animal husbandry, and gathering wild products. Some produce their own herbal remedies, skin products, and cleaning products and provide their households with water, power, and electricity. Other activities might include such practices as composting, recycling, renovating, and repairing. Yet, the term "subsistence farming" remains indistinct, as practitioners and commentators define the practice in various ways, while the term itself invokes a range of images, from poverty to romantic country escape to anarchistic lifestyles. The issue is further complicated by the fact that people who live a rural lifestyle of self-provisioning do not necessarily refer to themselves as subsistence farmers, while others might identify with the idea rather than with the practice.

The current research grew out of an earlier study of the volunteer program World Wide Opportunities on Organic Farms (WWOOF) in Austria and New Zealand. My continued interest in practices of self-provisioning took me to several small-scale farms across Europe, and in particular around the province of Styria. I met the Styrian farmers portrayed here in greater detail through social events of the WWOOF organization of Austria and arranged to stay with each of them for a week, helping out as a farm volunteer while carrying out my research. I extend this research by including (online and offline) autobiographic accounts of Austrian, Swiss, and German authors who document their everyday lives as subsistence farmers. The four farms I illustrate in more detail below are all situated in mountainous or so-called less favored agricultural areas in Styria. They are registered as farms and are largely if not exclusively engaged in self-provisioning. The five respondents portrayed below are middle-aged parents who came to their current farms and lifestyles as adults, although through various pathways. As the ethnographic examples illustrate, the backstories of contemporary subsistence farmers in Styria and their motivations are diverse. Yet, they also share many characteristics, including their attitudes toward nature, animals, natural resources, and food.

Historic context

Historians Karl Kaser and Karl Stocker (1986: 42) define subsistence farming as agriculture that produces predominantly for the consumption of the household members. Up until the twentieth century subsistence farming was a common agricultural practice in Styria (Groier 1999; Kaser and Stocker 1986). A poorly developed road and railway system isolated especially the mountainous areas. The farming population was no homogenous group, but the majority were small-scale subsistence farmers with two hectares[1] of land or less (Kaser and Stocker 1986). Kaser and Stocker warn against romanticizing the historic living conditions on these subsistence farms, where work was hard, food was often scarce, and material standards of living were low.

For bread, a staple food of the population, farmers predominantly grew rye. This is a major difference to modern-day subsistence farmers in Styria, who rarely grow their own grain. Historically, the farmers also grew large quantities (although few varieties) of vegetables, particularly cabbage and turnips, beans and, since the nineteenth century, also maize and potatoes. The farms included orchards of apples, pears, and plums. These fruits and vegetables were popular because they kept well through the winter. Poppies were commonly grown and their seeds used for seasoning, as well as for herbal remedies. Farmers produced their own beer, wine, and cider, and collected their own honey. They kept chicken, pigs, sheep and cows for eggs, meat, and milk (Tremel 1963). The large forests of Styria were, until the mid-nineteenth century, commons that those farmers entitled to them used for grazing their livestock, firewood, and logging (Kaser and Stocker 1987).

After the First World War, intensification of farming began in Styria, like elsewhere, with new state policies trying to combat the nationwide food scarcity (Kaser and Stocker 1986). Nonetheless, subsistence farming in Styria continued and even regained its importance during and between the First and Second World War. In the early twentieth century, the life reform movement spread from Germany to Austria, in particular to members of the middle class. As a reaction to industrialization, overcrowding and poor living conditions in the cities, life reformers promoted a return to a "natural way of life" that included a range of concepts such as vegetarianism, alternative medicine, and subsistence farming based on manual labor, providing people with a healthy diet and physical exercise. Yet, only a few life reformers ever attempted this lifestyle themselves by relocating to the country (Vogt 2000; Zimmerl 2002). A large body of research has emerged exploring past and present back-to-the-land experimentations, particularly of the 1960s/1970s politically motivated movements (Halfacree 2006; Komoch et al. 2003; Marsh 1982; Sargisson and Sargent 2004; Wilbur 2013). However, respondents in this ethnographic account did not identify themselves with this tradition of back-to-the-land experiments.

Modernization of farming practices began during the National Socialist period, leading to further intensification, specialization, mechanization, and increased use of chemicals. While farmers were reluctant to give up their traditional ways of life, government policies in the 1950s moved Austria toward the so-called "Western way"— the market economy (Kaser and Stocker 1986). Over the next twenty years subsistence farming, stigmatized as backward and anti-modernist, was systematically eliminated through state policies and bank investors favoring production for the market. Food should no longer be produced for use but predominantly, if not exclusively, for sale. By the 1970s and 1980s farming in Styria had become "modern." Many small-scale farmers gave up farming as they were unable to compete on the global market, and the rural population—their workforce no longer required on mechanized modern farms—moved to the cities in large numbers (Eberhart 1991; Schermer 2015).

Informal food production has since largely disappeared off the economic records. "Only industrial food traded in formal markets counts, in this worldview, and everything else is relegated to the traditional 'subsistence' sector of the economy" (Wilk 2006: 18). Yet, some aspects of self-provisioning continued to exist even on modernized farms, like the kitchen garden—historically the sphere of the female farmer (Heistinger 2001; Wahlhütter 2011). Many women who left their family farms continued this practice where they could, in order to support their households with home grown produce. From the mid-1970s on, some politically motivated middle-class urbanites joined back-to-the-land experimentations, although with declining degrees of political engagement and community orientation over the following years (Groier 1999).

A different practice of urban-rural cooperation in self-provisioning emerged in the late 1980s, whereby farmers would lease small plots of land to urban gardeners. The farmers would prepare the soil and plant the seeds, but otherwise leave the fields to the gardeners. The idea has since spread across Austria and to other countries (Groier 1999; Heistinger 2018). With Austria joining the European Union in 1995, the government support system "shifted from producer price subsidies to agro-environmental payments and diversification measures" (Schermer 2015: 126), which can provide subsistence farmers with some additional income. The small-scale family farm, where the members of the household are predominantly engaged in producing food for their own subsistence, had become an anachronism by the later twentieth century. Yet, this does not mean that practices of subsistence farming have disappeared in Styria all together, as the following four cases illustrate.

Subsistence farming continued

Theresa (in her late fifties) spent her early childhood in a small town in Styria. When her uncle passed away unexpectedly, her father inherited the family farm. Theresa completed an apprenticeship in a nearby wildlife park, got married to a civil servant and lived in Graz (the largest city in Styria) for fifteen years. After her divorce, she returned to the family farm with her son, where her parents still lived and her unmarried brother had taken over as farmer. On their 45 hectare farm (including forest), the family produced a large amount of food for their own consumption (meat, milk, eggs, potatoes, vegetables, fruits and berries, herbs and honey), as well as providing fodder for their animals. Apart from government subsidies, they received as mountain farmers the organic milk of fifteen cows and logging provided some cash income. This was the brother's domain, while Theresa's responsibility (who also jobbed as a gym instructor in the village) was the self-provisioning of the household. Not only did she do all the housework, look after her ailing parents, cook and bake (dark bread for weekdays and white bread on Sundays, as a special treat), she also processed the foodstuffs and honey, made her own skin products, teas and a range of herbal remedies, collected wild mushrooms and herbs, and even sewed some of her own clothes, which she proudly showed to me.

Andrea (in her late forties) grew up on a small-scale farm that her parents had bought in a Styrian village. Andrea was sent to an urban boarding school when she was ten years old, where she finished high school. She continued an urban life, working as a medical assistant in a nearby town for ten years. When she got married to her parent's neighbor, also a farmer, she brought a son with her. At the time of my visit, the farm (at 1250 meters altitude and in the middle of a forest) was no longer operated commercially. The pastures were leased to neighboring farmers. Andrea's husband derived some income from logging, but, as Andrea said: "He only appreciates the material side of things,"[2] by which she meant the financial aspects of forest industry. Andrea and her husband did not share the same ideas about nature and environment, leading to tensions between them and a refusal to work together. Instead, Andrea had a part-time office job in the nearby town and occasionally ran forest education programs for children. Andrea grew and processed vegetables and herbs from her kitchen garden, and fruits from their orchard. She gathered mushrooms and berries in the forest, where she also collected other wild products, like formic acid, and produced her own herbal remedies with it, as well as other ointments, oils, and creams.

The cases of Andrea and Theresa illustrate gendered labor as an aspect of the subsistence-oriented rural lifestyle. By extension of their household and family-related duties, activities of self-provisioning became their responsibility. Feminist researchers have long explored subsistence work as "women's labor," while emphasizing its economic value (Gibson-Graham 1996; Meyer-Renschhausen 2016; Müller 2011b; Werlhof et al. 1988). Contemporary lifestyles of self-provisioning do not necessarily challenge normative practices of gendered labor (DuPuis and Goodman 2005; Wilbur 2014). This also becomes apparent in autobiographic accounts of middle-aged couples new to the lifestyle of subsistence farming who routinely adopt these practices (Dolsperg 2014, 2016; Haß 2016; Weber 2015). Yet, where family (or group) dynamics are different to begin with, subsistence work can be shared, like in Nadine and David's case. Or the entire farm might be operated by a single person alone, as in Richard's case.

After traveling the world in a caravan for almost two years, Nadine and David (both in their forties) sold their big house in Vienna that Nadine had inherited from her father. They could not bear to return to an urban life with their three children and instead bought an abandoned farmhouse with seven hectares of land and forest in

Styria. There, they grew vegetables and herbs in raised beds and a glasshouse, planted orchards with a variety of fruit and nut trees, build a fishpond, and kept chicken, ducks, four pigs and a small flock of sheep at different times. They collected wild vegetables and beechnuts in the forest, and water from birch trees. Much of their land was covered with young nut trees, which Nadine and David considered their retirement fund. They were members of the Austrian branch of Via Campesina and used to be as a registered organic farm, although at the time of my visit they were not anymore as they no longer sold any produce. David and Nadine engaged in various formal, informal, and self-employed labor: both of them worked as tutors for school children and as tour guides in a local heritage museum; David (who had a higher degree in sports science) had seasonal work as a lifeguard and produced wooden bows, while Nadine (who had studied acting for a while and worked in television for several years) now wrote self-published novels and performed as a storyteller. Their favorite occupation was to provide workshops on their farm, such as how to bake bread and weave baskets, how to use a scythe, build a mudbrick oven, and construct bows. Yet, after eight years living on their subsistence farm and trying hard to provide much of their own food, Nadine found that she did not enjoy the lifestyle as much as she thought she would. They found animal husbandry too demanding and growing their own vegetables more difficult than they had expected. Self-critically, Nadine observed: "We belong to those naïve people who imagined living on the land as the simple life."[3]

Richard (in his early fifties) grew up in the suburbs of Graz, in a house with a large garden where the family grew vegetables and kept rabbits. As a child Richard loved to be outdoors and had his own little garden. His uncle inherited the family farm and Richard enjoyed helping out at his and other neighbors' farms, although he remembered that even as a child he disliked conventional farming methods. When he got married at eighteen, he leased some agricultural land near his house, just for their own subsistence needs, while Richard worked full-time as a technician. His wife, however, did not share his enthusiasm for farming and eventually they separated. Richard lived and worked in Vienna for several years. He spent a summer in the Alps, tending cows and learning how to make cheese. When the company he worked for closed down, he received a settlement and a regular pension that allowed him to finally fulfil his long held dream and become a small-scale organic subsistence farmer. Eleven years ago he returned to Styria where he bought and leased eighteen hectares of land with two vacant farmhouses. Richard produced his own fruits and vegetables, meat, eggs and honey, preserves and teas, as well as his own herbal remedies, skin and cleaning products. He bought grain to make flour and bake his own bread with it. By selling surplus produce, seeds and saplings, and with the help of government subsidies he kept the farm going.

Getting to know my respondents and their stories, I became cautions of classifications such as modern "peasants" in Alpine regions (Harris 2005; Seiser 2012), "smallholders" (Holloway 2000), and "back-to-the-landers" (Halfacree 2006; Wilbur 2013) or *Aussteiger* in German (Groier 1999). As people move back and forth between rural and semi-urban settings, small towns and cities, it seems forced to apply—in any way vaguely defined—concepts such as "counter culture" and "traditional" farming (Halfacree 2007). Rather than drawing an arbitrary line according to how my participants arrived at a rural lifestyle of self-provisioning, I will focus on their shared experiences of subsistence farming. Yet, that does not mean that there were no differences between them. Andrea as well as Theresa, for example, who grew up on family farms, did not refer to their smallholdings as subsistence farms, despite recognizing that what they produced was almost exclusively for the subsistence of their own households. I would suggest that this is a result of historic development that stigmatized subsistence practices as backward and anti-modern, sidelining in particular women's subsistence labor as economically insignificant (Meyer-Renschhausen 2016).

In comparison, Nadine and David as well as Richard referred to themselves as subsistence farmers, displaying a positive attitude toward the term. Apologetically, Nadine described how they had given up first on animal husbandry and later on vegetable growing when they discovered, after several years of subsistence farming, that their true passion, as she described it, lay with writing and archery, which did not leave them enough time to tend to their farm. As Hilal Sezgin, a German freelance journalist and writer who moved from the city to a farm, states in her autobiographic account, extensive subsistence farming is a full-time job. Like Nadine and David, Sezgin found that her many occupations did not leave her much time for gardening. "And yet, I believe that we others also have a right to bring a little bit of this seasonal rhythm into our everyday lives, the pride (and toil) of do-it-yourself" (2011: 115; my translation). In another autobiography, subsistence farming is defined as the ability to make it through the winter with home-made produce (Dolsperg 2016). Richard related subsistence farming to production volume, expressing his definition in exact numbers. "True" subsistence farmers, he explained, would produce at least 70 to 75 percent of their own staple foods. He estimated that he produced about 50 percent, calling himself a partial subsistence farmer. However, toward the end of my stay, after many conversations, he decided that he indeed produced most of his own food, spending on average an additional €10 per week on store-bought organic food. This was necessary because his new partner, who came to stay with him every weekend, liked a greater variety of foodstuff that Richard did not produce on his farm, such as dairy products.

While self-provisioning generally refers to food produced on the farm and in the household, many of the respondents extended the notion of a subsistence-oriented lifestyle to include foodstuffs produced within the local area. Buying food produced in their vicinity took away the pressure on the individual subsistence farm to supply all the food that was needed for the household. At the same time, this practice also supported regional food suppliers. Nadine calculated, "Why toil for months for a few kilograms of mutton when there is a sheep farmer in the next village you can support."[4] Authors of autobiographic accounts of subsistence farming similarly describe how they appreciate their neighbor's free range beef (Fischer 2001), or campaign for the local supermarket to sell local farmers' produce (Moor 2011). The promotion of regionally produced products to consumers has a long tradition in Austria (Sassatelli and Scott 2001; Schermer 2015). However, participants in my research framed their support for the region in somewhat different terms than political actors and retailers would have it—as "consumer patriotism," "sustaining the rural population and a more competitive national agriculture" (Sassatelli and Scott 2001: 234). Respondents in my study *are* the rural population who make a point of buying from their neighbors, the local farmers' market, the village supermarket (that might very well belong to a multinational chain but still offer some regional products, or at least offer jobs to the local population), and participate in local exchange networks. They do so with the expressed intention to stop depopulation and the decline of infrastructure in their own home regions that would directly affect their lifestyles, their families and children, and not least the availability of food produced (and sold) in their vicinity.

At the same time, farmers' priority for buying local produce was a way to address their environmental concerns, "supporting the purchase of local seasonal foods to cut food miles" (Schermer 2015: 127). Subsistence farmers share a belief that food should travel as short a distance as possible. In this regard, terms like local and regional become fluid concepts, their range depending on the circumstances. Austrian subsistence lifestyle blogger Lisa Pfleger relays her concerns regarding the environmental cost of long-distance haulage in the introduction to her cookbook on vegan, regional, and seasonal cooking. But "regional" does not end at the national border; living far in the east, regional products for Pfleger necessarily include foodstuffs from Hungary (2014: 12). Priority is given to the nearest producer.

Living with nature

That the food they produced for themselves and their families had to be organic was taken for granted among my respondents. They all were, or used to be, registered with the Austrian organic certification body, except for Andrea who did not sell any produce. Austria's organic sector has been thriving since its beginning in the 1990s (Michelsen 2001; Sassatelli and Scott 2001; Schermer 2015). In 2018, organic farms cover 22 percent of the total agricultural area in Austria,[5] and 47 percent of consumers in Austria claim that they eat organic produce more than once a week.[6] Yet, the subsistence farmers' "farming philosophy" had little to do with organic standards for production processes and instead embraced a holistic vision of organic (Guthman 2004), as they intend to live permanently, and healthy, off their own land. This resonates with the tradition of earlier back-to-the-land experiments that embraced and developed organic farming techniques and promoted a self-sufficient lifestyle close to nature (Halfacree 2006; Vogt 2000). Theresa described how she spent a lot of time watching and listening to nature, particularly to her bees. "I don't keep the bees for their honey," she said, "but because I want to give something back to nature."[7] It was Theresa who had introduced the bees and a greater variety of plants to the farm with the intention to increase its biodiversity. Her brother shared her sensitivities toward nature and had converted their farm to organic, against their parents' wishes. The parents did not share their children's ideals and mocked Theresa when she talked about the usefulness of her bees beyond creating additional income. For Theresa, everything on the farm was to be organic. The farm animals were treated homeopathically and Theresa was in constant dispute with her neighbor who, she believed, contaminated her kitchen garden with conventional chemicals.

Richard spoke of farming as a "circular flow of energy," a self-sustaining environment where plants, insects, livestock, and humans nurture each other. The idea has roots in the organic movement, such as in Rudolf Steiners' anthroposophy (Vogt 2000). Even so, Richard stated that he did not follow any established organic farming method. He reproduced seeds and used composting and biological pest control. His farm animals recreated in natural ways. "I have my fun, why shouldn't they have their fun too?"[8] he quipped. Andrea described her own activities and aspirations for the farm as sustainable, referring to the careful use of natural resources. A friend of hers, with an interest in New Age ideas, had taught her how to "read" natural signs as oracles, a practice that was also adopted by Nadine and David. Like Theresa, Andrea described how she spent much time watching and listening to nature. She did her work in the forest and in her kitchen garden according to the lunar and astrological calendar. "You have to see the whole thing," she said, "what we plant today is for the benefit of the next generation."[9] The next generation and a sustainable future was a common concern. Theresa similarly spoke of her work on the farm as doing something for the benefit of future generations, and Richard stated: "If my children and grandchildren should ask me, not that they would because they know anyway, but if they would ask me—what did you do? I can answer them that I made a difference, in my own way."[10]

For subsistence farmers, living in close contact with nature, natural resources, and food is an important aspect of their lifestyle. A lot of the labor on subsistence farms is done by hand, in direct contact with the soil, plants, and animals—whether farmers are working in the kitchen garden or gathering chanterelles in the forest. Bodily practices also extend to other aspects, such as not shielding oneself from the sun with chemical sunscreen, walking barefoot, or sticking to a raw-vegan diet.[11] None of the four farm households I describe here had a microwave. Instead, they cooked daily meals fresh from unprocessed products. Richard expressed his dislike for the microwave in regard to his ideas of flows of energy, while using a microwave "is not cooking." Similarly, Theresa disliked all electronic household tools, but she included environmental concerns in her reasons, since many things could be done by hand and without using electricity. The main meal of the day—which in Austria is lunch—was a synchronized family meal for most of them, prepared by one or more members of the household. From growing to processing, cooking and eating, food played a significant, time-consuming role in subsistence farmers' lives.

Living-off-the-land implies leading a lifestyle according to the rhythms of nature, the weather and seasons, the growth and reproductive cycle of plants and animals. Therefore, it also implies a seasonal diet (Gross 2009; Mintz 2006). The experience of not having access to all food items at all times of the year seems particularly noteworthy to those who are new to the lifestyle. For subsistence farmers, this is a positive experience, underlining their lifestyle as close to and dependent on nature. Their diet does not so much reflect individual choice, as it consists of what nature provides. In a society over-saturated with foodstuffs, this experience marks out those committed to a rural lifestyle of self-provisioning. Even informal exchange does not necessarily provide a greater variety of foodstuffs, as Nadine observed when all the members at her local exchange scheme had the same products on offer at the same time of the year. Factors outside of human control and non-human actors can also determine the diet of the subsistence farmer. In her self-published book Cordula Von Dolsperg (2014), a subsistence farmer from Germany living in rural Sweden, writes how her diet was dictated by the attack of a hawk that slew a chicken but fled when she approached it. Not wanting to be wasteful, Von Dolsperg had the chicken for dinner.

Distrust and independence

A healthy diet of unprocessed, chemical-free foodstuffs played an important role in participants' everyday practices, and genetically modified organisms were universally rejected.[12] That the food industry does not have the consumers' best interest at heart was taken for granted by the subsistence farmers in my study. Only by producing their own food could they be sure to know what they consumed. Richard was especially candid about his distrust of the food industry, and in particular of the markers placed on food items which, he insisted, lack transparency in regard to ingredients and supply chains, quite possibly hiding health hazards, and concealing unsustainable production methods. Richards's main motivation in becoming a subsistence farmer was his wish to gain independence from the food industry. His distrust also extended to the organic label—a sentiment that other subsistence farmers share, even though they continue to buy organic as the lesser of all food industry evils. Richard has been a member of the Austrian organic association since 1994, "back when it was still really organics."[13] In particular it is the organic meat industry that he considered as insignificantly better in regard to animal welfare than the conventional meat industry. Other subsistence farmers share this perspective. They provide their own farm animals (mostly poultry and rabbits, but also pigs and cows) with free range living conditions and appropriate fodder, and slaughter their animals at the farm. Subsistence farmers in my study agreed that because of this treatment the meat was of considerably better taste and quality than store-bought produce (also Weber 2015).

For Nadine and David, the dream of living in the country came first. But once they owned a farm, Nadine said, "it just seemed common-sense to be independent"[14] by growing their own food. As Nadine's quote from earlier demonstrates, producing her own meat however became too much of an effort for them, so they chose to buy meat from a neighbor, extending her trust based on personal relationships. Where insufficient or possibly false information on goods, transactions, and actors leads to distrust, the dilemma is solved by personalizing exchange relationships (Seiser and Thalhammer 2017). Indeed, personal relationships with producers can be of greater important to health- and eco-conscious consumers than the organic label (Campbell and Liepins 2001; Darnhofer et al. 2005). Anthropologist Gertraud Seiser states in regard to Austrian farmers, how their exchange practices are based on personal relationships even if that means paying more for the goods they want to obtain. Seiser demonstrates that this is particularly true in regard to large investments that are needed to support the farm for a long time (Seiser 2012). I would argue that for subsistence farmers the same applies to their food practices. Personal health, as well as social and environmental concerns, involve a perspective of long duration and are therefore too important to be left to the food industry.

Today, consumers in Europe buy and eat food independently from nature's seasons, from weather and soil conditions, droughts and crop failures. Subsistence farmers in Styria exchange this independence from nature for independence from the food industry. At least, what they seek is a balance that suits their lifestyle, between self-provisioning and provisioning through the market. As Richard stated: "I never wanted to be a slave to the system, but I never wanted to be a slave to the farm either."[15] Activities of self-provisioning also offer independence in the sense of self-determination. For Theresa and Andrea it was in particular their work in the kitchen garden, gathering wild foods, or tending to the bees that offered them greater personal autonomy, spaces where they were left to their own devices. Historically, the kitchen garden was indeed regarded as the domain where women were utterly independent in their decisions and even found a retreat from the crowded farm household (Heistinger 2001). For subsistence farmers, similar to urban gardeners (Müller 2011a), the activities of self-provisioning also provide an opportunity to experiment with foodstuffs and natural remedies and to be creative and try out new ideas. Subsistence farming means to live and eat according to farmers' own food and nature beliefs, but also to enjoy the pleasures of a do-it-yourself lifestyle, "the sense of satisfaction to be found in one's own competence" (Mintz 2006: 6).

Conclusion

This account of contemporary subsistence farming in Styria might almost appear too positive. Indeed, subsistence farming, as respondents described it, can at times also be stressful, particularly when, as Richard expressed it, everything demands your attention at the same time. It is difficult and time-consuming work, too time-consuming as some like Nadine and David found out after several years of self-provisioning. Subsistence farmers also stated that life on the farm could become monotonous and even boring, being tied down to the farm and making it difficult to meet new people. A lifestyle of subsistence farming should also not be romanticized as necessarily a space of social equality, as some cases demonstrate the upholding of conservative gender roles, questioning the voluntary character of subsistence labor.

For subsistence farmers living in contemporary Western societies, there is in general no economic necessity for a lifestyle of self-provisioning. Subsistence farming in capitalist market societies is not a lifestyle of bare survival born out of poverty. Rather, it is a lifestyle choice based on material security (Alber and Kohler 2008). Subsistence farmers come to this lifestyle in various ways, maybe because of family ties, or because circumstances provided them with the financial capital to begin a new life. What they have in common is their choice to feed themselves and their families through production for consumption. Self-provisioning refers to food produced on the farm and in the household, although some subsistence farmers extend the notion of a subsistence-oriented lifestyle to include foodstuffs produced within the local area. This takes away the pressure on the individual farming household to produce all staple foods for themselves. Buying food from neighbors, local farmers' markets, and village supermarkets, as well as participating in local exchange schemes, supports the local infrastructure that makes locally produced food available. The concept of local, however, remains a matter of individual definition.

Self-provisioning is not a hobby for determined subsistence farmers. It is part of their reproductive activities, valued for the benefit of providing the household with fresh, healthy food grown according to the farmers' personal agricultural philosophies, providing them with the bodily experience of close contact with their food sources. Dependence on the food industry is thereby exchanged for dependence on nature's rhythms and seasons. Practices of self-provisioning in themselves can also provide subsistence farmers with a sense of independence. They find pleasure in these do-it-yourself activities that allow them to experiment and be creative, even granting them autonomy within otherwise restrictive household structures. In this sense, subsistence farms continue to exist in advanced capitalist societies of the twenty-first century, providing people with their everyday foods, and contradicting dominant narratives of modernity and progress.

Notes

1   Less than five acres.
2   Fieldnotes from research diary, August 25, 2009, my translation. All quotes are originally in German.
3   Fieldnotes from research diary, May 17, 2016.
4   Personal communication, April 6, 2018.
5   Bundesministerium für Nachhaltigkeit und Tourismus, https://www.bmnt.gv.at/land/bio-lw/zahlen-fakten/Bio_Produktion.html (accessed on April 25, 2018).
6   RollAMA Motivanalyse Jänner 2018/ AMA-Marketing, Konsumverhalten Bio https://amainfo.at/ueber-uns/marktinformationen/?L=0 (accessed on April 25, 2018).
7   Field notes from research diary, September 4, 2009.
8   Field notes from research diary, August 14, 2017.
9   Field notes from research diary, August 25, 2009.
10 Field notes from research diary, August 15, 2017.
11 Hanna Benker and Bruno Weihsbrodt, Austrian bloggers documenting their vegan subsistence lifestyle; www.issgras.at.
12 Genetically modified organisms are legally restricted in Austria, even beyond EU standards. http://www.greenpeace.org/austria/Global/austria/dokumente/Factsheets/gentechnik_FS_Gentechnik-in-Oesterreich.pdf (accessed on June 17, 2015).
13 Field notes from research diary, August 15, 2017.
14 Personal communication, April 6, 2018.
15 Field notes from research diary, August 14, 2017.

References

Alber, J., and U. Kohler (2008). "Informal Food Production in the Enlarged European Union." *Social Indicators Research*, 89 (1): 113–27.

Baier, A. (2017). "Zwischen Schattenexistenz und Utopie. Subsistenz als Inspiration für eine neue soziale Praxis." In K. Poehls, L. Scholze-Irrlitz, and A. Vetter (eds.), *Strategien der Subsistenz: Neue prekäre, subversive und moralische Ökonomien*. 14–30, Berliner Blätter. Ethnographische und ethnologische Beiträge, 74. Berin: Panama Verlag.

Campbell, H., and R. Liepins (2001). "Naming Organics: Understanding Organic Standards in New Zealand as a Discursive Field." *Sociologia Ruralis*, 41 (1): 21–39.

Darnhofer, I., W. Schneeberger, and B. Freye (2005). "Converting or Not Converting to Organic Farming in Austria: Farmer Types and Their Rationale." *Agric Hum Values*, 22: 39–52.

Dolsperg, C. von (2014). *Ohne Strom und Fliessend Wasser: Unsere ersten Jahre in Schweden*. Norderstedt: BoD (Books on Demand).

Dolsperg, C. von (2016). *Mit Ökostrom und Fliessend Wasser. Leben auf unserem WWOOF-Hof in Schweden*. Norderstedt: BoD (Books on Demand).

DuPuis, M. E., and D. Goodman (2005). "Should We Go 'Home' to Eat? Toward a Reflexive Politics of Localism." *Journal of Rural Studies*, 21: 359–71.

Eberhart, H. (1991). "Bäuerliche Alltagskultur zwischen Autarkie und marktorientierter Produktion." *Schweizerisches Archiv für Volkskunde*, 87: 28–45.

Fischer, W. F. (2001). *Das Haus am Fjord: Inselleben in Schweden*. München: Sierra.

Gibson-Graham, J. K. (1996). *The End of Capitalism (As We Knew It): A Feminist Critique of Political Economy*. Oxford: Blackwell.

Groier, M. (1999). *"Mit'n Biachl Heign." Soziokulturelle und Ökonomische Aspekte von Aussteigerlandwirtschaften in Österreich*. Wien: Bundesanstalt für Bergbauernfragen.

Gross, J. (2009). "Capitalism and Its Discontents. Back-to-the-Lander and Freegan Foodways in Rural Oregon." *Food and Foodways*, 17 (2): 57–79.

Gudeman, S., and C. Hann, eds. (2015). "Introduction." In *Oikos and Market: Explorations in Self-Sufficiency after Socialism*, 1–23, New York and Oxford: Berghahn Books.

Guthman, J. (2004). "The Trouble with 'Organic Lite' in California: A Rejoinder to the 'Conventionalization' Debate." *Sociologia Ruralis*, 44: 301–16.

Halfacree, K. (2006). "From Dropping Out to Leading On? British Counter-Cultural Back-to-the-Land in a Changing Rurality." *Progress in Human Geography*, 30 (3): 309–36.

Halfacree, K. (2007). "Back-to-the-Land in the Twenty-First Century: Making Connections with Rurality." *Tijdschrift voor Economische en Sociale Geografie*, 98(1): 3–8.

Harris, M. (2005). "Peasants." In J. G. Carrier (ed.), *A Handbook of Economic Anthropology*, 423–38. Cheltenham and Northampton, MA: Edward Elgar.

Haß, K. (2016). *Bärenspeck mit Pfeffer. Mein kleines Stück Sibirien*. München: Piper.

Heistinger, A. (2001). *Die Saat der Bäuerinnen. Saatkunst und Kulturpflanzen in Südtirol*. Innsbruck: Loewenzahn.

Heistinger, A. (2018). *Basiswissen Selbstversorgung aus Biogärten: Individuelle und gemeinschaftliche Wege und Möglichkeiten*. Arche Noah. Innsbruck: Löwenzahn.

Holloway, L. (2000). "'Hell on Earth and Paradise All at the Same Time:' The Production of Smallholding Space in the British Countryside." *Area*, 32(3): 307–15.

Kaser, K., and K. Stocker (1986). *Bäuerliches Leben in der Oststeiermark seit 1848: Band I. Landwirtschaft von der Selbstversorgung zum Produktivitätszwang*. Wien: Böhlau.

Kaser, K., and K. Stocker (1987). *Bäuerliches Leben in der Oststeiermark seit 1848: Band II. Die verspätete Revolution.* Wien: Böhlau.

Komoch, A., S. Hagmaier, and M. Kirchner (2003). "Intentional Communities in Germany, Austria, and Switzerland." In K. Christensen and D. Levinson (eds.), *Encyclopaedia of Community: From the Village to the Virtual World*, 719–24. Thousand Oaks, CA: SAGE.

Langreiter, N., and K. Löffler, eds. (2017). *Selbermachen: Diskurse und Praktiken des "Do it yourself."* Bielefeld: Transcript-Verl.

Marsh, J. (1982). *Back to the Land: The Pastoral Impulse in England, from 1880 to 1914.* London: Quarter Books.

Meyer-Renschhausen, E. (2016). "Von der Allmende zur Urban Agriculture. Kleinstlandwirtschaft und Gärten als weibliche Ökonomie." *L'Homme,* 27 (2): 73–91.

Michelsen, J. (2001). "Recent Development and Political Acceptance of Organic Farming in Europe." *Sociologia Ruralis,* 41 (1): 3–20.

Mintz, S. (2006). "Food at Moderate Speeds." In R. Wilk (ed.), *Fast Food/Slow Food: The Cultural Economy of the Global Food System*, 3–11. Lanham, MD and New York: Altamira Press.

Moor, D. (2011). *Was wir nicht haben, brauchen Sie nicht. Geschichten aus der arschlochfreien Zone.* Hamburg: Rowohlt.

Müller, C. (2011a). "Einleitung." In C. Müller (ed.), *Urban Gardening: Über die Rückkehr der Gärten in die Stadt*, 9–18, München: Oekom-Verl.

Müller, C. (2011b). "Urban Gardening. Grüne Signaturen neuer urbaner Zivilisationen." In C. Müller (ed.), *Urban Gardening. Über die Rückkehr der Gärten in die Stadt*, 22–53. München: Oekom-Verl.

Murton, J., D. Bavington, and C. Dokis (2016). "Introduction: Why Subsistence?" In J. Murton, D. Bavington, and C. Dokis (eds.), *Subsistence under Capitalism: Historical and Contemporary Perspectives*, 3–36. Montreal and Kingston: McGill-Queen's University Press.

Pfleger, L. (2014). *Vegan, regional, saisonal: Einfache Rezepte für jeden Tag.* Stuttgart: Ulmer.

Roelvink, G., K. St. Martin, and J. K. Gibson-Graham, eds. (2015). *Making Other Worlds Possible. Performing Diverse Economies.* Minneapolis: University of Minnesota Press.

Sargisson, L., and L. T. Sargent (2004). *Living in Utopia. New Zealand's Intentional Communities.* Hants: Ashgate.

Sassatelli, R., and A. Scott (2001). "Novel Food, New Markets and Trust Regimes. Responses to the Erosion of Consumers' Confidence in Austria, Italy and the UK." *European Societies,* 3 (2): 213–44.

Schermer, M. (2015). "From 'Food from Nowhere' to 'Food from Here:' Changing Producer–Consumer Relations in Austria." *Agric Hum Values,* 32: 121–32.

Seiser, G. (2012). "Kooperationen in der Landwirtschaft kontextualisiert. Ethnografische Fallstudien von der Mühlviertler Alm." *Österreichische Zeitschrift für Soziologie,* 37 (4): 385–402.

Seiser, G., and M. Thalhammer (2017). "Von der Produktion zum Austausch. Begriffe und Konzepte der Ökonomischen Anthropologie begreifen." In G. Seiser (ed.), *Ökonomische Anthropologie: Einführung und Fallbeispiele*, 56–85. Wien: Facultas.

Sezgin, H. (2011). *Landleben. Von einer, die raus zog.* Köln: DuMont Buchverlag.

Tremel, F. (1963). "Die Bäuerliche Wirtschaft." In F. Posch (ed.), *Das Bauerntum in der Steiermark: Ein geschichtlicher Überblick*, 26–34. Graz: Selbstverlag des Historischen Vereines für Steiermark.

Vogt, G. (2000). *Entstehung und Entwicklung des ökologischen Landbaus im deutschsprachigen Raum.* Bad Dürkheim: SÖL.

Wahlhütter, S. (2011). "Lokales Wissen über Boden zwischen Praxis und Theorie. Eine kulturanthropologisch-ethnopedologische Studie im südlichen Burgenland und in der Weststeiermark." *Erstausgabe* 4: 43–52.

Weber, I. (2015). *Aussteigen für Anfänger.* Einwandern im Südburgenland: novum.

Werlhof, C. von, M. Mies, and V. Bennholdt-Thomsen, eds. (1988). *Frauen, die letzte Kolonie. Zur Hausfrauisierung der Arbeit.* Reinbek bei Hamburg: Rowohlt.

Wilbur, A. (2013). "Growing a Radical Ruralism: Back-to-the-Land as Practice and Ideal." *Geography Compass*, 7 (2): 149–60.

Wilbur, A. (2014). "Back-to-the-House? Gender, Domesticity and (Dis)empowerment among Back-to-the-Land Migrants in Northern Italy." *Journal of Rural Studies*, 35: 1–10.

Wilk, R., ed. (2006). "From Wild Weeds to Artisanal Cheese." In *Fast Food/Slow Food: The Cultural Economy of the Global Food System*, 13–27. Lanham, MD and New York: Altamira Press.

Zimmerl, U. (2002). *Kübeldörfer. Siedlung und Siedlerbewegung im Wien der Zwischenkriegszeit.* Vienna: Österreichischer Kunst- und Kulturverlag.

Part Two

Calculating Values

5

The Moral Price of Milk: Food Values and the Intersection of Moralities and Economies in Dairy Family Farms in Galicia

Bibiana Martínez Álvarez

Introduction

In April 2015 EU milk quotas that assumed control of the production came to an end. This meant the liberalization of the dairy market. From this moment, producers from across Europe started a series of protests and demonstrations. Among them small dairy farmers in Galicia, a region in the northwest of Spain. These Galician farmers are the center of my research.

My aim in this chapter is to analyze, through the study of these protests that occurred in Galicia as a result of the elimination of milk quotas, the different forms of value that these farmers mobilize. The study of this milk price crisis reveals both power relations and economic dynamics that hamper the productive process of small family farms and even jeopardize their survival, revealing the difficult relation that they maintain both with the dairy industry and with the institutional context that regulate their activity.

I use the work of J. C. Scott (1976) and related approaches (Edelman 2005) based on the notion of moral economy to examine how different stakeholders define and negotiate concepts associated with food values and food ideology, such as just price, quality and sustainability. Through the use of these concepts, it will be possible to see moral values as central to the definition of economic practices.

The results presented in this chapter are part of my larger research project which explores the tensions among different concepts of sustainability (economic, social, and environmental) as well as the difficulties and contradictions in the economic relations of small dairy farms. These are family farms, from small to medium size (around 50 to 150 cows), which have experienced profound transformations in the last half of a century as they moved from being part of subsistence polycrop farming to operating under a market-based productive logic.

Several historic milestones are essential to understanding the transformation of these farms. One of them was the Green Revolution, which took place during the developmental period of the Franco dictatorship, and brought about the "modernization" and specialization of agrarian productive systems, as well as an obsession with the increase in productivity. Another important milestone was joining the European Union, which involved very important changes that would transform the entire productive process of these farms.

I carried out fieldwork with these family dairy farmers between 2013 and 2015, documenting the protests and demonstrations that were occurring in Galicia due to the social upheaval created by the fall of prices following the liberalization of the sector and the elimination of milk quotas. I undertook in-depth interviews, participant observation, and happen-chance conversation with farmers and other relevant stakeholders in the dairy sector. At present, the farmers that my research focuses on are struggling to survive in the dairy sector, especially after liberalization policies and the end of European milk quotas in 2015. Since then, one family farm is disappearing per day in Galicia.

Milk price crisis and the just price

It's 2015. August is almost over. After a whole summer of tensions and social unrest among farmers due to the sudden drop of milk prices following the elimination of the EU milk quotas, I am spending some time in one of the Galician family farms that are part of my research. It is Amelia's dairy farm, of small-medium size and located in the interior of the province of Coruña. This farm is owned by two young women who are sisters. Three older family members (two women and one man) also live there, and despite having retired, they contribute a great deal to farming work, especially Amelia, the mother of the sisters. I am told that a big *tractorada*—a demonstration where farmers block the street with their tractors—has begun in Lugo, one of the main urban centers in Galicia and head city in a primarily farming province. My informants feel gloomy and pessimistic about it. The main demand of those taking part in these demonstrations in Lugo, and elsewhere in Galicia, is a just price that would allow them to have a decent life and to continue being farmers. To this end it is necessary, they argue, to create a state-based mechanism of mediation that would guarantee the adequate negotiation of prices between the farmers and the industry.

In dairy farming, every day is a work day. There is no time for resting, no chance to take a day break. Day after day, and during the whole year, work never ends. In the evening, after a long day of work, in addition to the usual preoccupations (getting their subsidies paid, dropping milk prices, new and growing requirements from the government and the European Union), new ones arise: those deriving from the tensions and protests that have been affecting the milk sector for the last couple of months. Thus, when the news arrived at Amelia's farm on the first Friday of September, saying that the participants of the *tractorada* in Lugo had decided to continue with it indefinitely, it was met with mixed feelings: both hope and unease. On the following Monday, farmers are still in Lugo, blocking the city with their tractors. Once the work is finished at Amelia's farm, Julia, Angela, and I decide to go into the city to see what is happening. When we arrive, a large number of farmers are coming together. It's getting dark but more and more tractors are joining the *tractorada*, coming from other parts of Galicia. People on the streets applaud the passing tractors, and many farmers cannot help feeling emotional. They say they have never felt such kind of popular support. But despite this, there is a generalized feeling of tension and pessimism. They fear being on the brink of an unstoppable process that began with the elimination of quotas, when the industry started to drop the price paid to producers. To understand this situation and these feelings, we must look at the context where the EU milk quotas first appeared as well as the history of the milk industry.

The process of implementing milk quotas, which started in 1993, created a great deal of controversy throughout the Spanish state, and in particular in Galicia. The countries that were among the biggest producers in the European Union imposed on smaller producers such as Spain a quota of 4.5 million tons per year (which later on went up to 6.5 million). Yet the total annual demand of milk in Spain was 9 million tons. This forced the country to import milk from others with biggest surplus in milk production.

In Galicia, which produces 40 percent of the total milk in the country, this process was marked by a lack of information and growing fears among farmers that the application of milk quotas would mean higher agricultural taxes for them. This fear may have had roots in past experiences and struggles, such as the important protests during the 1970s to refuse state imposition of higher taxes for the Agrarian Social Security. Although for different reasons, both issues—the lack of information and the fear among farmers—caused the artificial manipulation of data on milk production not only by farmers but also by the dairy industry and other relevant stakeholders. As a result, estimates of production capacity, which was used as a reference for the designation of milk quotas, dropped. This caused the assigned quota to become much lower than the actual production capacity.

This manipulation of production capacity generated the need for large investments by the producers to purchase a bigger amount of milk quota. In addition to this purchase, farmers also found a way to either rent or transfer quota between different producers. This process intensified just before quotas were removed in April 2015, mainly because the amount of quota of producers was the reference that industries would have in order to know how much milk should be collected. In fact, the quantities of milk delivery that are reflected in the contracts between industry and farmers are based on supplies made in the last two years. In addition to people who would transfer or rent quota for temporary use, there was also the possibility of keeping the subsidies related to that quota. Yet sometimes producers would transfer quota for other reasons, such as in cases of farms that were being dismantled.

In the months prior to the elimination of the milk quota, the dairy industry in Galicia started to lower the price in the contracts offered to the farmers. They threatened not to collect the milk of farmers who refused to sign these contracts and accept lower prices. At that time, the price of milk in Galicia was already the lowest in Spain. This situation was exacerbated when the quotas came to an end on March 31, 2015, generating a profound sense of uncertainty and unease among farmers, since they felt weak and vulnerable as they could not negotiate with the industry.

This feeling was partly due to existing agreements among big dairy companies, which had been taking place for years. In these agreements, the companies fixed milk prices and parceled out milk collection areas between themselves, leaving farmers without the possibility of changing companies if they were not satisfied with the conditions.

To understand the origins of this situation, it is important to know some details of the history and structure of the dairy industry in Spain and in Galicia. The development of this industry started during the first three decades of the twentieth century. However, due to the civil war and the postwar period, in the 1950s the degree of commercialization and transformation was still very low; most of the milk was produced in family farms for self-consumption. The few existing industries at that time were mostly dedicated to the processing of milk products (such as butter and cheese). It is also in this period when foreign companies, such as Nestlé (which was already present in other regions in Spain), began to operate in Galicia and to promote a more market-oriented form of milk production (Iturra, 1988: 39).

There were two other historic milestones in the dairy sector in this decade. The first was the creation of the Dairy Plan (*Plan de Centrales Lecheras*) in 1952, which introduced the prohibition of selling raw milk in populations with more than 25,000 inhabitants and promoted the supply of pasteurized milk by allocating its production to dairy industries—small companies that would process and sell the milk, but would not produce it. This plan fostered the creation of small dairy industries in areas of consumption outside the traditional areas of production. These small industries became the leading collectors of milk and began to compete fiercely with each other and with larger dairy products industries (butter and cheese mostly) (Langreo Navarro, Alicia, 1995). Alongside the implementation of this plan, growing consumption of milk was causing considerable shortfalls. This revealed that the small-scale form of milk production in family farms, which was dominant in the north of Spain (the main area of production historically, where Galicia is located), was unable to meet the demand of milk. Import of milk from abroad began, but only through the dairies.

The second milestone in the dairy sector in the 1950s occurred as part of broader changes caused by the Stabilization Plan of 1959: a set of economic measures launched by the Franco regime to promote the industrialization of the country, which caused a mass demographic move from the countryside to the cities. This period (early 1960s) brought about a growing commodification in the context of family farms (with regard to the selling not only of milk but also of the entire productive process), which ensured a growing presence of transnational companies (from the agro-industry in general, both supplying and processing) and the progressive dependence on them. Although this plan caused the revitalization of the dairy sector, it also subordinated it to the interests of the agro-industry. Alberte Martínez López in *Terra e Progreso* (2000) notes how, unlike what happened in the first three decades of the twentieth century (the period in which the process of modernization was carried out by farmers associations), the modernization process that started in the 1960s was led by industries (from the 1980s onward, these industries were mainly of foreign capital) (2000: 373). The transformation that occurred in the dairy sector in Spain and in Galicia meant that the work carried out in family farms was relegated to just the initial stages of the productive process, disconnecting these farms completely from the processing and the supplying of the product.

Since the postwar period, family farms have constantly increased the volume of milk sold to the processing and supplier industries, leading to a growing dependence and more complex relationship between small farmers and the dairy industry. Currently, this relationship could be defined as an oligopsony, wherein a small group of buyers (the industry) has the power to control prices and volumes of production, generating a situation that is disadvantageous for the milk producers. Among other reasons, this power and control derives from the prohibition on selling raw milk in Spain.[1] Producers do not have the resources to sell pasteurized milk directly to consumers (bypassing the industry) because most Galician family farms are already heavily indebted as a result of the advance purchase of milk quotas, among other reasons.

Contracts are one of the most controversial issues in the relationship between the dairy industry and the farmers. This issue emerged repeatedly in the producers' conversations during my fieldwork. For them the way these contracts are managed by the industry show the producers' low capacity for negotiation. During fieldwork, I was able to observe regularly hard and frustrating negotiations of contracts, which caused anger, disappointment, and a considerable strain sometimes, especially when the employee of the dairy industry arrived with the contract for the farmer ready to be signed, where they had already decided on the price of milk unilaterally.

It is important to note that the use of this kind of contract was not compulsory in Spain until 2013. The obligation to sign a contract between farmers and the industry appeared as part of the Milk Package (*Paquete Lácteo*)[2] during the negotiation of the new Common Agricultural Policy (2014–20), to compensate milk producers for the elimination of quotas. These contracts were meant to end the anachronistic way that the relationship between farmers and the industry was regulated up until that point.[3] In August 2013, I was at one of these family farms when they received the first standardized contract from the industry. They did not feel enthusiastic about this because the new situation failed to give them a stronger capacity to negotiate prices. Despite the promise of a fairer contract, it turned out that prices were fixed in advance by the industry without consulting producers. This has been an important bone of contention since the industry can threaten producers by not buying their milk if they do not accept such fixed price. Moreover, even if the price is usually detrimental to the interest of producers, the industry knows that, as above mentioned, producers don't have the possibility of changing companies if they are not satisfied with the conditions imposed on them because of internal agreements in the industry.

Another conflictual issue that generated frustration among my informants was the duration of this standardized contract. At first, it was expected to last for one entire year but this goal was never met. However, the actual contracts turn out to be for less than a year, usually for three months only. Farmers were left speechless when they first encountered this, because it created the same uncertainty as the previous, non-standardized contracts. Another similar trick was introduced by the industry, especially after April 2015 when the milk quotas ended. Farmers unions start denouncing that some industries were offering one-year contracts for 20 cents per liter, and once farmers rejected it because of being extremely low, the dairy industry counter offered with a three-month contract for 26 cents. After the protests in 2015 because the end of the quotas, a new standardized contract appeared in 2016 that forced the industry to maintain their agreement with farmers for a minimum of one year. Despite this, the industry found new instruments to release itself from such obligation, such as the "voluntary renunciation" clause, whereby farmers agree on a shorter duration of the contract.

For years, agricultural unions and producers have denounced the passivity of the state with regard to these agreements among the big dairy companies. They argue that the state, which has the responsibility to ensure that the industry offer contracts to farmers, has not introduced any mechanism to guarantee that these contracts are properly negotiated. The state should therefore be a mediator to avoid having contracts between the industry and the farmers arranged unilaterally, as has actually happened.

In June 2015, three of the major industries in Galicia ceased to collect milk of several producers arguing that the required quality standards were not met. The tension was growing in the sector. The politicians from town councils in the regions with bigger productions carried out meetings to find a solution. The main agricultural unions together with organizations of producers, political parties, unions and other social organizations created the Platform for the Defence of the Dairy Sector. From this time until mid-September demonstrations and protests in the form of *tractorada* took place, including blockades by farmers in major industries and logistics centers to prevent the transportation of milk and dairy products. Attempts to reach an agreement were also made by milk producers, dairy industry, distribution companies and the government, which did not conclude satisfactorily for the producers.

The main claims of farmers throughout this process hinged on the necessity to create a free and public mediation system. This system would ensure that the selling agreements no longer reflected only the interest of big corporations. Above all, what farmers were demanding was the payment of a just price (*prezo xusto*) for the milk that they produce. This just price is the price that should permit them to live their life with dignity and maintain their way of life in rural areas. As one of my informants pointed out in an interview, this way of life in Galicia is really important not only "as an economic, but also as a social model." In fact they consider the situation of the dairy sector in Galicia as a "social disaster."

The *prezo xusto* is not a new demand for these farmers. They have used it constantly to protest against the dependence that, in their opinion, Common Agricultural Policy subsidies entail. And even before, during the 1970s, farmers sought to guarantee minimum prices to cover production costs. With the concept of just price, a certain contradiction of the term "value" is also expressed; one that addresses the tension between what, in such context, is considered market value and social value. On the one hand, farmers talk about their dependence on market-based notions of value. On the other hand, they point out the need for this income (obtained via the market) to cover the reproduction of the family and the environment. So justice or equity of price obtained in the market should not be established, in their view, only in terms of the market, but also in terms of the social sphere.

This ambiguity and ambivalence was present all the time when I was doing fieldwork during the protests in Galicia, even if it is not at all easy for Galician farmers to talk about price in general or to stick to one single definition, as they usually could talk about price in terms of market or in terms of subsistence (or social justice) depending on the context. What farmers consider just price should be seen in the context, not as a free market price, but as a market price managed or controlled, as Polanyi noted (2014). In the same way, analyses around Thomas Aquinas ideas suggest the possibility of combining market price and subsistence price to establish a just price. Factors such as labor and expenses are still central to this analysis, but also "the representation of human need and utility" and the importance of price for the continuity and reproduction of society as a whole (Baldwin 1959).

The concept of "just price" used in the demands of the farmers clashes with the other key concept that developed during the price crisis after the elimination of the milk quotas: the concept of "sustainable price." This new concept is used mainly by the central and regional governments, and also by other relevant actors in the context such as the dairy industry and distribution companies. It appeared mostly in the moments when all actors in the sector were gathered together to carry out pre-agreements and agreements that guaranteed a solution to the situation of milk price crisis. At first, during the pre-agreements where farmers were looking for a guarantee minimum price by law, this sustainable price was defined in a vague way, as a price that would guarantee the end of production below the cost price. But between this pre-agreement and the final agreement (which in the end was not signed by the main agricultural unions), the National Commission of Markets and Competition (CNMC) started saying that it was not reasonable to prohibit or criticize selling at prices that would be lower than the costs of production, because in certain situations this could encourage competition and even bring benefits to the consumer. These statements of the CNMC were reflected in the final agreement, in which initial allusions at prices covering production costs disappeared and were replaced by something as vague as payments of the industries should contribute to the "sustainability" of farms.

Throughout this process, farmers considered that this "sustainable price" was not defined clearly, and that it was used by the government in a way that the dairy industry and distribution companies could eventually avoid to ensure a fair minimum price. This situation, in which the concepts of "sustainable price" and "just price" are opposed to each other, reflects an important tension between economic and social sustainability, since both concepts are based on completely different and opposed moral universes in which moral values of farmers are completely different from their "antagonists," using Scott's parlance.

Farmers' "antagonists" are in this case the dairy industry and the state. The use of the "sustainable" concept in this context (both for the concept of "sustainable price" and for the idea of the "sustainability" of farms) is based on the idea of a price that ensures the existence of farms that supply the market and consumers with the product, without specifying if these must be family farms or, on the other hand, big farms that produce in an industrial way. While with the use of the concept of "just price," farmers are claiming the need of a price that allows them to live with dignity for what they produce, while also enabling the reproduction of their domestic groups as well as their particular way of life, which is present in a relevant way in the Galician rural context.

Furthermore, the process of liberalization of the milk market through the elimination of quotas unearth another underlying process: the attempt to move milk production from Galicia to other areas in the Spanish state. This relocation would be made to places of the state that are oriented toward industrial production and farms closer to the main centers of consumption, for example, Andalusia (south of Spain). This would eliminate a production model such as the Galician one which is based on small family farms. This is deduced primarily from the frustrated attempts to negotiate a just minimum price, and from the vague way in which both the government and the industry defined the concept of sustainable price, which mainly harms farms of smaller size (family farms) with lower production capacity, which does not allow them to survive under current prices.

Another evidence that suggests that there is an attempt to relocate and re-orientate production toward an industrial model is the implementation of government subsidies, arising specifically out of the context of this crisis. In these the bottom-line profitability (for farms) that determine the amount of subsidies to be received by a producer is based on a model that varies according to the geographical area of the country. In this model, Andalusia (with an important number of big industrial farms) is the region which receives a larger amount of subsidies and Galicia receives fewer in spite of being, as explained above, the community that produces more milk across the state.

Quality

Although milk quality was not an important bone of contention in the recent milk price crisis, it is nevertheless a key concept to understand conflicts between various stakeholders in the dairy sector. The quality of milk produced in family farms is defined very differently by the actors involved. Quality is also one of the areas where economic activity is regulated by procedures that go beyond price. Yet, at the same time, within the dairy sector, quality is directly related to the price paid to the producers. The analysis of this concept also connects with certain food values.

Convention theory is essential to analyzing these quality issues. This economic theory considers productive activity as a form of collective action that depends on the coordination of different entities within some framework for action or convention. Marie-Christine Renard (2003) considered quality as an endogenous and social construct that contributes to coordinate the economic activity through two routes: on the one hand, through the introduction of collective institutions that established rules or standards for the quality, and the means to hold them, and on the other hand, through the recognition of social links among the different stakeholders that allow them to negotiate and communicate.

In the context of family dairy farms in Galicia, the relevant stakeholders that establish rules and standards for quality are mainly the state and supranational institutions (regional, state and European authorities), industry (dairy, but also biotechnologies that facilitate genetic improvement of livestock), and associations at both the regional and state level, on the genetic improvement of livestock. They, along with farmers, negotiate the quality of milk. These negotiations are carried out among different conventions around quality and these are not exempt from power relations.

Marie-Christine Renard (2003) in her article distinguishes different types of conventions around which quality is negotiated and does so by taking the types of coordination that Bertil Sylvander uses to explain the different ways of defining quality in the agri-food sector. These types of coordination include (a) industrial coordination, based on standards, objectified rules, and test procedures; (b) domestic coordination, focused on face-to-face relationships and trust; (c) civic coordination, which is based on the adherence of groups of actors to a set of collective principles that structure their economic relations; and finally (d) market coordination or coordination through the laws of market, that is to say basically through mechanisms of prices.

In the context of conflicts and disputes studied, although there is also this constant negotiation and re-definition of quality, power relations, as described by Renard, occur among the different conventions, most notably within the industrial convention, commercial or market convention, and domestic convention. Among these, domestic convention is the one that has greater difficulties to channel their interests, given the imposition of quality criteria of the other two. To define the relationship between these three types of conventions, it is first necessary to explain why actors are represented and how they are coordinated.

The domestic convention is represented within the Galician dairy sector by the farmers. Despite not showing a clear definition of quality, from their conversations and ideas around it, I have been able to observe that the issues to which the farmers attach the greatest importance: (a) the possibility of providing the consumer with a product that is "healthy and clean" and which is in optimum conditions for consumption; (b) a clear traceability, so that the origin of the product can be known and consumers are aware that the milk they consume comes from a farm where a family tries to make a living by producing food in the best possible way.[4] In a way, this view is opposed to industrial production, since the concept *da casa* (products that come from a domestic group, a home which is also a farm where milk is produced) is valued as the ideal origin of food.

Industrial conventions, as mentioned above, are based on objective standard test procedures, and are represented in the dairy sector by different actors that are located in the dairy industry and in different institutions, in most cases of public character, or officially recognized organisms. Within the public institutions, both the regional and state authorities are relevant in the industrial conventions. However, the most relevant agent has been the measures implemented by the European Union (especially those in place at the time Spain joined the European Union), and the changes in sanitation that try to promote certain concerns for hygiene and healthiness. In addition, these conventions are also endorsed by the extensive legal regulations at the regional, national, and European levels. These legal regulations contain numerous rules and standards that prevail in the definition of the quality of milk. Within the officially recognized organizations we find those that support the abovementioned standards, such as

LIGAL.[5] Furthermore, various organizations recognized by the European Commission on Agriculture develop programs aimed at livestock genetic improvement.[6] For this purpose, one of the main mechanisms that they use is milk testing (Control Lechero).

Milk testing is a set of actions aimed at the genetic evaluation of dairy breeders to improve milk production by systematically checking the quality of milk produced and its components. It is important to emphasize that livestock farmers that undergo this test also had in the past the possibility of obtaining points to benefit from subsidies from the Common Agricultural Policy. The product is analyzed in LIGAL, and this analysis precisely focuses on the elements related to quality that are relevant for the standards used by these institutions as well as by the dairy industry which are proteins, fat, bacteria, and somatic cells.

The dairy industry is the last of the stakeholders who coordinate and evaluate quality in the framework of the Galician dairy sector through industrial conventions. But it also does this from commercial or market conventions, since it uses precisely the standards endorsed by public institutions and by officially recognized organizations, although by setting prices in relation to standards for proteins, fat, bacteria, and somatic cells. That is, the evaluations that the dairy industry carry out on quality focus on the price and the commercial quality of the goods. Based on this, the price paid to farmers for the milk they produce varies according to the levels obtained in these four elements on which the quality standards used hinge on. Both fat and protein means better price for the producers if the concentration of these elements in milk is higher. The levels of bacteria and somatic cells should be low, as they could mean a decrease in the price paid for the product. Premiums can also be granted if these levels are very low.

Taking into account these characteristics of industrial and commercial conventions, it is easy to understand their dominant position and the tensions with domestic conventions. Despite not expressing a clear definition of quality, Galician farmers highlight the impossibility of finding other ways of measuring quality, other than via industrial and commercial conventions. They feel forced to follow these two conventions under premises that they do not understand and which they find certainly arbitrary and guided mainly by a search for economic benefits.

In a conversation with an employee of the dairy industry, when asked about quality, he responded with a technical language and focused on standardization. He explains that the standards are those that are reflected at the national level and gives some detailed figures, adding that the less bacteria the better. Finally, he relates the quality of milk to productivity: "Farms are becoming larger, therefore there is better milk." Most farmers do not agree with this idea, and often relate quality to the management and feeding of animals. They argue that the intention of dairy companies is not primarily the search for quality, but commercial interests and the pursuit of profitability. That is why farmers usually point out that being at a suitable point in the collection route of the cisterns that carry the product to the processing plant is one of the key criteria for dairy industries when they select the farms supplying them with milk.

The clash between domestic conventions and industrial conventions and, above all, commercial or market conventions, can be deducted, among other things, from the persistent insistence of the farmers that the interest of the dairy industry in quality is mainly focused on other issues that have more to do with the market. One producer stated, "I believe the industry think in profitability and nothing else." Another elaborated, "There was a time when quality was one thing, and now it is something else. . . . Now is not about quality but rather commercial interest." Generally, farmers claim that the industry requires quality levels that directly and arbitrarily influence the price paid to producers, but these quality standards are not reflected in the middle and final part of the chain. They believe that industrial processing reduces their milk's properties and content. On many occasions, I have heard them comment that *cartón* milk (milk sold in Tetra Paks) in supermarkets is like water and has no taste. But they also point out that the quality requirements that must be met as producers, which determine the price paid, do not correlate with differences in price and product differentiation when the milk is sold in supermarkets.

It is important to keep in mind that, despite feeling that they do not fit into the system of standardization created within the framework of industrial and commercial conventions, and despite finding them arbitrary, for these farmers there is also a continuous "in and out." They are routinely governed by these industrial and commercial conventions and they use them in day-to-day work, but these are intermingled with domestic conventions and their own quality standards. In the area of the dairy sector in Galicia, despite links between different quality conventions, these are not exempt from power relations.

With regard to food values in the context of milk quality, we can conclude that quality is a contested issue that embodies the different values that underpin the main demands of farmers. Quality makes reference to the origin of the product (a product that is *da casa*, which means something produced in a family farm, and not industrially) and this has important implications: it means the survival not only of the family farms but also of a particular livelihood that permits the survival of rural communities. This kind of value collides with those ideas of quality from commercial and industrial perspectives which are linked to standardization. Because they are directly linked to price, farmers consider these values as something negative that only seeks the maximization of economic benefits.

Sustainability

Sustainability is another important concept in the context of these family farms and their disputes with other stakeholders. The analysis of sustainability must be framed not only within the tension between the three types of sustainability (economic, social and environmental) but also with regard to how farmers define this concept vis-à-vis their own idea of a sustainable livelihood. To understand these different issues, we need to focus on the vision that farmers have of their work in relation to nature. Farmers view themselves as caretakers of the environment, and this connects with ideas of a common good. As one farmer, Antonio, says: "In spite of what politicians say, we are the ones that care for the environment, if we have to leave, everything will disappear."

This form of understanding human-environment relations are entangled in an institutional context in which Common Agricultural Policy (CAP) policies, among others, try to combine a competitive agriculture with an extensive way of producing food that is respectful of the environment and supported by family farms. This model is an unresolved contradiction for farmers because they are perfectly aware, as McMichael puts it, that "there is a substantial distinction between appropriating green practices into current political-economic structures and developing methods of social production driven by an ecological, rather than a market principle" (2011: 804).

Another dimension of care relates to caring for the family (the household) and the rural community. This makes social and environmental sustainability to be understood somehow as an inseparable unit. If the environment deteriorates there will not exist the possibility of maintaining the care of the family and of the community. This takes us to the field of economic sustainability. Economic issues are central to these family farms as a key element to maintain both their way of life and livelihood while they cope with the reproduction of the household; these are the elements that farmers really value. Regarding the way of life, they value the quality of life in rural community as opposed to the urban environment: a quality of life that allows them to reproduce and take care of the family while they carry out the production tasks to get the farm off the ground. They insist that this way of life permits them to have more time for raising up their children and "live life" in general.

In the context of these farms, such complex idea of sustainability—related to values like the care of the environment but also of the family and the rural community— underpins the concept of *prezo xusto*. This is because, for these farmers, a *prezo xusto* is the tool that would permit them to live life with dignity and maintain their way of life in rural areas.

As I explained above in the just price section, the conflict that arose in the protest after the elimination of the milk quotas also reveals the different food values that the stakeholders involved give to the concept of sustainability. The clash between the concepts of "sustainable price" and "just price" reflects the tension between two moral universes (Booth, 1994). From the point of view of the farmers, the values that move them in the production of food are the search for the social reproduction and the maintenance of their way of life. On the other hand, they consider that the values that move the food industry and the authorities are the maximization of economic benefits and the possibility of industrializing food production.

In short, what we can see is a parallelism between the issues analyzed with regard to different views of sustainability and those analyzed in the context of different views of quality and price. In sustainability, like in the other two concepts analyzed, the notions held by small family farms, in opposition to the notions of other stakeholders, are linked to the social reproduction of these small households and, more broadly, of their way of living in rural Galicia. It is a dispute connected to the power relations between groups that defend different social models: one that wishes to preserve their current way of living, and other that wants to maximize economic benefits, regardless of their social impacts.

Conclusion

The milk price crisis reveals certain food values in the context of family farms in Galicia. The center from which these values radiate is the claim of a just price that should permit these farmers to live life with dignity and maintain their way of living in rural areas. These ideas are also present through a central element in the context of these family farms, which is directly related to price: the quality of milk. Both price and quality shows the clash with other values present in the Galician dairy sector. Through these other values, represented mainly by the dairy industry and regional, state, and European authorities, it becomes clear how their primary intention is the pursuit of productivity and the maximization of economic benefit through the industrialization of food production.

A third key element that comes into play in the analysis of food values is sustainability. Like quality, sustainability is also directly related to price, and this relation is embodied, as described above, precisely in the clash between the concepts of "just price" and "sustainable price" that was revealed during the protests that took place during the milk price crisis after the elimination of milk quotas in 2015. The use of the term "sustainable" here is based on the idea of a price that ensures the existence of farms that supply the market and consumers with the product, without specifying if these must be family farms or big farms that produce in an industrial way. But for these family farms the concept of sustainability, seen from a social point of view, cannot be separated from the concept of "just price." This is because they understand that only just price allows them to maintain their way of living, while preserving the rural environment and also avoiding what they consider not only an economic but also a social disaster: the disappearance and extinction of family farms. These ideas are clearly visible in the words of one of these Galician farmers: "What is valuable to me is to have more time to live life (*hacer la vida*), and live it with dignity. For that you don't need to produce like a madman. I think the ideal is that you are able, more or less, to live with what you have; to follow, in some way, the cycle of life." In short, the values— maintaining their way of living and the continuity of the rural community—which they oppose those of the industry, the state or CAP are defended by what farmers consider their main claiming tool: the just price.

Notes

1   It is important to note that the Spanish government is currently finalizing a measure (since 2017) to adjust the direct sale of meat and raw milk.

2   The Milk Package is an instrument created in 2009 in response to the crisis that was affecting the milk sector at that time. It consists of series of measures that aimed to stabilize the sector.

3   Before 2013, the industry used non-standardized contracts or even oral and informal agreements. In fact, farmers usually ignored the amounts that they were going to be paid per liter of milk in advance.

4 Farmers usually consider that, above all, the dairy industry makes it difficult for both issues to be implemented properly. They believe that, on many occasions, it is the dairy industry itself that makes it difficult for consumers to obtain a clean and healthy product through some of the techniques that they use in the processing of milk. Furthermore, it also impedes traceability.

5 Laboratorio Interprofesional Galego de Ánalise do leite (Galician Interprofessional Laboratory for the Analysis of Milk).

6 In this case Holstein-Friesian cattle considered the most suitable for milk production.

References

Baldwin, J. W. (1959). "The Medieval Theories of the Just Price: Romanists, Canonists, and Theologians in the Twelfth and Thirteenth Centuries." *Transactions of the American Philosophical Society, New Series*, 49 (4): 1–92.

Booth, W. J. (1994). "On the Idea of the Moral Economy." *The American Political Science Review*, 88 (3): 653–67.

Edelman, M. (2005). "Bringing the Moral Economy back in . . . to the Study of 21st Century Transnational Peasant Movements." *American Anthropologist*, 107 (3): 331–35.

Fernández Prieto, L., ed. (2000). *Terra e Progreso: Historia Agraria da Galicia Contemporánea*. Vigo: Edicións Xerais.

Iturra, R. (1988). *Antropología Económica de la Galicia Rural*. Santiago de Compostela: Consellería de Presidencia de Administración Pública, Servicio Central de Publicacións.

Langreo Navarro, A. (1995). *Historia de la Industria Láctea Española: Una aplicación a Asturias*. Madrid: Ministerio de Agricultura, Pesca y Alimentación.

McMichael, P. (2011). "Food System Sustainability: Questions of Environmental Governance in the New World (Dis)order." *Global Environmental Change*, 21: 804–12.

Polanyi, K. (2014). *Los límites del mercado: Reflexiones sobre economía, antropología y democracia*. Madrid: Capitán Swing.

Renard, M. C. (2003). "Fair Trade: Quality, Market and Conventions." *Journal of Peasant Studies*, 19: 87–96.

Scott, J. C. (1976). *The Moral Economy of the Peasant: Rebellion and Subsistence in Southeast Asia*. New Heaven, CT, and London: Yale University Press.

6

From Milk Price to Milk Value: Sardinian Sheepherders Facing Neoliberal Restructuring

Filippo M. Zerilli and Marco Pitzalis

The great sheep massacre: Shepherds between non-agency and freedom

While writing this chapter we were shocked by newspaper headlines concerning a sheep massacre: in October 2017 a flock of 135 sheep and 4 sheep dogs were found brutally slaughtered and abandoned in a plot of land near Ploaghe, Sassari district, northern Sardinia, while the shepherd vanished.[1] According to rumors and early investigations, the owner of the flock, a 62-year-old shepherd, was exasperated by the local dairy cooperative's refusal to buy his milk because it contained too heavy a bacterial load. Unquestionably, this could be hardly considered a reason or a justification for such a bloodbath, an extreme gesture "of a madman," as one of our interlocutors suggested. However, as in the case of the celebrated—and anthropologically inspired— "great cat massacre" (Darnton 1999), this tragic episode may be a vantage point to explore the economic sociocultural context in which sheep milk production and its commercialization takes place in contemporary Sardinia. Interestingly, while most online commentators of the sheep massacre vehemently condemn and stigmatize the shepherd for his "brutality" and "primitiveness," according to many others, his gesture needs a nuanced contextualization in order to understand the genuine motives, beyond the fact that it was presumably performed by a mentally disturbed individual. As one anonymous commentator suggested: "This poor guy has gone insane after seeing the fruit of so much work downgraded to waste, simply because they should pay him more than what they pay for imports. The shepherd is a victim along with his sheep, but you cannot understand it."[2] As this comment and others imply, a number of important issues are at stake here, namely the current undervaluation of the shepherd's labor, the fair price of Sardinian sheep milk in a context in which its market price is formed in a global, competitive capitalist economy influenced by import-export transactions, and, last but not least, the relation between the shepherd and the sheep, both considered victims of a local system of practices difficult to explain to non-shepherds. Like Darnton's cat massacre, the sheep massacre may be seen as a political act, a desperate gesture of rebellion against a system of regulations and market dynamics that are impossible for small producers to challenge.

In a recent contribution, Hadas Weiss distinguishes "between value and values in the context of a uniquely capitalist confrontation between freedom and nonagency." According to Weiss (2015: 240),

> Freedom issues from the individual freedom to buy and sell work and commodities according to personal capacities and preferences. Nonagency marks dependence on market exchange for goods and services, and lack of control over their production. . . . People partaking in this relation might nevertheless exert a measure of influence over their immediate surroundings, and thereby attempt to reconcile their freedom with their nonagency. Values are their means of doing so, because they extend freedom by surmounting self-interest, and meet necessity on more normatively palatable terms.

We are not persuaded that it is always possible in actual practice to distinguish clearly between non-agency ("value" in Weiss' terms) and freedom ("values" according to Weiss). However, in Weiss's challenging theoretical framework the sheep massacre may be seen as the ultimate deliberate act of a person (the owner of the flock) who is no longer able to face the violence of the current capitalist mode of production in which he is partaking—as a producer, marketeer, and consumer. In other words, the shepherd had lost the ability to reconcile his non-agency—his dependence on global market exchange and lack of control on his production—with his freedom to express shared social values to contest relations of domination or make them more acceptable.

All shepherds we have met so far in Sardinia are well aware of being incorporated and actually dominated within a capitalist mode of production and by its global and local market rules and constraints. They also show their ability to articulate shared values that challenge the dominant mode in the course of their everyday social life and practices. Interestingly, a number of them have decided to organize a wider, collective project of social mobilization in order to make the voice of the shepherds and their claims be heard in the public sphere through different forms of engagement and political activism. We draw upon ethnographic fieldwork conducted with shepherds of *Movimento pastori sardi* (MPS), a social movement of Sardinian sheepherders mobilizing to protect their economic interest and affirm their political agency in the context of the global financial crisis of 2008 and beyond.[3] We explore tensions and intersections of two related processes: the setting of market prices for sheep milk in Sardinia and the market and non-market value(s) associated with producing sheep milk and its products according to the producers themselves.

The rest of the chapter is organized in three sections. In the first, we provide a short summary of Sardinian "pastoralism" from its incorporation into capitalist market economy to its current transformation under neoliberal restructuring. Combining the conversations we have had with many Sardinian sheepherders—notably with those affiliated to MPS—with recent socioeconomic analysis of milk price volatility, we try to disentangle the puzzling issue of the monetary value of milk and its historical fluctuations, showing how Sardinian sheepherders feel—and to different degrees actually are—structurally subjected to local and global agro-industrial capitalist market logics and pressure. We explore shepherds' discourses and practices concerning the value of milk, namely the social, economic, and political value given to the action of producing milk, including a number of parallel labor activities such as forest and environmental protection, animal care, and sustainable agricultural development. Finally, we suggest how while engaging in a highly publicized struggle to reconcile the market price of sheep milk and the value of producing milk, the shepherds of MPS imagine themselves as an emergent social class driving Sardinia toward alternatives sovereignties, claiming to challenge neoliberal global policies, ideologies, and values.

Sardinian pastoralism: From capitalist incorporation to neoliberal globalization

Different scholarly traditions have shown how Sardinian pastoralism was incorporated within capitalist market economy at least since the late nineteenth century (Le Lannou 1941; Ortu 1981; Angioni 1989; Pulina et al. 2011). As Karl Polanyi cogently argued, the modern capitalist market economy is nothing "natural," in Sardinia or elsewhere (Polanyi 1944). In fact, this is rather a political economy project; in the Sardinian case, it was implemented by the Italian and local, regional ruling classes as agrarian reforms show (Brigaglia 2004). The transformation of Sardinia's pre-capitalist pastoral economy was promoted by state powers and industrial elites, notably through deforestation policy for meeting the demands of the flourishing mining industry (Caterini 2013). Deforestation created the ideal "natural conditions" of available land for sheep grazing. In this context, commercial cheese-makers (*casari*) from continental Italy (notably from the Lazio region) established and developed Sardinia's *Pecorino romano* cheese industry (Di Felice 2011). These two interwoven processes—deforestation and the development of a dairy industry—have radically transformed the Sardinian landscape and pastoral economy by encouraging the monoculture of the sheep and the production of the *Pecorino romano* cheese for foreign markets (Vargas-Cetina 2000).

Another significant set of changes occurred between the Second World War and the late 1960s, years in which the national industrialization plan for southern Italy also affected Sardinia, albeit in specific ways. In this context, the key features of what Weingrod and Marin (1971) define as the Sardinian "post-peasant society" were the persistence of traditional technologies in parallel with the adoption of technological innovations, along with "an expansion of non-farming tertiary occupations, the spreading consumer economy, the bureaucratisation and politicisation of rural life, a closer integration of countryside and city, and the spreading influence of mass culture" (Weingrod and Marin 1971: 320). Concerning sheepherding, three important and related phenomena developed during the following decade: the gradual decline of the transhumance system (Caltagirone 1986), the parallel move of a great number of sheep farmers from inland Sardinia to the Campidano regions (Murru Corriga 1990), and the migration of many of them to continental Italy, notably to Lazio, Umbria, and Tuscany (Solinas 1990). The adoption of new national land legislation, especially Law n.11/1971 (also known as "De Marzi-Cipolla law") contributed to creating a new social class of small landowners, attenuating the historical opposition between shepherds and agriculturalists.

Since the 1980s, due to the adoption of national and supranational legislation, including EU regulations facilitating access to credit and promoting investments, several sheep farms were restructured, introducing significant technological innovations, specializing in milk production and its commercialization as their core business (Idda et al. 2010; Vargas-Cetina 2000). Notwithstanding the regime of quasi-monopoly of the regional milk industry and the more minor role of dairy cooperatives, shepherds were able to make good revenues, aspiring to an Italian middle-class lifestyle, consumption patterns, and increased social mobility (Mientjes 2010). From simple owners of a relatively small number of sheep (e.g. 50 to 100 animals), many shepherds became owners of larger flocks (200 to 500 animals) and extended pasture land, in some cases hiring migrants from former socialist countries such as Romania and Albania as wage laborers. In short, many shepherds today might be well described as "petty capitalists," namely "individuals or households who employ a small number of workers but are themselves actively involved in the labour process" (Smart and Smart 2005: 3). From this perspective, like "peasants" (Narotzky 2016) "shepherds" have progressively "vanished" as they were incorporated into wider social formations.

Another significant ongoing transformation in sheepherding concerns the ways in which the relationship between capital and labor have changed paralleling neoliberal global policies and processes (e.g. Gledhill 2004; Edelman and Haugerud 2005; Shore et al. 2011; Narotzky 2016), along with the increasing influential role played by mobility, migration, and mass mediation (Inda and Rosaldo 2008), both in urban and rural contexts (Ploeg 2008). Digital technologies have immensely extended communication opportunities, also disclosing new forms of sociality.[4] Neoliberal restructuring and its core principles, namely the alleged self-regulation of the markets, the privatization of public goods and services, and the gradual dismantling of the welfare state have contributed to produce new forms of subjectivity (Ganti 2014), even among people in the most remote areas of the world (Gledhill 2004: 340). Paradoxically, as emerging neoliberal subjects our "petty capitalist" Sardinian shepherds are ideologically consistent with neoliberal values, being at the same time among its first victims. Actually, their first social mobilization in the early 1990s developed against the abrogation of European agricultural subventions, while few years later MPS activists joined the anti-globalization movement at the 2001 G8 Summit held in Genoa, Italy. Later, their public demonstrations targeted especially the stagnation of milk price, and were particularly intense between 2010 and 2012, when their protest included occupation of strategic infrastructures such as roads, airports, and commercial harbors and received wide media coverage, at the local and national level. It is in fact the struggles against the recursive crisis of sheep milk that emblematically represents MPS with its many facets and contradictions, from anti-globalization attitudes to tacit complicity with neoliberal regime and policies (Pitzalis and Zerilli 2013a; Zerilli and Pitzalis 2018). As an activist of MPS remarks during a conversation:

We demand everything related to milk price. When we started to protest in 2010 the milk was paid from 40 to 50 cents. . . . If you consider that the cost of production is 1.00 € per liter. . . . Now they are paying 70, so there are still 30 cents missing, 30 cents covered by the European subsides. . . . But it is not enough, because there are several expenses. . . . At the end you're working to create debts, you know. The costs today are too high: animal feed, electricity, gasoline. . . . Then to these you add the rent of the land, because the land is not all yours, maybe you own part of it, you bought it and have to pay a mortgage rate. . . . The food, the cost of food, forage and feed, all of which are too expensive compared to the price of milk! (Gianmario, MPS delegate, January 2013, emphasis added)

Interestingly, it is within these contentious, porous social spaces where neoliberalism shapes and is shaped by consent and critique that MPS shepherds have developed their most recent political mobilizations, notably around the struggle for a fair price for sheep milk.

The price of milk: Global fluctuations and local arrangements

Following Max Weber, we assume that "money prices are the product of conflicts of interest and of compromises; they thus result from power constellations" (Weber 1978: 108). In order to explore and frame such power constellations, one needs to move back and forth between global and local contexts, actors and practices. Taking inspiration from Weber's astronomical metaphor, we suggest that *Pecorino romano* cheese is a bright star refracting its light on multiple constellation scenarios.

Volatility in milk prices has a daily concern of Sardinian shepherds from at least since 2009 to today. In their Facebook groups, they regularly discuss milk prices, the variations of which are told to be connected to the price of the *Pecorino romano* cheese with significant consequences for their revenues. In fact, the world market price of this global commodity—the majority of which is exported to the United States—directly affects the price of the milk paid to the producers. According to Leonardo, another MPS activist, variations in milk prices are a mysterious issue, especially because it is perceived as something "established elsewhere." But where, in fact?

Price volatility in the dairy market is also the object of concern and political intervention at global level. Through its Dairy Price Index, the Food Agricultural Organization (FAO) is systematically documenting and monitoring its evolution.[5] Looking at the FAO Dairy Price Index historical series, the global dairy market appears quite stable until 2005–06. That year marked a significant increase in price volatility directly connected to new regulations and agreements adopted by the World Trade Organization (WTO) that broke down protectionist barriers and limited subsidies that were considered market distortions. In this framework, European subventions dropped, exposing producers to the chance fluctuations of weather and markets. According to a recent report presented to the European Parliament, four main factors explain increased price volatility: market factors, climate and weather factors, policy decisions, and financial speculation. At present, the European Union is elaborating policies in order to avoid the risks of price volatility. The same report indicates the direction of the new Common Agricultural Policy (CAP) for 2014–20, "which is mainly aimed at compensating farmers for the negative effects of price volatility and at tackling income volatility, rather than directly addressing price volatility itself."[6]

If the price of *Pecorino romano* cheese is negotiated on the global market, the price of the sheep milk necessary for its production is established at the regional and local level. However, the price of *Pecorino romano* represents a benchmark, namely a standard on which milk price is decided annually. Accordingly, the wavering of global stock markets has a direct impact on Sardinian dairy industry, a "social field" (in Pierre Bourdieu's meaning) dominated by a small industrial elite that rules the entire process, from milk collection and commercialization to milk processing and foreign export. Currently, few corporate actors in Sardinia act locally as market gatekeepers, controlling strategic information, restricting market access to other local players, and limiting if not obstructing competition. This industrial elite maintains dominance thanks to its ability to operate across different marketplaces and contexts, at local and global levels. While it commands well-established connections with the international network of dairy farmers and partners, its position at the local level is boosted by its capacity to play the role of a financial institution, offering loans to small producers through a system of "down payment" (discussed a little later in this chapter), while also overseeing a capillary, door-to-door system of milk collection and transportation.

Alongside the private industrial elite, the cooperative sector is another historically important player of Sardinian dairy industry (Porcheddu 2004). Established to counterbalance the power of the industrial elite, a significant number of cooperatives of producers also operate in the process of collection and milk transformation. However, given a number of structural difficulties—from a high degree of indebtedness to a low level of market penetration and product innovation—and due to their limited ability to protect the interests of their associates, most of these cooperative institutions function on the corporate model (Ruju 2011; Vargas-Cetina 2011), and respond to corporate logics often in explicit agreement with the dominant industrial elite. At the same time, their governance is strongly influenced by local politics and trade unions. For all these reasons, producers' cooperatives are often subject to contestation from within and outside.

Down payments: A noose around a neck

The MPS mobilization originates within capitalist relations of production, and in particular as a result of the tensions between milk producers and the processing industry in a market in which milk pricing depends on multiple global and local actors and factors, as we have just seen. At the local level, however, decisions are made by a limited number of processing companies from the corporate and cooperative sectors which operate in a quasi-monopoly, as recognized by MPS activists and academics alike (e.g. Pulina et al. 2011). During a conversation, Giovanni and Leonardo, two MPS activists, both explicitly identified the leadership of Fratelli Pinna Industria Casearia SpA, the main global corporate actor of Sardinia dairy industry:

> Giovanni: As far as industrialists are concerned, the one who has the power in Sardinia is Pinna . . .
>
> Leonardo: Pretty much for the last thirty years, Pinna has managed the export market
>
> Giovanni: For Pecorino Romano cheese . . .
>
> Leonardo: The presence of the Protection Consortium is useless when the person who . . . the exporter, *the only one who does the pricing, is Pinna* . . . if he has another product . . . even though it doesn't carry the PDO label, which is what we want, and that isn't guaranteed by the Consortium, he sells, because he can make a lower price than the others and sell because he's well-known. . . . Even if the Pecorino [Romano] cheese was Romanian instead of Romano, he would sell it! (conversation with Giovanni and Leonardo, January 2013, emphasis added)

The affirmation that Pinna is "the one who does the pricing" is confirmed by many other sources, and especially from the informal conversations we had with industrialists and herders of the cooperative sector.

Anticipi (advance partial payments) and *caparre* (down payments) are conventional and well-established systems of payment. The contract is effectively fixed only at the end of the year, when the annual price of the *Pecorino romano* has been fixed on the international market. These contracts/agreements represent an advantage for the industrialist, insomuch as they ensure the loyalty of the milk producers each year. The system is also advantageous for the shepherds, especially if they are behind with their payments. Notably during the summer, when the cycle of sheep milk production is interrupted, shepherds are often short on the cash they need in order to pay the bills for their farms and animal feed. Loans received as advance or down payments are the object of a formal contract and/or informal agreement between individual shepherds and the industrial elite and/or the cooperative sector. In this framework the actual price paid for one liter of raw milk may also vary considerably, even in the same local context.

However, as Gianni, an MPS delegate clearly explains, this kind of arrangement seriously challenges the freedom of the milk producers, especially the smallest ones:

> *There is a monopoly*, because if you go to see here there is just a monopoly, in practice there are these 4 or 5 big industrialists that monopolize the milk market. . . . The price, is made by them, in practice . . . I'm not saying that . . . it is not an accusation towards an industrialist, because he does his job correctly, he has to do this, he has to capitalize for himself, however, he keeps a lot of people on a leash . . . and the more the shepherd is in crisis the more is better for him. . . . In fact, he acts as a sort of bank, he has the power to finance the producer, the shepherd. . . . If I am in trouble, I go to the industrialist and say "look, I need 20,000 €."

... It's a hypothesis. . . . Just to say, *he finances me, but at the same time he puts the noose around my neck,* and he pulls me when he wants . . . I mean, it's sort of . . . I don't say it is usury (*usura*), but a kind of. (Gianni, MPS activist, January 2013, emphasis added)

As many other conversations would show, most shepherds feel expropriated of their products and especially in their role of producers. While they use the term *pastori* to designate themselves, they are actually *produttori, imprenditori, allevatori,* namely producers, entrepreneurs, herders. Milk price dynamics, however, are out of their control, and they feel reduced to the status of simple workers. Many shepherds perceive themselves as dominated by a social and economic structure of relations they cannot engage with or escape from. On the one hand, milk prices might drop down unexpectedly, even below production cost; however, they have no power to negotiate and must sell at market price. On the other hand, the cost of keeping their farms alive are continually growing. For some, the annual financial report may result in a loss, for others the final balance turns out to be far less favorable than fifteen or twenty years ago. In addition, as MPS delegate Gianmario remarks, it is impossible to close down or sell a sheep farm from one day to another. And when a farm is exposed to a considerable degree of indebtedness, as it is often the case, its ability to resist is seriously challenged.

As such, shepherds feel caught between two fires: the local market quasi-monopoly and the obligation to sustain the living costs of their farms and feeding their flocks. As a banner shown during a protest meeting in Cagliari ironically suggests, shepherds are not milking anymore, in fact they are being "milked" (see Figure 6.1).

The banner shows a shepherd on all fours milked by a wolf embodied by the industrialist Pinna (i.e., Fratelli Pinna SpA) on the one side, and by sheep on the other, illustrating the impossibility to evade from a condition of dispossession and

Figure 6.1 Sardinian shepherd "milked" by an industrialist wolf and a sheep. Banner at MPS protest meeting, Cagliari 2014 (©Filippo M. Zerilli).

immobilization at the same time. In fact, such structural constraints make it also difficult to take action in many important ways. For instance, the "milk strike" (*lo sciopero del latte*), namely the organized interruption of making sheep milk available on the local market is a measure many times discussed among MPS activists during their assembly meetings, but never achieved. In fact, the actual power to negotiate, namely, to collect, to store, and eventually to export and sell the milk is strictly limited to few existing producers' organizations (*Organizzazioni di produttori*). Moreover, as we have seen, most milk producers have already sold part of their milk production in advance through the down payment system, before actually producing it.

In short, price volatility with its uneven global dynamics and the local system of payments undermine shepherds' ability to successfully manage the product of their work. This may be well described in terms of exploitation and alienation, a condition that, according to Marx himself, is possible to overcome because we "know that human labour is the source of the commodities we exchange for money" (Hart 2005: 167). Hence, instead of further exploring how the price of milk is formed between global markets and local arrangements, in the next section, we focus on the ways MPS activists elaborate on milk value as a social process entangled with the labor of the shepherd.

The value(s) of milk and the shepherd's "noble work"

In a brilliant contribution toward an anthropological theory of value, David Graeber (2001: xii) suggested that value may be considered "as the way in which actions become meaningful to the actor by being incorporated in some larger social totality." Challenging the notion of "regime of value" developed by Appadurai in his 1983 introduction to the seminal collection *The Social Life of Things* (now also in Appadurai 2013: 9–60), positioning his perspective beyond the reconfiguration of the formalist/ substantivist economic anthropology debate, and taking inspiration from Nancy Munn's insights, Graeber proposes to frame value—"values" in Weiss terms—as "the power to create social relations" (Graeber 2001: 47). As Graeber himself recognizes, his main argument is indebted to Marx's ideas and understanding of value. The most important contribution provided by Marx's value theory is perhaps its ability to indicate value from different sources in order to denaturalize the capitalist notion of value, and what Marx called "the fetishism of commodities" (Turner 2008: 52–53). We find Graeber's contribution to value theory especially provoking in order to frame the dialectics of monetary value and non-monetary value in relation to social mobilization and collective action. In fact, it seems productive to apply Graeber's discussion of value and its political implications (Graeber 2001: 229–61; see also Pratt 2007: 297–99) to MPS's attempt to redefine the work of the shepherds as a source for political action and mobilization. As Graeber's approach to value may be ultimately considered as a way "to imagine people being able to change society purposefully," and "to look at social systems as structures of creative action, and value" (Graeber 2001: 230), MPS activism and its cultural work on value may be read as a tentative effort to challenge the hegemony of current relations of production, recognizing first "the shepherd's social role." This is in fact a crucial concept formulated by MPS leaders since the early 2010s, when a major mobilization was organized around the crisis generated by a milk price collapse in late 2009.

During a well-attended public meeting held at the municipality of Siliqua, near Cagliari, Sardinia's largest city, MPS organizer Fortunato Ladu argued:

> The milk may also be paid 1.00 € [per liter], however, that would be not a solution, for us. The issue that we want to bring forward is to ensure that society gives us really what we are entitled to, namely *the role of the Sardinian shepherd that really belongs to us, which is not merely the economic role, but the social role of the man who stays in the countryside and protects the countryside.* (emphasis added)[7]

Accidental stewards of the countryside

Felice Floris, founder and MPS's undisputed leader to date, has elaborated on the idea of the shepherd's social role in many public and private endeavors. In fact, capitalizing MPS's remarkable public success and subtly using his own political sensitivity and ability to navigate across traditional media actors and practices, as well as within new social media networking such as Facebook and WhatsApp, Felice is often invited in public meetings to represent the position of the Sardinian shepherds together with public and private actors such as trade union representatives, scientific experts, policy makers, and politicians. On one such occasion, at a conference organized and sponsored by Hon. Giovanni La Via, a member of the European Parliament at that time in charge of the report of the new Common Agricultural Policy, Felice intervened to defend the traditional work of small agro-pastoral enterprises, complaining against the organization of European agricultural subsidies currently privileging large, agri-food corporate actors:

> In Sardinia we live of sheep farming. It's an economy rooted in time and history, which has always produced culture and quality products. It's a sector that employs thousands of people, we say more than 100,000 people work in dairy farms. It is *a noble work*, a work that in addition to creating culture, environment, and defending tradition, it is a democratic economy.[8]

Few moments later he explicitly addressed the main political actors seated next to him at the speaker's platform:

> Commissioner, Minister, EU representative, you should hear our voices as well because we do not have interests to defend beyond our work, we have no income to maintain and protect, we do not have a bureaucracy to defend, *we only have our noble work. We, accidental stewards of the countryside, who work free, who have always worked for free, we ask for nothing, we ask for everything, we ask for dignity.* (emphasis added)

The "accidental steward" is a powerful, imaginary character Felice has developed and refined in the last few years in order to capture the authentic value of sheep farming (Pitzalis and Zerilli 2013b). While for many sheepherders, the main activity and source of revenues is milk production, inspired by the evocative image of the accidental steward, MPS suggests that the shepherds' work cannot be reduced to the role of milk producers. In fact, according to Felice and his colleagues, milk production is just one aspect of shepherds' "noble work." As they convincingly argue, the production of milk implies a number of related tasks which are integral part of the agro-pastoral work in which shepherds have always been and actually are involved in their daily life. Environmental protection and territorial control represent specific tasks that the shepherds claim they have traditionally undertaken without any monetary compensation. If you look at the Sardinian landscape from an airplane, Felice suggested once, you see how the countryside is well preserved and designed, and you understand the shepherds' contribution to preserving the order and organization of the natural environment. During a conversation, Francesca, another influential MPS delegate, stressed how shepherds have always contributed to taking care of the territory. She recounts a story of her father once risking his life to save a burning tree. According to Francesca, "If Sardinia is preserved as it is today, it is not due to forestal management. It is thanks to the shepherds, you know. It is thanks to the shepherds who care about the territory, because to me, if a tree burns it does not hurt the forest management, it hurts *me*!"(emphasis in original). According to Francesca, it is important to recall that the shepherd is always present with his flock; he is often the owner of the land, and if not, he nevertheless "manages it, he controls it, he takes care of it in all details." Accordingly—Francesca implicitly argues—national and supranational policies and regulations should recognize "*a new social position. That is, the role of the shepherd. Which in fact already exists, and actually has always existed!*" (Francesca, MPS delegate, January 2013, emphasis added). Interestingly, recognizing the stewardship role of farmers in protecting the environment is common within the European Union's current system of "direct payments" for ecological services promoted in the framework of the new CAP.[9]

"If you eat cheese you keep on living, if you eat plastic you die!"

MPS discourses on the shepherd's noble work also extend to a "typical" Sardinian product, sheep's milk cheese (*pecorino*). As it will immediately become apparent, this should not be confused with the *Pecorino romano* cheese, the manufactured industrial product mentioned in previous section. Although several MPS activists do not produce cheese as their core business, some of them still make it for family use, informal trading and/or as a part of a multifunctional productive strategy as opposed to specialization (Ploeg 2008: 121–22). The value of this artisanal, handmade *pecorino* cheese is built in opposition to the *Pecorino romano* cheese, the production of which represents roughly 70 percent of the cheese produced by Sardinian cooperatives and corporate actors.

While shepherds consider the *Pecorino romano* "inedible" because its taste is deemed too salty and suitable only for export, they prize artisanal *pecorino*, and especially the variety named *Fiore sardo*, as a typical Sardinian product, recently protected as "the cheese of the shepherds" (*il formaggio dei pastori*) by a dedicated Slow Food *presidia* (Siniscalchi 2013, 2014).

An example of the cultural value attached to handcrafted *pecorino* cheese is given by Giovanni, a militant for Sardinian independence and MPS activist supporting the struggle for the recognition of the shepherd's social role. Within MPS, Giovanni is among those who, during a street demonstration, are always on trenches, ready to take part in the riots against the police when these occur. While he is not a cheese producer himself, Giovanni often helps other shepherds make cheese. One day, while brushing several wheels of *Fiore sardo,* he recalled the strong police repression against MPS shepherds protesting in Civitavecchia and observed: "Instead of giving an award to the shepherds, who produce life—no, they hit them with a truncheon!"[10] Soon after, moving another cheese wheel, Giovanni exclaimed: "This is life, *life!* If one eats a piece of this, life continues. We are not producing plastic, this is not plastic, this is cheese, and *if you eat cheese you keep on living, if you eat plastic you die!*" (emphasis added).[11]

If we had more space, we could elaborate more on MPS discourses about the cultural value attached to shepherd's "traditional" products (cheese, but also meat and wool) and how they filter and translate environmental global concerns like food quality and food safety into features intrinsic to pastoral identity and culture. In particular, anti-globalization and environmentalist rhetorics are appropriated and assembled with ideas about shepherds' identity and "millennial culture" as a model for alternative developments (Zerilli and Pitzalis 2018). From this perspective, MPS work of cultural production is in many ways comparable to forms of engagement promoted by other social movements and diverse kinds of "food activism" (Siniscalchi and Counihan 2014), including Slow Food movement (Siniscalchi 2013, 2014), organic farming (e.g. Leutcheford and Pratt 2011), clandestine food networks (Koensler 2018), and, more generally, processes of "repeasantization" (Ploeg 2008) or, as we have suggested,"repastoralization" (Pitzalis and Zerilli 2013b).

Conclusion

In this chapter, we have explored tensions and intersections between the price, or "market value," of Sardinian sheep milk and the "value(s)" of milk understood as the ensemble of practices and operations associated with the shepherd's work. We have mapped these complex local and global dynamics, focusing on recent social mobilizations and political discourse of the MPS, which elaborates and popularizes the idea that milk value is linked to the shepherds' "noble work" and their unrecognized social role as environmental stewards. Within this framework the crisis generated by the stagnation of milk prices in 2009–10 gave an opportunity for MPS shepherds to develop and promote a discourse on shepherd's labor aimed at generating new social relations of production while trying to challenge the hegemonic market structures and ideologies.

Long objectified in academic and popular representations, entangled in local and global markets, and constrained by the state and non-state institutions and agencies, the shepherds of MPS succeeded in creating new spaces for maneuvering and campaigning for their social recognition. Their struggle intentionally undermined a number of stereotypes (such as "banditry," "familism," "individualism," and "backwardness") that have characterized scholarly work and discourses concerning "pastoralism" for decades (Pitzalis and Zerilli 2013a). Creating a system of beliefs and a network of solidarity and trust, MPS activists provided ground for an emerging political subject promising the coming of a new cultural hegemony (Zerilli and Pitzalis 2015). Regardless of the actual outcome—the inconsistencies and contradictions—of this ambitious political project, MPS could be considered not simply as a platform from which shepherds could claim a fair price for their milk and other commodities they produce but also as a space of sociality and collective action where shepherds build and experience the consciousness of their political agency and elaborate on the meaning of being a shepherd today. Ultimately, the shepherd's movement is a social space of creativity and *value production* where shepherds affirm the dignity of their work, recasting the role of primary food producers as a blueprint for future and alternative development consistent with current global environmental concerns.

Acknowledgment

Filippo M. Zerilli acknowledges research funding from the Italian Ministry of University and Research (MIUR), within the project Eco-frizioni dell'antropocene (PRIN 2015, Prot. n. 20155TYKCM).

Notes

1   Cf. Sgozza l'intero gregge e fugge: Ploaghe, strage in campagna [Slaughters the whole flock and runs away: Ploaghe, massacre in the countryside], *L'Unione sarda*, October 18, 2017, http://www.unionesarda.it/articolo/cronaca/2017/10/18/sgozza_l_intero_gregg e_e_fugge_ploaghe_strage_in_campagna-68-656944.html (accessed December 25, 2017).
2   Cf. G. Drugo, La storia del pastore di Ploaghe che uccide il suo gregge perché il latte non è buono [The story of Ploaghe's shepherd who kills his flock because the milk is not good], *neXt quotidiano*, October 19, 2017, https://www.nextquotidiano.it/pasto re-ploaghe-uccide-gregge/ (accessed December 25, 2017).
3   *Movimento pastori sardi*, literally "Sardinian shepherds movement" (hereafter glossed as MPS), was born in the early 1990s (cf. Pulina and Biddau 2015: 77–85). Since 2011, we have carried out an ethnographic research project focusing on the sociopolitical and cultural life of this social movement (cf. Pitzalis and Zerilli 2013a, 2013b; Zerilli and Pitzalis 2015, 2018).
4   The recent mobilizations of MPS are hardly intelligible without considering the crucial role played by digital technologies, notably the cell phone and the social media networking such as Facebook (Casula 2013).

5 The FAO Dairy Price Index displays the situation of dairy global exchanges, where cow milk represents more than 80 percent of all exchanges. Sheep and goat milk is barely a fraction of the total (goat with 2 percent and sheep with 1 percent). However, a large part of that fraction (almost 75 percent) is provided by the European sheep and goat dairy sector, a significant portion of which is represented by Sardinian production. See http://www.fao.org/economic/est/est-commodities/dairy/en/ (accessed December 25, 2017).

6 Cf. F. Tropea and P. Devuyst, "Price volatility in agricultural markets. Risk management and other tools," EPRS (European Parliamentary Research Service) Members Research Service PE 586.609 http://www.europarl.europa.eu/RegData/etudes/BRIE/2016/586609/EPRS_BRI(2016)586609_EN.pdf (accessed December 25, 2017). Beyond its presumed neutrality, like all policy the EU Common Agricultural Policy itself is a field of conflicts and negotiations among state and non-state actors representing diverse economic and political interests.

7 Introduction by Fortunato Ladu at MPS meeting held in Siliqua, June 19, 2010 ((cf. http://vimeo.com/12873804), accessed December 25, 2017).

8 Speech by Felice Floris at the conference *La PAC dopo il 2013. Il processo di riforma della nuova Politica Agricola Comune* (The PAC after 2013. The reform process of the new Common Agricultural Policy), Centro Fieristico "Le Ciminiere," Catania, Sicily, December 14, 2012.

9 Annoyed with the politics of Italian agricultural trade unions such as Coldiretti, MPS directly engaged with EU policies. In 1996 a delegation of more than 1,000 MPS shepherds went to Brussels in order to ask EU representatives recognition for the special features of the sheep and goat sector.

10 Giovanni refers here to a harsh confrontation MPS had with the police at the Civitavecchia harbor in 2010, which was the object of a publicized court case.

11 The scene and Giovanni's words are taken from *Capo e Croce*, a brilliant ethnographically inspired documentary film on MPS struggles (cf. Pani and Carboni 2013).

References

Angioni, G. (1989). *I pascoli erranti: Antropologia del pastore in Sardegna*. Napoli: Liguori.

Appadurai, A. (2013). *The Future as Cultural Fact: Essays on the Global Condition*. London and New York: Verso.

Brigaglia, M., ed. (2004). *Per una storia della riforma agraria in Sardegna*. Roma: Carocci.

Caltagirone, B. (1986). "Lo studio della transumanza come dispositivo di analisi del mondo pastorale." *Etudes Corses*, 14 (27): 27–44.

Casula, C. (2013). *Comunità online e offline: contributo all'etnografia del Movimento Pastori Sardi*. Unpublished MA dissertation. University of Cagliari.

Caterini, F. (2013). *Colpi di scure e sensi di colpa: Storia del disboscamento della Sardegna dalle origini a oggi*. Sassari: Carlo Delfino editore.

Dartnon, R. (1999). *The Great Cat Massacre and Other Episodes in French Cultural History*. New York: Basic Books.

Di Felice, M. L. (2011). "La 'rivoluzione' del pecorino romano. Modernità e tradizione nell'industria casearia sarda del primo novecento." In A. Mattone and P. F. Simbula (eds.), *La pastorizia mediterranea: Storia e diritto (secoli XI-XX)*, 949–93. Roma: Carocci.

Edelman, M., and A. Haugerud, eds. (2005). *The Anthropology of Development and Globalization: From Classical Political Economy to Contemporary Neoliberalism*. Oxford: Blackwell.

Ganti, T. (2014). "Neoliberalism." *Annual Review of Anthropology*, 43: 89–104.

Gledhill, J. (2004). "Neoliberalism." In D. Nugent and J. Vincent (eds.), *A Companion to the Anthropology of Politics*, 323–48. Oxford: Blackwell.

Graeber, D. (2001). *Toward an Anthropological Theory of Value: The False Coin of Our Own Dreams*. New York: Palgrave.

Hart, K. (2005). "Money: One Anthropologist's View." In J. Carrier (ed.), *A Handbook of Economic Anthropology*, 160–75. Cheltenham and Northampton, MA: Elgar.

Idda, L., R. Furesi, and P. Pulina (2010). *Economia dell'allevamento ovino da latte. Produzione, trasformazione, mercato*. Milano: Franco Angeli.

Inda, J. X., and R. Rosaldo, eds. (2008). *The Anthropology of Globalization: A Reader* (2nd ed.). Oxford: Blackwell.

Koensler, A. (2018). "Reinventing Transparency: Governance, Trust and Passion in Activism for Food Sovereignty in Italy." *Ethnologia Europaea: Journal of European Anthropology*, 48 (1): 50–66.

Le Lannou, M. (1941). *Pâtres et paysans de la Sardaigne*. Tours: Arrault.

Leutcheford, P., and J. Pratt (2011). "Values and Markets: an Analysis of Organic Farming Initiatives in Andalusia." *Journal of Agrarian Change*, 11 (1): 87–103.

Mientjes, A. C. (2010). "Pastoral Communities in the Sardinian Highlands (Italy): A View on Social Mobility." *Ethnos*, 75 (2): 148–70.

Murru Corriga, G. (1990). *Dalla montagna ai Campidani: Famiglia e mutamento in una comunità di pastori*. Cagliari: EDES.

Narotzky, S. (2016). "Where Have All the Peasants Gone?" *Annual Review of Anthropology*, 45: 301–18.

Ortu, G. G. (1981). *L'economia pastorale della Sardegna moderna: Saggio di antropologia storica sulla soccida*. Cagliari: Edizioni della Torre.

Pani, M. A., and P. Carboni (2013). [Film] *Capo e croce. Le ragioni dei pastori*, Italy.

Pitzalis, M., and F. M. Zerilli (2013a). "Pastore sardu non t'arrendas como! Il Movimento pastori sardi: alterità, resistenza, complicità." *Rassegna italiana di sociologia*, 54 (3): 379–400.

Pitzalis, M., and F. M. Zerilli (2013b). "Il giardiniere inconsapevole. Pastori sardi, retoriche ambientaliste e strategie di riconversione." *Culture della sostenibilità*, 6 (12): 149–59.

Ploeg, J. D. van der (2008). *The New Peasantries: Struggles for Autonomy and Sustainability in an Era of Empire and Globalization*. London: Earthscan.

Polanyi, K. (1944). *The Great Transformation: The Political and Economic Origins of Our Time*. Boston, MA: Beacon Press.

Porcheddu, D. (2004). *Le cooperative casearie in Sardegna. Modelli teorici, verifiche empiriche e casi di studio*. Milano: Franco Angeli.

Pratt, J. (2007). "Food Values: The Local and the Authentic." *Critique of Anthropology*, 27 (3): 285–300.

Pulina, G., and G. Biddau (2015). *Pascoli, pecore e politica: 70 anni di pastorizia in Sardegna*. Sassari: EDES.

Pulina, G., S. P. G. Rassu, G. Rossi, and P. Brindano (2011). "La pastorizia sarda nell'ultimo secolo." In A. Mattone and P. F. Simbula (eds.), *La pastorizia mediterranea. Storia e diritto (secoli XI-XX)*, 1111–31. Roma: Carocci.

Ruju, S. (2011). "I caseifici cooperativi nella Sardegna del Novecento." In A. Mattone and P. Simbula (eds.), *La pastorizia mediterranea. Storia e diritto (secoli XI-XX)*, 994–1010. Roma: Carocci.

Shore, C., S. Wright, and D. Però, eds. (2011). *Policy Worlds: Anthropology and the Analysis of Contemporary Power*. Oxford: Berghahn.

Siniscalchi, V. (2013). "Pastori, attivisti e mercato. Pratiche economiche e logiche politiche nei presidi Slow Food." *Voci*, 10: 173–82.

Siniscalchi, V. (2014). "Slow Food Activism between Politics and Economy." In C. Counihan and V. Siniscalchi (eds.), *Food Activism: Agency, Democracy and Economy*, 225–41. London: Bloomsbury.

Siniscalchi, V., and C. Counihan (2014). "Ethnography of Food Activism." In C. Counihan and V. Siniscalchi (eds.), *Food Activism: Agency, Democracy and Economy*, 3–14. London: Bloomsbury.

Smart, A., and J. Smart, eds. (2005). *Petty Capitalists and Globalization: Flexibility, Entrepreneurship, and Economic Development*. Albany: State University of New York Press.

Solinas, P. G., ed. (1990). *Pastori sardi in provincia di Siena*. 3 vol., Siena: Laboratorio etno-antropologico, Dipartimento di filosofia e scienze sociali.

Turner, T. (2008). "Marxian Value Theory: An Anthropological Perspective." *Anthropological Theory*, 8 (1): 43–56.

Vargas-Cetina, G. (2000). "From Handicraft to Monocrop: Pecorino Cheese Production in Highland Sardinia." In A. Haugeraud, M. P. Stone, and P. D. Little (eds.), *Commodities and Globalization: Anthropological Perspectives*, 219–38. Lanham, MD: Rowman and Littlefield.

Vargas-Cetina, G. (2011). "Corporations, Cooperatives, and the State. Examples from Italy." *Current Anthropology*, 52 (3): S127–36.

Weber, M. (1978). *Economy and Society: An Outline of Interpretive Sociology*. Guenther Roth and Claus Wittich (eds.). Berkeley, Los Angeles, and London: University of California Press.

Weingrod, A., and E. Marin (1971). "Post-Peasants: The Character of Contemporary Sardinian Society." *Comparative Studies in Society and History*, 13: 301–24.

Weiss, H. (2015). "Capitalist Normativity: Value and Values." *Anthropological Theory*, 15 (2): 239–53.

Zerilli, F. M., and M. Pitzalis (2015). "Pastoralismo, neoliberalismo e identità di classe in Sardegna." In F. Bachis and A. M. Pusceddu (eds.), *Cose da prendere sul serio. Le antropologie di Giulio Angioni*, 97–116. Nuoro: Il Maestrale.

Zerilli, F. M., and M. Pitzalis (2018). "'They Cannot Teach Me How to Be a Shepherd.' Sheepherding, Neoliberalism, and Animal Welfare in Post-Peasant Sardinia." In H. Horáková, A. Boscoboinik, and R. Smith (eds.), *Utopia and Neoliberalism: Ethnographies of Rural Spaces*, 45–65. Münster: Lit Verlag.

7

"Small Farms, Better Food": Valuing Local Agri-Food Systems in Europe from the European Peasants Coordination to the Nyéléni European Forum for Food Sovereignty

Delphine Thivet

Nyéléni was a woman who left her mark on the history of Mali, as a woman and as a great farmer. . . . Nyéléni's reputation grew beyond the limits of her region; she became a living legend. Her struggle is for food, a struggle for food sovereignty. Nyéléni is synonymous with perseverance, engagement, success. . . . Each of you should be Nyéléni.[1]

Six thousand kilometers away from West Africa and "Nyéléni," a Malian peasant woman who became a legendary heroine of the global food sovereignty movement, about fifty snowy-haired activists, the former delegates to the European Peasants Coordination (CPE), gathered in February 2012 in an ancient monastery located in a small village in the northwest of France. They had come there from France, Norway, Italy, the Netherlands, Austria, Portugal, Germany, and Spain to take part in the commemoration of the thirtieth anniversary of the European peasant movement.[2] After a multilingual[3] slideshow on the history of the CPE, the participants—walking along the beautiful and tranquil rural setting of the valley—spent this commemorative weekend in informal discussions and sharing memories of their commitment to peasant activism at the local, national and European level. A significant amount of the remaining time was devoted to delectable lunches and dinners which were prepared from the produce brought from their farms and from the local farmers. The participants paid particular attention to how foods were produced and to the taste of the products. Far from being "food from nowhere," these diverse local and regional foods exemplified a "vernacular food cosmopolitanism" made possible through and by small- and medium-scale farmers of Europe.

The rise of a European movement for "food sovereignty" and of a critique of the agricultural policies in Europe is significant in the emerging food production and distribution policies of the states, which are often seen as within the immediate interests of the industrial agri-food system and transnational agrofood corporations. One of the effective movements to critique, and to offer alternative policy suggestions with due regard to the rights of the farmers, food safety and quality concerns of consumers, and environmental issues is the European Coordination Via Campesina (ECVC). Small- and medium-scale farmers and farmers' unions of various European states organized themselves into the CPE in 1986, which in 2008 was renamed as ECVC with its headquarters at Brussels in Belgium. The members of participating organizations involved in the CPE realized that the issues of the farmers of European countries alone would not suffice to address the agricultural crisis and farmers' issues. Consequently, the CPE, together with farmers' organizations and trade unions from other continents played a leading role in creating the international farmer movement La Vía Campesina. Since the 2000s, the CPE has adopted "food sovereignty" (Thivet 2014) as an alternative framework for organizing food and agricultural policies and has stressed for its implementation regionally and locally in Europe. The building of a European movement for food sovereignty exemplifies the challenges of combining different food discourses: notably, ones that emphasizes the farm producers' claim to ensure their social reproduction in a context of the decline of farming, then the environmentalists' concerns for sustainable food and agriculture systems and the consumers' demand for "quality" food and animal welfare. This process leads to rethinking the food, to paraphrase Gibson-Graham, as "a site of ethical interdependence" (2014: S152).

Drawing upon ethnographic, archival, and historical materials from my research (Thivet 2015), this chapter opens with an overview of the context of emergence of CAP, which directs agricultural production in the European Union since 1962. It then, in the second section, traces the history of the CPE, showing that it initiated a process of coalition formation among grassroots organizations and social agents coming from different backgrounds (farmers, NGOs, environmental and consumer groups, and so on) across Europe, so as to resist mainstream food chain and bring forth alternative production and distribution systems at the local scale. The third section shows how the CPE created space for public debate through various forums organized around the concept of "food sovereignty." The initial focus on food production issues diverged and opened to include all areas of food and agricultural systems from production to consumption and distribution. One of the more significant forums that emerged was the "Nyeleni European Forum for Food Sovereignty" launched in Austria in August 2011 and, more recently, in Romania in October 2016.

Common agricultural policy and the rise of agricultural productivism in Europe

Achieving self-sufficiency in food supplies and securing the incomes of farmers in postwar Western Europe

To understand better the integrated agricultural policy European countries adopted in the 1950s, one may need to take into account the food shortages during and after the

Second World War. The war imposed severe hardships and food scarcity on European populations (Federico 2012: 18). However, European agriculture recovered quickly in the 1950s and 1960s to become an exporter of agricultural products (Federico 2012: 23) thanks to the modernization of agriculture. Eventually in 1962 the Common Agricultural Policy (CAP) was adopted among the six original members of European Economic Community (EEC), that is, France, West Germany, Italy, the Netherlands, Belgium, and Luxembourg, by the Treaty of Rome (1957). Ludlow sees this as "the most complex, the most ambitious, and the most controversial undertaking by the European institutions" (2005: 347). The prominent objectives of CAP were to increase the domestic agricultural production and supply of food, to ensure a decent standard of living for farmers by guaranteeing minimum prices, and to adopt reasonable food prices for the consumers. Within the context of reconstruction of the countries affected by the war, these objectives, though undermined by liberal market mechanisms and paradigms, were seen "as a precondition for political stability" (Gerhard 2012: 204). These welfarist agricultural policies and the modernization of the farm sector through CAP coincided with the transition toward an agro-system characterized by the intensification, specialization, and concentration of agricultural activities especially through the use of chemical fertilizers and mechanization. Over the years, CAP also led to a common organization of agricultural markets by (a) the removal of trade restrictions in agriculture among the member states and the establishment of a common pricing mechanism for agricultural products; and (b) the erection of a common trade barrier on agricultural goods on international trade.

CAP's ambivalent effects

While CAP realized most of its objectives, notably ensuring food security in Western Europe and securing farmers' incomes, it was not able to fulfil all of its promises. CAP was criticized by a wide range of actors (including farmers' unions, governments of "developing" countries, international solidarity NGOs, consumers, and environmentalists) on three counts.

First, the agricultural sector deflated from 25 percent of the workforce in the six original member states in the late 1950s to less than 5 percent in the 1990s. As Knudsen points out CAP "created new cleavages among Europe's farmers" (2009: 274). It resulted in what Mendras called "la fin des paysans" (the end of peasants) (1967). CAP tended to channelize most of the subsidies to the "farmers"—the new agricultural professionals with large, technologically advanced farms seen as responsible for feeding the nation and as fitting into the category of those promoting modernization of agriculture.[4] Thus, CAP failed to protect small- and medium-sized farms that were considered economically unviable or less efficient.

Secondly, the national agricultural protection, high common minimum prices for agricultural commodities,[5] and modernization of agriculture stimulated production leading to mounting food and agricultural surpluses and overproduction of key agricultural commodities. This coupled with negative demand for food saturated the national markets of European countries for agricultural products (Gray 2000). The international and European press reported this phenomenon as "butter mountains" and "lakes of wine and milk." This compelled the states to buy up the surpluses to maintain prices. Thus, CAP tended to become more and more expensive. The only outlet for this "embarrassment of plenty" (Knudsen 2009: 278) was the absorbing of national surpluses by the world market. Thanks to the increasing export subsidies enabling Western European farmers to be competitive, the EEC, after having been an overall net importer of agricultural products earlier, now became a net exporter of agricultural commodities such as grains, beef, sugar, and wine. However, in the context of famines especially in Sahel and in other parts of the world in the 1970s, the EEC's decision to reduce surpluses by feeding animals with wheat and milk powder came under severe criticism both within Europe and from outside the EEC (Gerlach 2009). This raised questions about EEC's model of export and its participation in international trade.

Thirdly, the expansion of the industrial and intensive model of agriculture led to an ecological crisis in the European countryside. The intensive use of fertilizers and pesticides as a means of maximizing income left their devastating ecological footprint. Loss of biodiversity, contamination of water, air, and soil, leading to human health and ecosystems hazards were seen as a failure of CAP's model of agricultural development. Today's farmers and food movements in Europe have endorsed environmental values and included in their agendas the need for sustainable and more ecological agricultural practices.[6]

In search of an alternative to EU CAP

The birth of the European Peasant Coordination

In the above delineated context of decline of agricultural working population, production surpluses, loss of biodiversity due to agricultural intensification, and a heavy reliance on commodity support for agriculture, several progressive farmers' organizations from around Europe opposed CAP after almost twenty years of its inception. These organizations came together as an alternative voice, and attempted to break the hegemony of the agricultural lobbies and, in particular, the Committee of Agricultural Organizations on the Common Agricultural Policy (COPA) at the European level. Meanwhile, small- and medium-sized farmers from these organizations realized that they "should be linked as partners and not competitors" and create a "European farmers movement" defending "a new kind of agricultural policy in the service of farmers" (CPE 1986). Nicolas Duntze, a vine grower from the south of France and a member of the Peasant Confederation and the sustainable agriculture and seasonal migrant workers' group of the ECVC,[7] remembers,

> For us, it meant to give up on the competition between agricultural producers that used to be organized in the 1970–80s, especially at the very moment of European enlargement. . . . Dominant farm union in France used to empty trucks of tomato

shipments that arrived from Spain, used to have French and Spain peasants think they were mutual enemies. . . . The CPE on the contrary told them to look higher, farther, deeper into the European and international agricultural policies . . . to make them understand that, of course not officially, a war has been declared on peasant agricultures at various levels, and that, we, the peasants from Europe, had to recover our common identity, work and savoir-faire. (interview, Bagnolet, June 2010, my translation from French)

While dominant and industrial farmers have been closely associated to the orientation of CAP at the European level, many of these European farmers' organizations had been excluded from the official domestic systems of political representation or only had a marginalized position. Nevertheless, after more than six years of networking between small and medium farmers' organizations, starting in 1981 in Austria (see Chapter 4 by Kosnik), the CPE was set up in 1986, emerging out of opposition to mainstream farming (Choplin 2017). As Paul Nicholson, a small-scale dairy farmer in the Basque region of Spain and former president of the Basque Union of Livestock Breeders and Small Farmers (Euskal Herriko Nekezarien Elkartasuna, EHNE) and former international secretary of La Vía Campesina (1993–96), states:

Farmers in Europe . . . began to understand that the CAP is the main instrument to promote an intensive agricultural model that is moving towards concentration and destruction of peasant employment, and in this context of negotiations in Brussels, EHNE and other farmers unions in Europe began to understand that the peasant struggle is not only in a local context, but that agricultural policy is being decided further away from the farms. (interview, Basque country, Spain, April 2010, my translation from French)

With the initial financial help from the French Peasant Confederation (Confédération Paysanne), CPE established its headquarters in Brussels in 1989. Since 1998, CPE is represented in the Agricultural Advisory Committees of the European Commission. In parallel, realizing that other groups and organizations around the world shared similar ideas relating to agricultural trade liberalization and problems associated with industrial agriculture, the CPE was greatly stimulated. This furthered the development of new alliances with "peasant" and landless movements in other countries of the Global North and the Global South. The farmers' unions taking part in the CPE were indeed very critical of the export-oriented CAP and its inequitable effects, especially the damage caused to the rural economies of developing countries and to the incomes of their *frères de métier* from the Global South who were unable to compete with agricultural exports of European surplus at prices below the costs of production in their markets ("dumping") (Thivet 2015). In 1993, the CPE, in association with Central, South, and North American farmers' movements set up La Vía Campesina at Mons, Belgium, and held the international operative secretariat during its first three years of existence (1993–96).

Small-scale farmers forging alliances with environmental and consumer groups

The CPE rapidly became a driving force in the establishment of alliances between small-scale farmers and "other social forces" (CPE 1986) such as non-farmers, environmental groups, and consumers. While the growing distance and disconnect between the spheres of food production and food consumption are the result of an historical process, the necessity to redefine the role of agriculture and the, mostly, declining role of farmers in European societies led the latter to open relations with non-farming interest groups. Alliances with non-farming groups were indeed seen by farmers' organizations as a middle ground between the defense of their "right to existence" as small-scale farmers and a response to a growing societal understanding of the health implications of food and of environmental issues in the agricultural and food sectors.

The first effective alliance was established in the early 1980s, which coincided with increasing concerns about the negative environmental and other impacts of postwar agricultural development especially around food safety and quality issues. These concerns and issues were underscored due to a series of food scares associated with productivist agriculture and the crises within conventional food systems. In 1980, the hormone-infected veal scandal—that is, the illegal injection of prohibited anabolics into the edible tissues of calves—illustrated the growing public attention paid to the health consequences of the model of agriculture promoted in Europe through CAP. The Federal Union of Consumers appealed to boycott French veal. Fearing more boycotts which could harm farmers economically and a growing collapse of consumer confidence, the French Peasant Confederation—one of the founding member of the CPE—abandoned the old farming corporatist discourses and aligned with those of consumer groups by developing a stark critique of "agricultural productivism" meant for producing more and cheaper lower quality food products destined for low-income households.

At the end of the 1980s, learning about the introduction of a genetically engineered Monsanto growth hormone to boost milk production (*Bovine Somatropin*) (BST) in the United States, the CPE together with the European Green Group (Rainbow Group) initiated a successful campaign against the introduction of the BST[8] to Europe since it grievously impacted human and animal health (CPE 1987). This campaign would later form the base for the rise of a European social movement opposing genetically modified organisms (GMOs). The CPE was particularly in tune with the agenda of the Greens. For instance, the socioeconomic impacts of the BST on the dairy and meat industry was not the main discursive frame of the CPE. Whereas the other farming groups and the European Commission itself emphasized "the idea that approval for market introduction of a new technology should be based in part on its likely socio-economic impacts and the consistency of these impacts with existing policy determinations and the values underlying those policies" (Kleinman and Kinchy 2003: 390), the CPE primarily emphasized on environmental impacts and food safety—an agricultural and ecological "equilibria." Jean Cabaret, an organic chicken farmer in the west of France—also a former national secretary and spokesman for the Peasant Confederation and a former member of the Coordinating Committee of the CPE—explained it thus:

I have always been very proud to belong to the CPE, representing, I thought, a social category that has their place in society, being the main producers of food. We have always worked on the farms to develop alternative agricultural practices. We were fighting on both fronts: we were fighting for our rights, and we were also fighting to produce food without endorsing productivism. So both were absolutely important to us. (interview, Brittany, July 2010, my translation from French)

In the 1990s, health, safety, and sustainability concerns became even more pivotal for European consumers (Harvey et al. 2002). The outbreak of bovine spongiform encephalopathy (BSE) (known also as "mad cow" disease) (Zwanenberg et al. 2003) resulted in a loss of confidence in food supplies and prompted the consumers to progressively turn away from industrial food provisioning toward quality. The alliance and convergence between the CPE and other social groups therefore appeared even more visible, both at the national and at the European level, in the 1990s. The context of abundance and plenty in the EEC indeed allowed, as Mara Miele writes, a "new sensibility" and a "new morality of food" (2001: 46), that is to say, a concern for the quality of food but also, increasingly, the particular social relations that have been involved in its production and distribution. In May 1992, as a result of external pressures from General Agreement on Tariffs and Trade (GATT) negotiations on agriculture (Uruguay Round, 1986–94) and from an internal budgetary crisis, CAP underwent a liberalizing reform under the leadership of the EU commissioner for agriculture, Ray MacSharry. The reformed CAP moved toward a realignment of agricultural product prices within the European Union closer to those of world markets. This liberalization of the agricultural sector was meant to address the trade-distorting effects of various types of domestic subsidies, which led to the decrease in farmers income. To compensate the loss of income, direct compensatory aid payments were made to farmers. The CPE contested this CAP reform, which according to them would favor neoliberalism, that is, promote accumulation of farms in fewer hands and serve the interests of agro-industry and supermarkets (Dufour 2002). Following the example of the member organizations at the domestic level[9]—the members of the Coordinating Committee of the CPE conceptualized an alternative CAP reform proposal based on the promotion of self-sufficient domestic markets and small-scale farming across Europe as a necessary precondition for food quality, environmental sustainability, and biodiversity conservation. Furthermore, in continuation of the Second European Social Forum 2003 held in Paris,[10] the CPE launched a "European and international campaign to change the European agriculture policy." Standing in a circle in front of the European Parliament in Brussels, Belgium (May 2004), members of the CPE from various European countries represented the "CAP clock." The clock in one part depicted the hand of the clock eliminating a farmer every three minutes in the European Union; and in another a young man representing himself as a new farmer raises up the fallen farmers as a symbol hope and unity of the European farmers. They concluded this presentation explicating their motive with the slogan: "Together, we will achieve to save the farmers and to settle down young people in farming" (CPE 2004).

In 2008, CAP entered again into a phase of renegotiations and reforms (CAP post-2013). This offered an opportunity to the ECVC for broadening their base of support to

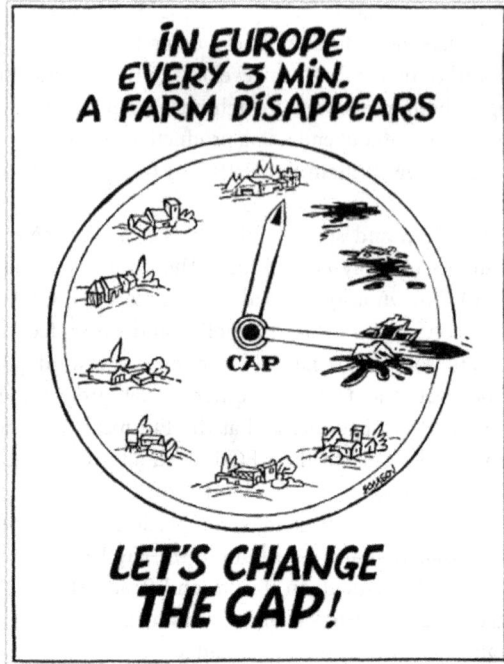

Figure 7.1 Cartoon depicting the "CAP clock" (Illustration by Pierre Samson).

non-farming actors and developing an alternative CAP reform proposal resonating with concerns of both environmental and consumer groups. The ECVC organized a European campaign to challenge the European Commission's and various governments' vision of keeping the global "competitiveness" of Europe's food industry as the chief objective of CAP. In September 2008, during an informal council of European agriculture ministers held at Annecy in the east of France, farmers, rural and environmental organizations, and international solidarity NGOs organized a rally under the banner "Let's change the CAP!" and drew up a manifesto calling for the re-orienting of agricultural policies and modes of production by the agriculture ministers of the European Union.

However, these coalitions with consumer groups, Greens, and development NGOs tended to remain as short-term alliances, and did not succeed in overcoming the individual demands of each of the organizations. A poster in the ECVC headquarters in Brussels emphasized their claim: "*No farmers, no food.*" One of the main difficulty for farmers was to increase consumers' awareness about the economic and social sustainability of food production:

> It is an encouraging sign that consumers are more interested in the quality of food, in the amount of pesticides used. But, from time to time, they should also be more curious to know how this stuff has been cultivated. Really, somehow consumers activating a social switch, it would lever us greater advantage with criticising industrial agriculture. (interview with Nicolas Duntze, Bagnolet, June 2010)

Toward a "common food policy" for Europe?

The promotion of a "food sovereignty" agenda

The ECVC's alliances with non-farmers groups, especially the environmental groups, successfully strengthened the advocacy of "food sovereignty" agenda in Europe. The concept of food sovereignty was first publicly proposed in international arenas in 1996 at the sidelines of the World Food Summit in Rome by the international farmers movement La Vía Campesina (Thivet 2014). This coincided with the completion of the Uruguay Round of the GATT trade negotiations and the creation of the World Trade Organization (WTO). Stemming from the idea that the WTO deprived the European Union and all other countries of the right to shape their own agricultural policies, the farmers used the term "food sovereignty" instead of "food security," and thereby stressed the right of the people to not only have control over their food systems but also to decrease the power of the transnational agri-food corporations and increase the power of the states over agricultural and food policies. The range of issues contained in the definition of food sovereignty was steadily widened and deepened over time, especially during the 2000s after the "Nyéléni Forum for Food Sovereignty" took place in Sélingué, Mali (2007), a village located about 140 kilometers south of the capital city Bamako. The choice of location was made to allow the debate on food and agriculture to take place in a rural and agricultural context. As the coordinator of the forum, Jean-Marc Desfilhes, an agricultural engineer and former coordinator of the French Peasant Confederation's Committee on International Relations, explained it:

> We decided not to meet in an international luxury hotel of Bamako, but rather to meet in the countryside because we thought that the best thing was to take advantage of this opportunity to create a structure that could serve the social movements afterwards. We wanted it also to be a center built with local and traditional materials and methods, local knowledge. . . . We were looking for consistency between what we say and what we do in practice: for example, not drinking coca-cola or Heineken beer, in other words, doing things differently, so that it really makes sense. . . . We organized ourselves to provide all participants with peasant food and peasant beverages locally produced in Mali. It was important for us to show that it works, that there is no need for industrial food produced by multinationals firms. We were successful, we really did things differently. (interview, Brussels, June 2010, my translation from French)

The "Nyéléni 2007 Forum for Food Sovereignty"[11] was indeed a landmark event in the food sovereignty movement for it took the concept beyond the confines of the farmers to the other social groups. Around five hundred people from more than eighty countries gathered in Mali, including peasants, fisherfolk, indigenous peoples, migrant workers, environmentalists, youth, and family farmers.[12] Organized by the Friends of the Earth International, La Vía Campesina, the International NGO/CSO Planning Committee for Food Sovereignty (IPC), NGO members of the Food Sovereignty Network, the

World March of Women, the Network of Farmers and Producers Organisations of West Africa (Réseau des Organisations Paysannes et de Producteurs de l'Afrique de l'Ouest, ROPPA), the World Forum of Fish Harvesters and Fishworkers (WFF), and the World Forum of Fisher Peoples (WFFP), this forum clearly reflected the enhancing strategic alliances beyond the agricultural sector. It considerably enlarged the concept of food sovereignty. The deepened and widened definition included not only the production of food but also other concerns such as health and ecological impacts, culture, distribution, and consumption (Forum for Food Sovereignty 2007).

Agarwal rightly points out that the definition of "food sovereignty" moved away "from the right of self-reliance of nations (1996), to the rights of people to define domestic production and trade, as well as determine the extent to which they want to be self-reliant (2002)," while embracing "everyone who is involved in the food chain—from producers to distributors to consumers (2007)" (2014: 1248). In spite of the many contradictions encountered especially in the new definition, the extension of the "food sovereignty" understanding helped to link producers and consumers and build a movement toward strengthening local food systems. For Jean Cabaret from the Peasant Confederation, "food sovereignty" is indeed

> a way to advocate, beyond the interests of the peasants themselves, the interests of the people: that is, getting quality food, diversity of food. It means articulating food quality with how many jobs we can save for peasants, how they produce food, how they work, in which conditions, etc. And it means also building a strong relationship with consumers: we can't anymore mislead them in thinking they can eat tomatoes here, in Brittany [west of France] in February. It is almost like heresy. We need to help people understand where their food comes from and who grows it, we need to teach them to eat locally grown fruits and vegetables in season: relocation of food production is part of the food sovereignty. (interview, Brittany, July 2010)

The movement for food sovereignty in Europe

Representatives of the ECVC, attending the forum in Mali in 2007, decided to replicate a similar meeting in Europe. Two years after the "Nyéléni Forum for Food Sovereignty" in Mali, the ECVC, together with the NGO Friends of the Earth Europe, the European ATTAC (Association for the Taxation of financial Transactions and Aid to Citizens) network, and the European Group of the International Federation of Organic Agriculture Movements launched the European movement for food sovereignty and another common agricultural policy with the name "FoodSovCap." This campaign resulted in the European food declaration: "Towards a healthy, sustainable, fair and mutually supportive Common agriculture and food policy" of March 2010. This was endorsed by more than 300 organizations from all over Europe. The ECVC and its allies agreed "to build a broad movement for change towards food sovereignty policies and practices in Europe, including the EU," and called for a comprehensive reform of EU policy for food and agriculture. The "FoodSovCap" then merged with another project, the "Nyeleni European Forum for Food Sovereignty," conceived by the ECVC's members as a forum discussing all areas of food and agricultural systems from production to distribution and consumption in Europe.

In the beginning, the ECVC planned to organize the forum in Hungary because of its geographical position in the middle of Europe, as a symbol of the linkage between Western and Eastern Europe. ECVC's members thought that this location could also involve more farmers organizations from Eastern Europe that were still being under-represented in the movement. The purpose of the meeting was to build a shared understanding of the issues related to food sovereignty for different Europeans actors involved in driving changes in the food system from the bottom up. After three years of preparatory process, the forum was finally held in Krems (Austria) in August 2011 under the auspices of the Austrian Association of Mountain Farmers (Österreichische Bergbauern und Bergbäuerinnen Vereinigung, ÖBV—Via Campesina Austria). More than 400 women and men from thirty-four European countries attended the forum.[13]

At the forum, the "diversity of the movement" (diversity of the participant movements) was valued and celebrated. For example, at the opening of the plenary sessions the national delegations from across Europe and beyond (Mali, Nigeria, Mozambique, India, Peru, Guatemala, Canada, and the United States) expressed their cultural diversity through traditional music and songs. The commitment to food sovereignty was symbolized by decorating the podiums with local summer vegetables and fruits. It was also accompanied by excursions within Krems, including visits to a farmer's shop and an organic food store selling regional organic food, a bio-dynamic farm with vineyards, and an organic farmers cooperative linking agricultural producers and urban consumers. Finally, at mealtimes, fresh, local food products supplied from neighboring farmers[14] were cooked and served to the forum participants by about fifteen volunteers forming the "People's Kitchen." The volunteers giving their feedback pondered:

> We didn't see ourselves as a service station but as part of this movement towards food sovereignty and autonomous food production. Most of us are in some way or the other linked to the active scene of agrarian activists here in Austria and also for us the Nyeleni was a possibility to network, refreshing contacts and see what is going on in other countries. The kitchen was our way of supporting a political concept in our own very practical and radical way. . . . This was food sovereignty in action. (Nyéléni Europe 2011: 42)

The forum resulted in the "Nyéléni Europe Declaration for Food Sovereignty," outlining the common vision and commitments of the participants, as well as the first steps taken toward implementing food sovereignty agenda in Europe. Five months after the forum, in February 2012, a steering committee drew up an action plan. The five thematic axis discussed in the forum became working groups and led to the implementation of the specific actions (see Table 7.1).

The forum was followed by the organization of a "Good Food—Good Farming" campaign launched in 2012. Organized along with the European Milk Board, ECVC, Friends of the Earth Europe, IFOAM EU Group, Meine Landwirtschaft, PAC2013, and Slow Food, the event saw farmers, consumers, and young people from across Europe

Table 7.1 Working groups, objectives, plan of action, and actions undertaken following the first Nyéléni European Forum for Food Sovereignty (Krems, Austria, August 2011)

Working Groups	Objectives of the Nyéléni Europe Declaration (2011)	Main Plan of Action	Actions Undertaken
Models of production	"*Working towards resilient food production systems, which provide healthy and safe food for all people in Europe, while also preserving biodiversity and natural resources and ensuring animal welfare*"	Promoting agroecology in Europe	Collective non-GMOs seed-banks; local seed-exchange markets; campaign for seed sovereignty; direct nonviolent action against GMOs, etc.
Changing how food is distributed	"*Work towards the decentralization of food chains, promoting diversified markets based on solidarity and fair prices, and short supply chains and intensified relations between producers and consumers in local food webs to counter the expansion and power of supermarkets . . . work to ensure that the food we produce reaches all people in society, including people with little or no income*"	Promoting community-supported agriculture and alternative distribution networks	Creation of a European network of CSA named URGENCI (Urbain-Rural: Générer des Echanges Nouveaux entre Citoyens) in 2012; publication of a *European Handbook on CSA* (2013)
Improving work and social conditions in food and agriculture systems	"*Work towards public policies that respect social rights, set high standards and make public funding conditional upon their implementation*"		Support the struggle of migrant workers to realize their rights

Table 7.1 (*Continued*)

Working Groups	Objectives of the Nyéléni Europe Declaration (2011)	Main Plan of Action	Actions Undertaken
Access to land and other resources	*"Oppose and struggle against the commodification, financialisation and patenting of our commons, such as: land; farmers' traditional and reproducible seeds; livestock breeds and fish stocks; trees and forests; water; the atmosphere; and knowledge"*	Advocating for agrarian reform in Europe and for institutional mechanisms for securing access to land for those who don't have it	Organizing an "access to land" meeting in Cluj (Romania) in December 2012
Public policies and the reform of the CAP	*"Changing public policies and governance structures that rule our food systems— from the local to the national, European and global levels—and to delegitimize corporate power"*	Lobbying decision markers, entering the debate on policy formulation at the European (CAP) and global level (FAO)	Participation in the European subregion of the Civil Society Mechanism of the UN Committee on World Food Security (CFS) hosted by the FAO and lobby to include Food Sovereignty principles in the Global Strategic Framework

travel to Brussels (many by bikes) for a day of action on September 19, 2012. A second forum of the "Nyéléni European Movement for Food Sovereignty," meant to update the first and extend the movement to Eastern Europe and Central Asia, which still hase large peasant populations, was held in Cluj-Napoca, Romania (October 26–30, 2016).[15] One of the results of this second forum was to prepare the ground for reflection on a European "common food policy" that goes beyond the proposal of a reformed CAP.

Noting that "food systems are . . . affected and impacted by a wide set of related policies: agriculture and rural development, public health, consumer protection, climate and energy, social cohesion policies, environmental protection, etc.," the participants asserted the "need for a holistic approach to European food systems, reaching from production to consumption of food in Europe" (Nyéléni Europe 2016: 9).

Above all, they emphasized that food and agricultural policy should express a "commitment to social values and agroecological principles" (Nyéléni Europe 2016).

Conclusion

Faced with scarcity of food during and after the Second World War, Western Europe planned for an abundance of food in the immediate and she did succeed. However, in the long term, CAP turned to be dangerous. It alienated the farmers from the land and food production, the farming activity became a business in the hands of the multinational agro-industry corporations and brought environmental and health hazards. The alienated farmers regrouped themselves to reclaim and protect farming and thus gave birth to the CPE. Gradually it dawned to the farmers that their activity and their struggle are not isolated but mutually dependent on other forces and movements not closely related to farming. Furthermore, CAP had far-reaching consequences not only in the countries of its origin but also in other countries through the commercialization of agriculture. Consequently the CPE united the farmers movements across Europe. Nearly three decades after its birth, the coordination has maintained its leading role in advocating an alternative CAP and in bringing and networking alternative food movements based on food sovereignty. Its members have succeeded in articulating, through different alliances, different coexisting regimes of values by linking the social role of small-scale farming issues, fair prices for both producers and consumers, respect of the environment, and "quality" food.

The building of a European movement for food sovereignty is now well under way. The two Nyéléni European Forums for Food Sovereignty helped to foster and strengthen alliances with actors of different origins and with different interests toward a fairer, more inclusive and sustainable food system. Both consumers and agricultural producers have assessed their responsibilities differently, considering food as a political site for experiencing reflective democratizing practices while taking into consideration its broader societal implications without overlooking the environmental, health, agricultural, and socioeconomic issues. The European movement for food sovereignty questions the social, cultural, and political values embedded in food practices and contributes to cultivate what Gibson-Graham and Roelvin call "ethical economies," meaning "more diverse, people and environment centered economies" (2011: 29). However, the question arises to what extent these alternative localized agrofood systems can develop beyond a "discursive field" (Pratt 2007) and across certain social classes, without a strong political will and support of the European states.

Notes

1 Nyéléni is a legendary thirteenth-century Malian peasant woman who became a renowned farmer and cultivator. Cf. Massa Koné from Mali, secretary-general of the Union of Associations and Coordination of Associations for the Development and Defence of the Rights of the Deprived and spokesperson of the Malian Convergence Against Land Grabbing, "Nyeleni European Forum for Food Sovereignty," Cluj-Napoca (Romania), October 2016: "Nyéléni was a woman who left her mark on the history of Mali, as a woman and as a great farmer. . . . Nyéléni's reputation grew beyond the limits of her region; she became a living legend. Her struggle is for food, a struggle for food sovereignty. Nyéléni is synonymous with perseverance, engagement, success. . . . Each of you should be Nyéléni."

2 This commemorative weekend entitled "30 years of European peasant movement, 30 years of European agricultural policy: what lessons for the future?" (Saint-Léonard-des-Bois, February 2012) was organized at the personal initiative of Gérard Choplin, coordinator of the CPE from 1986 to 2008 and of the ECVC from 2008 to 2013.

3 All participants were at least able to understand either French or/and English.

4 In 1968, the Mansholt Plan called for a replacement of family farms with "modern agricultural enterprises."

5 From 1965, common minimum prices for agricultural commodities were based on German prices which were the highest in Europe. Support prices far above the world market prices and tariff protection on the European level provided incentives for excessive production.

6 Such as, in France, organic farming (Christen and Leroux 2017) and the Associations for the Support of Peasant Agriculture (Ripoll 2009) in Italy, *Slow food* (Siniscalchi 2013), and, in many European countries, the revival of environmentally sustainable food self-provisioning through home gardening or "urban agriculture" (Veen et al. 2012) and the diffusion of GMO-free regions (Tosun and Shikano 2015).

7 In 2008, the CPE merged with the Coordination of Farmer and Livestock Owner Organisations from Spain (COAG) to form the European Coordination Via Campesina.

8 After a ten-year moratorium, it was finally banned in the European Union in 1999.

9 In 1992, the French Peasant Confederation initiated an alliance between peasants, consumer associations, and environmentalist groups named "Alliance Paysans, Ecologistes, et Consommateurs" (Heller 2007; Roullaud 2013).

10 The ECVC organized several panels such as: "For a sustainable and fair agriculture in Europe. Time to change the common agricultural policy!" and "For food sovereignty in Europe."

11 The word "Nyéléni" comes from the organizations in Mali that wanted to give to the forum a name that would have meaning to the farmers of their country.

12 Nevertheless, no consumers association nor labour unions attended this forum.

13 The forum was organized with a system of quotas and constituencies: food producers (farmers, fisherfolk, pastoralists, urban gardeners, CSA); workers (agricultural workers, migrants, trade unions); consumers (food coops; urban poor); others.

14 The organizers had an agreement with local farmers one year in advance to provide several tons of vegetables and cereals for this forum.

15 The forum was attended by over 500 delegates from forty-three countries.

References

Agarwal, B. (2014). "Food Sovereignty, Food Security and Democratic Choice: Critical Contradictions, Difficult Conciliations." *Journal of Peasant Studies*, 41 (6): 1247–68.

Choplin, G. (2017). *Paysans mutins, paysans demain (Pour une autre politique agricole etalimentaire)*. Gap: Editions Yves Michel (collection Société civile).

Christen, G., and B. Leroux (2017). "Processus d'écologisation des pratiques agricoles: injonctions contradictoires et appropriations multiformes." *Regards sociologiques*, 50–51: 7–21.

Dufour, F. (2002). "Le grain de l'avenir." *L'Humanité*, December 11, 2002, p. 11.

European Farmers Coordination (CPE) (1986). "Platform," Madrid, Spain.

European Farmers Coordination (CPE) (1987). "Compte-rendu de la reunion CPE du 10–11 décembre 1987 à Bruxelles," Bruxelles, Belgium.

European Farmers Coordination (CPE) (2004). Internal document.

Federico, G. (2012). "Natura non fecit saltus: The 1930s as the Discontinuity in the History of European Agriculture." In P. Brassley, Y. Segers, and L. Van Molle (eds.), *War, Agriculture, and Food: Rural Europe from the 1930s to the 1950s*, 15–32. New York: Routledge.

Forum for Food Sovereignty (2007). *Nyéléni Declaration*. Sélingué, Mali.

Gerhard, G. (2012). "Change in the European Countryside: Peasants and Democracy in Germany, 1935–1955." In P. Brassley, Y. Segers, and L. Van Molle (eds.), *War, Agriculture, and Food: Rural Europe from the 1930s to the 1950s*, 195–208. New York: Routledge.

Gerlach, C. (2009). "Fortress Europe: The EEC in the World Food Crisis, 1972–1975." In K. K. Patel (ed.), *Fertile Ground for Europe? The History of European Integration and the Common Agriculture Policy since 1945*, 241–56. Baden Baden: Nomos.

Gibson-Graham, J. K. (2014). "Rethinking the Economy with Thick Description and Weak Theory." *Current Anthropology*, 55 (9): S147–53.

Gibson-Graham, J. K., and G. Roelvink (2011). "The Nitty Gritty of Creating Alternative Economies." *Social Alternatives*, 30 (1): 29–33.

Gray, J. (2000). "The Common Agricultural Policy and the Re-invention of the Rural in the European Community." *Sociologia Ruralis*, 40 (1): 30–52.

Harvey, M., A. Mcmeekin, and A. Warde (2002). *Qualities of Food*. Manchester: Manchester University Press.

Heller, C. (2007). "Techne versus Technoscience: Divergent (and Ambiguous) Notions of Food 'Quality' in the French Debate over GM Crops." *American Anthropologist*, 109 (4): 603–15.

Kleinman, D. L., and A. J. Kinchy (2003). "Why Ban Bovine Growth Hormone? Science, Social Welfare, and the Divergent Biotech Policy Landscapes in Europe and the United States." *Science as Culture*, 12 (3): 375–414.

Knudsen, A. C. (2009). *Farmers on Welfare: The Making of Europe's Common Agricultural Policy*. Ithaca, NY: Cornell University Press.

Ludlow, N. P. (2005). "The Making of the CAP: Towards a Historical Analysis of the EU's First Major Policy." *Contemporary European History*, 14 (3): 347–71.

Mendras, H. (1967). *La fin des paysans, innovations et changement dans l'agriculture française*. Paris: S.E.D.E.I.S.

Miele, M. (2001). "Changing Passions for Food in Europe." In H. Buller and K. Hoggart (eds.), *Agricultural Transformation, Food and Environment: Perspectives on European Rural Policy and Planning*, volume 1, 29–50. Farnham: Ashgate Publishing Ltd.

Nyéléni Europe (2016). *Report - Nyéléni Pan-European Forum for Food Sovereignty*, October 25–30, 2016, Cluj Napoca, Romania. https://handsontheland.net/wp-content/uploads/2017/04/Nyeleni-Europe-Report-2016_web-1.pdf (accessed April 2, 2019).

Nyéléni Europe Movement and European Coordination Via Campesina (February 2012). *Nyéléni Europe 2011: Forum for Food Sovereignty*, August 16–21, 2011, Krems, Austria, Synthesis Report & Action Plan.

Pratt, J. (2007). "Food Values: The Local and the Authentic." *Critique of Anthropology*, 27 (3): 285–300.

Ripoll, F. (2009). "Le concept 'AMAP.'" *Géographie et cultures*, 72: 99–116.

Roullaud, E. (2013). "La Confédération paysanne à la lumière de ses positionnements face aux réformes de la PAC (1991–2003)." In L. Jalabert and C. Patillon (eds.), *Mouvements paysans face à la politique agricole commune et à la mondialisation (1957-2011)*, 97–108. Rennes: Presses Universitaires de Rennes.

Siniscalchi, V. (2013). "Slow versus Fast: Économie et écologie dans le mouvement Slow Food." *Terrain*, 60: 132–47.

Thivet, D. (2014). "Peasants' Transnational Mobilization for Food Sovereignty in La Vía Campesina." In C. Counihan and V. Siniscalchi (eds.), *Food Activism: Agency, Democracy and Economy*, 193–209. Oxford: Bloomsbury.

Thivet, D. (2015). *Le travail d'internationalisation des luttes: le cas de "La Via Campesina."* PhD dissertation in sociology, Paris: EHESS.

Tosun, J., and S. Shikano (2015). "GMO-free Regions in Europe: An Analysis of Diffusion Patterns." *Journal of Risk Research*, 19 (6): 743–59.

Veen, E. J., P. Derkzen, and J. S. C. Wiskerke (2012). "Motivations, Reflexivity and Food Provisioning in Alternative Food Networks: Case Studies in Two Medium-Sized Towns in the Netherlands." *International Journal of Sociology of Agriculture and Food*, 19 (3): 365–82.

Zwanenberg, P. van, and E. Millstone (2003). "BSE: A Paradigm for Policy Failure." *Political Quarterly*, 74 (1): 27–37.

Part Three

Connecting Values

8

Solidarity, Calculation, and Economic Proximity inside the "Vegetable Basket" System in the South of France

Valeria Siniscalchi

Fieldwork

Friday at 6:30 p.m., the truck arrives on time at the social center in the eighth arrondissement. Robert gets out, greets the volunteers who have arrived early, and quickly greets the consumers who have already been waiting in line. Some of them leave the line and help Robert and those who have begun unloading the crates of vegetables from the truck. Others open the folding tables that Robert also keeps in his truck. He takes out the large blackboard that lists the products and quantities (in kilos or in number) of vegetables that each basket will contain. The four or five members who are assigned to distribute this evening install the crates and scales, and people approach the tables. Robert gives instructions, begins weighing, and the distribution begins. People arrive, one after the other, some of them with children or a partner; they take their place at the end of the line to wait their turn.

For fifteen years, most every Friday evenings, about ninety members of the group, *Fans de carottes*, come to an urban social center in the middle of Marseille to collect their weekly subscription of organic vegetables from the farmers who grow and deliver them. The cover of this book, shows some of the volunteers who are weighing tomatoes and other vegetables that fill the members' baskets. *Fans de carottes* is one of the local groups in the town of Marseille that compose the *Paniers Marseillais* association, built on the model of the AMAP (*Association pour le maintien de l'agriculture paysanne*).[1]

The first association in support of small (peasant) farmers in France was launched in 2001 in the Provence-Alpes-Côte d'Azur (PACA) region of southeastern France. Similar in some regard to community-supported agriculture (CSA) networks, the AMAPs started as small groups of consumers linked by an economic and privileged relationship with a local farmer producing fruits and vegetables (*maraîcher*). The main objective of this system was to provide stable and local markets for small producers who had difficulty being competitive with large (monoculture) industrial farms. The second goal was to develop local "peasant" agriculture through the direct management of distribution. Over a period of time, hundreds of similar associations spread throughout France, eventually growing into more structured networks of associations (Lamine 2008: 22–26), most of which adhere today to a national network.[2]

The core of the system is a "solidarity" contract with an annual subscription, directly linking the producer and the consumer without any middleman. Adherents—consumers and producers—often present this "alternative" system as a way to bypass dominant neoliberal logics and fight against the system of industrial agriculture. What types of economy and values do these "food activists" imagine or practice? How is the exchange imagined and achieved? What type of calculation do people use in this system? How do they realize and represent this dimension of solidarity? I will try to answer to these questions through the example of one of these associations located in the PACA region.

The core of my research concerns the association of the *Paniers Marseillais* (designated by the acronym PAMA) that includes around thirty local groups located in different neighborhoods in the urban area of Marseille. Legally, each group itself is an individual association, which is in turn a member of the umbrella association, PAMA. The analysis presented here is the result of ethnographic work based on participant observation and observant participation, informal follow-up of encounters, political instances of the association, preparation and distribution of baskets, and, finally, interviews with farmers, consumers, volunteers in local groups, and members of the association's governing board.[3] I explored the daily activities of farmers and the place that this system occupies in those activities, as well as the practices and the vision of consumer group representatives. This fieldwork allowed me to study the basket system through a qualitative approach over an extended period of time and to explore the relations between producers and consumers from a perspective that frames them as "food activists." The notion of "food activism" (Counihan and Siniscalchi 2014)—conceived as an operative concept—places the accent on the links between political commitment and critical economic practices in the field of food production and consumption. Some of the people involved in this kind of system see themselves as militants but many of them do not. Nevertheless, as in other examples of food activism, they are trying to gain some degree of control over the food supply system in order to change it. And they are looking for (new) values through a new relationship with food.

Food is a controversial object. It delineates social boundaries and represents a sphere of intimacy and sharing, but also of exclusion (Anderson 2005; DuPuis and Goodman 2005; Narotzky 2012; Siniscalchi 2018). Although food is an element of cultural uniformity, it can, at the same time, be a means for people to exert their opposition to the system (Douglas and Isherwood 1979; Dubuisson-Quellier 2009). It is a commodity that circulates and connects, and as commodity, it has a price, and that price can change according to the market. Food production and distribution are regulated by actors and institutions situated at different scales. These actors are charged with certifying quality through specific legal tools. As Marianne Lien (2004) pointed out some years ago, food is a political object found in arenas that we don't consider specifically as being political. Richard Wilk underlined the capacity of food to transform political issues into something extremely concrete (2006: 22): it is political and, at the same time, an object that is actually ingested and necessary for our survival. For these reasons, it's a powerful instrument for committed consumption and production, capable of linking political and economic dimensions, the latter of which embodies the concrete side of commitment. To quote Pratt and Luetchford, "Food has become a focal point for action (and reflection) on contemporary economic processes . . . the most prominent area in which people try to realize an alternative economy" (2014: 1–3).

In some respects the AMAP or "vegetable basket" (*paniers de légumes*) system constitutes an alternative economic and social space conceived as place of experimentation outside of the market, and a place where people can express their opposition or resistance to that dominant system. At the same time, the basket system is not completely detached from the market, as compared to some alternative forms of production or distribution (see chapters by Homs and Narotzky and Rakopoulos in this book). It functions as a parallel food provisioning system. This chapter discusses forms, ideas, and practices that are generated in the basket system, paying attention to the emerging values and to their connection with, and disconnection from, the market.

"Baskets" and "vegetable baskets"

Today, more and more forms of mobilizations in the field of food define themselves as organizations (associations, cooperatives, movements, etc.) of producers "and" consumers, even though much research continues to regard and analyze them as though they belong to different worlds. The "basket" systems provide an excellent way to study this connection and to understand what happens "between" producers and consumers. It is often represented as a consumer system (similar to the Italian GAS, *gruppi di acquisto solidale*, Grasseni 2013), but the "vegetable basket" system was actually "invented" by producers who conceived it as a way to circumvent wholesalers, traders, and other intermediaries and create new marketing opportunities for themselves as producers. Their inspiration came from the concept of CSA, that some of the producers in the area of Marseille had discovered in the United States (Lamine 2008: 17–21). Here I prefer to use the term "vegetable basket system," similar to the French term "*système de paniers de legumes*," rather than translating it as CSA (the term used most often in the literature) in order to underline the specificities of this provisioning system as compared to other similar forms.

In 2007, few years after the creation of the first AMAP, and after the system had already spread throughout France, internal schisms inside the association of the PACA region produced two distinct networks, the *Alliance Provence* (today *AMAP de Provence*) and the *Paniers Marseillais* (Marseille Baskets, PAMA).[4] Besides the personal tensions between some of the leaders of the structure, there were two main issues that stood out among the reasons for the schism. The AMAP's first projects were focused on local, family farms or small producers more than on agricultural methods (Dubuisson-Quellier and Lamine 2004). But progressively, a growing number of basket networks began to give preference to organic production. One of the main reasons for the creation of the PAMA association was the aspiration to restrict the network to organic producers and eliminate the ambiguity between "local" and "organic" products which some consumers often perceive as equivalent and interchangeable. The *Paniers Marseillais* are now defined as "a network of consumer associations in partnership with local producers of organic agriculture or agro-ecology."[5] The second important reason for the schism was the desire to focus the network exclusively in the town of Marseille, and create an umbrella association capable of expanding awareness and knowledge about the system and how to manage it. This includes ensuring support and follow-up among the established organic producers and those transitioning to organic farming. Today the umbrella association—known as the PAMA or simply the *Paniers* ("baskets") and represented by an elected board and two co-presidents (a consumer and a producer)—is in charge of the coordination of the network, the creation of new local groups, and the distribution of other products (meat, cheese, spices, citrus fruits, flours, etc.) which are offered for sale to members as an option. It is also in charge of relations with the municipality and other local institutions, particularly in terms of funding. With respect to most tasks, the association functions through voluntary work (representatives of products, leaders of local groups, members of the board of directors, working committees, etc.), but funding is required to pay the salary of an employee who works in the association's office.

The term "basket" (*panier*), besides being the unit of measure for the contracted weekly quantity of vegetables that members receive from their established local producer, is also used to identify the local groups that make up the network. Each local group is also identified by the name of the neighborhood (*panier d'Endoume, panier du Rouet, panier du Roy d'Espagn*, etc.) where the weekly distribution takes place at a social center, the courtyard of a school, or some public space.[6] Each "basket" is composed of roughly fifty consumer households[7] and has a privileged link to a local farmer with whom the members establish an annual or biannual contract.

Contracts and solidarity

Today, around seven farmers situated in the peri-urban area of Marseille (between 70 and 100 kilometers from the town) participate in the association. Each farmer can supply one or multiple groups depending on his productive capacity and the number of members in each group. He or she is free to sell excess production at other kinds of markets (farmers markets or farm sales) even if the ideal model is a farmer who only supplies consumers through this system, in a sort of exclusive relationship.

The contract that each family establishes with the farmer can have different formulations—each local group and/or producer elaborates its own model—but they all contain certain commons elements. First of all it is a "solidarity contract" that takes the form of an annual subscription: the consumers buy the products in advance and promise to collect them each week. The solidarity of the member is not simply expressed in the one-year subscription; it is also inherent in the agreement to accept the consequences of climatic vagaries and possible decreases in production.

In the case of a poor harvest or destructive weather, the consumers accepts the risk that their share of vegetables could decrease. The contract established between the producer and each family of consumers defines the commitments of the parties concerned:

> The member agrees to support (the producer) in his approach to organic, market farming (*production maraîchère*); to accept the consequences on production from difficulties inherent in this type of agriculture and to maintain solidarity with (the producer) in the case of adverse climatic events or pest damage up to the amount of the basket; to assist in the unloading and distribution of vegetables at least twice a year; to participate in the life of the association (information meetings, general assembly, visits to the farm, etc.); to collect his basket every week or have it collected by a person of his choice. (contract, PAMA)

Another contract example:

> The member agrees to respect the schedules and the day of distribution, to help with the installation and arrangement for the distribution and to participate in at least one distribution every three months; to show solidarity with producers, particularly in the case of an adverse climatic event; to participate in farm visits and/or workshops on the farm, in order to improve awareness of agrarian issues. (contract, PAMA)

The producers undertake responsibility to produce according to agro-ecology or organic methods (AB, *agriculture biologique*) and deliver a diversified basket of vegetables weekly in Marseille. The amount of vegetables in each basket is calculated to cover the weekly needs of an average household or family of four individuals. Some producers adapt the dimension of their baskets proposing smaller baskets for couples or single people; others offer the possibility of half a basket or a basket every two weeks.

Another characteristic of the system distinguishing it from a market transaction is that members cannot choose the varieties of products they receive every week. Their basket contains whatever seasonal products correspond to the calendar of crops established by the farmer in the contract: approximately six or seven different kinds of products according to some contracts. The various forms of contracts are intended to assure the consumers that they will enjoy a degree of variety among the vegetables and not be left with a basket of potatoes or cabbage. In some cases, the contract specifies other guarantees from the producer:

> The producer agrees: to provide a diversified basket each week having an average value of € 17.50 (value may vary more or less depending on the time of year); to compensate for any significant drops in the quantity, quality, or diversity of vegetables with alternative solutions (contribution by other organically certified local, market gardeners). (contract, PAMA)

At the same time, contracts are often designed to avoid abuse of member solidarity by producers: in the instance of climatic events, he should find alternative solutions to continue to provide high-quality baskets.

> The producer agrees, in the event of vagaries in climate, to do his best to meet his commitments and provide the baskets in the determined quantities or to foresee solutions to compensate the Member. The Producer will communicate any discrepancies between the foreseen and the actual basket content as events unfold. If need be, he will count on solidarity on the part of the Adherent. (contract, PAMA)

The basket has a fixed weekly price—generally lower than the market price paid by consumers for similar products, but higher than the typical wholesale price received by producers—decided by the producers in agreement with consumers at the beginning of the annual contract. The price is calculated on the basis of a certain amount of vegetable varieties that the producer commits to deliver every week, but this amount is not directly linked to the weight of the vegetables, which can change from one week to the other. This means that the basket could be lighter or less full during the "transition" periods (e.g., in autumn) or in the event of problems that can occur in agriculture, particularly organic agriculture. The underlying strategy is one of consistent compensation over the course of the year: the summer baskets will be richer and will compensate those in off-season periods.

Food values

Pratt and Luetchford use the expression "contesting food" to comparatively describe food movements. For them, this means challenging unsustainable farming methods that are based on exploitation of non-renewable resources, challenging producer remuneration that is below subsistence levels, and challenging agricultural prices that are below production costs. The two authors also see this as challenging the loss of knowledge, traceability, and food quality (2014: 3). Social relationships, autonomy, fair prices, and regulation are key words in these forms of resistance, even if their objectives vary. "These movements are concerned with monetary value, the way corporations in the food chain destroy livelihoods of small farmers or shopkeepers. But they are also concerned with the destruction of values in the plural, whether the social qualities of people or the aesthetic properties of things and places" (2014: 16).

What exactly does the vegetable basket system oppose? This system and the practices characterizing it are less mired in the conflict of opposition than in other forms of mobilization. Participants valorize both the quality of food and the social values which allow them to create a specific "alternative food space" in which people "contest" not only the agro-industrial food but also the economic system by introducing a new relationship to food, its production, and its distribution. The basket system, which brings together consumers and producers, is presented by participants as promoting the development of "fair" and "quality" agriculture (on a small scale) and "quality" food products with an accent on health and respect for the environment. The (good) quality is seen as a consequence of the direct exchange and the possibilities that it offers farmers and consumers in terms of varieties, freshness and seasonality:

> Above all, the advantage of local produce is keeping transportation to a minimum . . . you have products that are adapted, that are fresher. Locally you can also grow products that are more delicate with more flavor, more quality, ultra-fresh, that isn't done much anymore because of transportation, to be able to send them further. (R. R., farmer with PAMA, 2015)

"High quality vegetables" (*des beaux légumes*) does not mean "standardized" or calibrated to be the same size, coloration, and shape as often required for those sold in supermarkets. This kind of distribution system allows producers, for example, to return to heirloom varieties of tomatoes—*noire de Crimée, cerise noire, andine cornue, rose de Berne*—as Christian, a participating farmer, told me are "impossible to produce when you work with large distributers and when tomatoes have to travel on long distances" (C. P., farmer with PAMA, 2015).

Certainly, the members look for quality products, but they are also seeking more transparency in the production, traceability, and less transportation, fewer intermediaries, and even a direct relationship with the producer. Direct exchange, solidarity, and close proximity (a local dimension) are the main issues they defend (see also Lamine 2008; Poulot 2014). At the base of the basket system there is a critique of the market, the capitalist system itself, and its destructive effects on the economy, values, and the quality of farmers' work and life. Removing the factor of distance from the capitalist system is a means to experiment with "alternative" market practices.

The direct relationship between producer and consumer is presented as something that allows people to reconnect two links in the chain that have been separated by intermediaries and large retailers; in part, it's an alternative that creates new forms of exchange while, at the same time, reviving more or less historical practices. The expression "retro-innovation," used by Marion Stuiver (2006) in reference to agricultural development strategies, is useful for understanding these perspectives and overcoming the impasse of questioning the novelty—or not—in these economic propositions. "Retro-innovation is about developing knowledge and expertise that combines elements and practices from the past (before modernization) and the present and configures these elements for new and future purposes" (2006: 163).

Members are not merely consumers; they are actors in food choices (*consomm'acteur* in the PAMA/AMAP vocabulary), and also active actors in the system, particularly through their assistance and mobilization during the distributions. Occasionally, the producer may seek help from members of his group (e.g., to remove weeds). Even if not all members are involved to the same extent, and some are reluctant to participate in such a direct way, this involvement contributes to the construction of proximity that characterizes the relationships produced by the system. Proximity is seen as both spatial and social, and the direct weekly contact between the producer and the members, adds significant value to the relationship. This close proximity is in contrast to the distances typical of the dominant market system: distance in spatial terms (contrary to products transported over long distances) but also socially (contrary to products from unknown producers) and in terms of a gap in knowledge (contrary to unknown means of production). Therefore the notion of "local" contains all these dimensions (Siniscalchi et al. forthcoming; Pratt 2007).

> "Local" means here (the place of distribution), first of all it's that everything happens here, in a place favorable to the exchange. Then it's the proximity and the seasonality: we live with the vegetables of our garden, it's like we have a gardener that works with us. In reality it's more than that because we wouldn't know how to do it on our own. . . . It's the geographical proximity and the human proximity together. (C. S., consumer actor with PAMA, 2015)

The basket system provides the members with regular opportunities for discussions and exchanges with the farmer and among themselves.

> The advantage is the joy of producing for people; you don't have the impression being there just to feed the trucks and the refrigerators of the middleman. You have real contact with the people that tell you about their lives and talk about something other than your business, and finally you have this super strong social link, and this is one advantage that is worth several advantages. (T. G., farmer with PAMA, 2013)

The exchange is both economic and social, and the social dimension becomes a value to preserve and reintroduce. When members come to collect their baskets they benefit from a climate of familiarity. At the scene of Robert's distribution, that I initially described, some are discussing with each other or with Robert as they wait for the line to shrink. Others linger after they have filled their basket, taking time to interact with other members or with the volunteers at the signatures desk. They talk to the producer about production or the vegetables, the weather, or any other news more or less related to the agricultural system. The distribution of the products is in some respects a social event. Although many of the members take part in this opportunity for social interaction at the end of a work day, there are certainly some consumers who "come get their basket as if they were at the supermarket" (T. T. treasurer in a local group), which is to say, hurriedly, without helping or engaging in conversation. Another aspect of this *prix-fixe* system is the fact that the consumers accept a pre-determined selection of produce. Although some members find this constraint too limiting and eventually leave the system, others feel the absence of choice is replaced by the discovery of previously unfamiliar products and—through exchanges with other members—ways to prepare them. Members do not know in advance what they will have in the basket. Even when they participate in preparing their own basket according to the producer's instruction, they are not free to pick and choose among the products that are larger or prettier, and thus leaving a less desirable selection for those members who come after them.

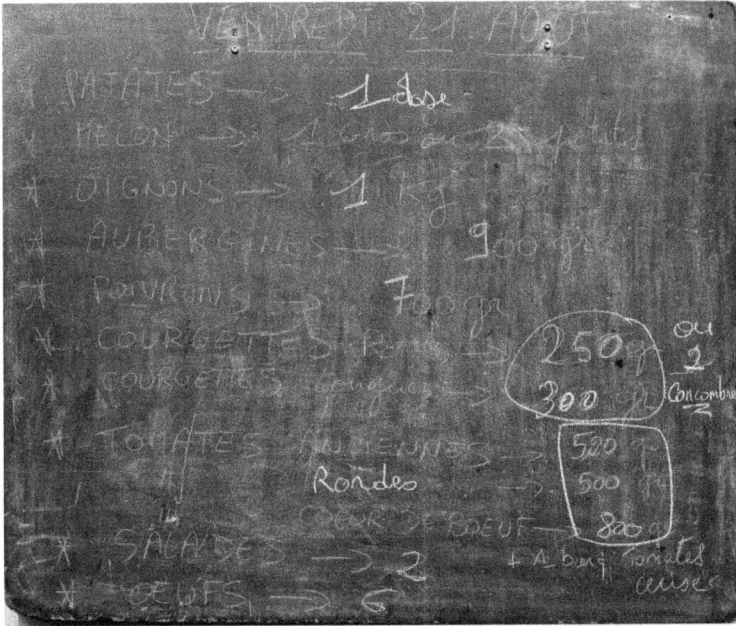

Figure 8.1 Producer's instruction to prepare the vegetables basket (©Franco Zecchin).

That sort of behavior reflects the impersonal aspect of the traditional market system that most supporters of the basket system seek to oppose via the solidarity within the group, and the direct relationship established between consumers and producers. The perceived impersonal and competitive character of the market represents the negative side of the exchange that these members seek to avoid within this protected, social space.

Through these elements of proximity, solidarity, and the elimination of intermediaries, the basket contracted directly from the producer without any intermediaries creates a system that is performed "outside the market" and escapes the constraints and the competition that large-scale distribution networks impose on producers. At the same time, while offering new ways to practice and conceive economic exchanges, the basket system maintains a relationship with the dominant (neoliberal) capitalist model at a different level.

Where is the money? The economic proximity

The basket systems' principle of subscription with a solidarity contract is an important element establishing consumer involvement over a much longer period than a simple market exchange. The system needs this contractual commitment to guarantee small producers the sale of their production for the entire year. The economic survival of the producers depends on the loyalty and commitment of the members over the long term. This extended time period contributes to the sense of the contractual relationship as, above all, a social relationship. At the same time, the contract implies an economic involvement over time, linking the producer and the consumer household in an economic relationship that is exclusive and in some respects, binding, while also creating a sort of reciprocal dependence. I am tempted to compare this type of relationship with the one established in the *métayage* or *mezzadria*, a specific form of sharecropping in which the farmer paid half of the farm's annual production to the landowner.[8] Historically, the *mezzadria* assumed various forms depending on the region and the period of time, and have since been the subject of contrasting analysis (Robertson 1980). The forms that I studied in southern Italy involved levels of sharing that are reflected in those established in the basket contracts. These include the contractual and relational dimensions, the social proximity, the sharing of production and risks, and the principle eliminating quantification of products (Siniscalchi 1995). In the ideal basket system model, the farmer would share all of the production with the consumers who pay in advance, and this actually happens for some of the network's producers. These farmers usually own their own land, and the relationship is therefore purged of the conflicts that traditionally characterized sharecropping types of contracts—even if other types of conflicts can still appear, as we will see later.

Producers are not paid directly by the consumers at the time of distribution. The members pay for their baskets in advance, with monthly, quarterly, or annual checks or bank transfers. This payment is routed through the treasurer of the local group who in turn makes monthly payments to the producer. The payment is therefore moved through a different channel and deferred in time. The apparent absence of money, or its invisibility, makes it possible to think of the transaction during the distribution as an exchange that is, to a certain extent, not economic. This allows members to valorize the social dimension of the exchange more than the economic one.[9] But the aspect of economics does not disappear completely.

> In the same way that there are family doctors, now in AMAP there are "family farmers," who are valued in much the same way as a family doctor: he is someone who knows the family, who knows the family history, who cares, and you trust him. (J. P., farmer with PAMA, 2013)

Along with social and geographical proximity, the system creates an "economic" proximity. Volunteers in charge of the contracts for vegetables or other products proposed inside the circuit meet with the farmer at least twice a year to take stock of the season. For example, Jean Marc produces vegetables for several local groups, and uses these meetings to explain situations on the farm, such as difficulties he has had with employees or how he plans to manage the harvest. In a close relationship established over many years with his groups, he has developed a level of trust that almost eliminates the need to ask for adjustments to the system. Whether it is a vacation break or a need to increase the price of the basket, the members are likely to propose a solution in advance, and in any case they almost always agree with his requests.

In this protected space, economic proximity means the possibility to discuss economic questions inside (increases in basket prices) and outside (increased labor costs for the farmers, taxes, etc.) the system. They discuss problems, possible forms of assistance, and costs that the producer must absorb. These include not only what

Figure 8.2 Members of a basket visiting the producer's farm (©Franco Zecchin).

is happening in the fields but also how these issues affect the "bottom line" of the producer. "Once all the expenses are deducted, we are left with a profit margin of 10%. If the number of baskets drops 10%, we lose our income" (M. C. farmer PAMA, 2016). The producer's income seems to be calculated on the basis of a certain number of baskets that his farm can provide. If the number of members decreases (i.e., the number of baskets "sold"), incomes also fall. The system also offers protection against fluctuations in the market, and associated speculation.

> In the classical market, when you sell to large-scale retailers, every day the strawberries are worth a certain price, the next day it goes down or it goes up, because it is the supply and the demand, the more strawberries, the less expensive they are. We are not in that system, we have a linear price during the year. . . . Even if the selling price is not very high and we are not going to become rich selling the baskets, we ensure regular sales. Our only issue is being able to grow the maximum of vegetables to fill the baskets, but [the basket] is already sold and that is really good point. (L. P., farmer with PAMA, 2013)

The price helps secure the loyalty of the members while providing small producers with a guarantee of the sale of their produce and protection from the vagaries of the market. At the beginning of the contract prices, varieties of vegetable, and other elements concerning the production or the distribution are expected to be decided by the producer "and" (or in agreement with) the consumers. As previously noted, the basket price is not directly related to the variety, quantity, or a per unit price, and one of the primary objectives of the system is to remove the transaction from the market, including this aspect of pricing. However, most producers actually calculate the quantity of weekly vegetables based, to some extent, on market prices.

> [The price] it's global, it's true that there isn't a relationship between the weight and the price. We establish [the price] by comparing, not by calculating our basket . . . instead, we get to have a sense of the value of a basket. . . . You make a comparison with, if our members had bought the same basket at the supermarket. Sometimes I [also] check the prices in the stores. (T. G., farmer with PAMA)

Regardless of the way the comparison or calculation is made, the prices for these exchanges, seen as "outside of the market," tend to be slightly lower but close to the market prices for comparable products. The dissociation (in principle) between the weight, the type of products, and the price of the basket is also true for other products (cheese, meat, fruit, flour, etc.) that are available to members as an option, from other local producers. In these cases even if the weight is a determining element for establishing the price, it isn't differentiated as a function of the type of product, contrary to a classic market system: the price per kilo of fish will be the same whether it is a sardine or a tuna, and the price of a *bleu* cheese is not different than a *tomme* cheese. The principle is the same: there is no choice, you receive the fish of the day in the fish basket, just as you receive a fixed quantity of vegetable varieties as a function of the season.

According to Lamine, the annual or six-month contracts (where the exchange takes place before the transaction is concluded), coupled with the absence of choice for the consumers, the space of discussion, and the collective involvement are the main elements forging the basket system as a real alternative to the classical market system (2008: 91). As in other forms of food activism, the basket system proposes new ways of conceiving economic exchange in the interstices of the dominant (neoliberal) model, while actually maintaining some type of relationship with it. At its heart, the system itself is a criticism of the capitalist economy and its destructive effects (in economics and values), but, at the same time, there are still direct links with this same market economy. For this reason, the basket system must be considered, from my point of view, as being both an alternative and a parallel system.

Crisis and calculation

The market can also enter the system by the back door, when the relationship enters a period of crisis. Cyril's farm is located east of Marseille, and for eight years Cyril brought his vegetables to a "basket" group of PAMA not far from the city center. During this time the difficulties accumulated. He pays monthly installments on the business loan attached to his farm, then there was a new tractor, a watering system, and then protection against the foxes that damage his salad production. His regular information bulletins often list his difficulties and his baskets are not always very "*beaux*" (beautiful): a "*beau panier*," a beautiful basket is one that is full of beautiful, fresh vegetables. The president of the PAMA association tried to help him to find other groups to increase his subscriptions and provide more income. A few years after he entered the system, he accepted a group from the other network, *Alliance Provence*. This group was closer to his farm and required less driving time. But the quality of its baskets—as noted by the members of the group in Marseille—gradually declined. The baskets of Cyril contained faded vegetables of lesser quality and sometimes damaged. Once the damaged produce was eliminated there was not much left. Whenever the basket board, composed of a few volunteers, met with him to discuss his situation, the discussions were tense. Even some of the "most loyal" members began to complain: "I feel like he's taking advantage of us," "we [virtually] paid for his new tractor, but now he abuses his position." The group members felt as if they had paid for his equipment because of the difference between the value of the basket received and the price paid. Suspicions began to grow. In fact, Cyril also sells his vegetables "on the farm" and the members began to wonder if the vegetables in their baskets were the leftover vegetables that he didn't manage to sell on the farm. And so, the controls began.

There is no official proscription preventing producers from selling part of their production in other markets (sales on the farm, farmer's markets) even if an ideal model exists where production is intended for the baskets exclusively thus allowing periods of low production to be compensated by produce from more abundant periods. The cases in which the producer combines several economic models are sometimes the origin of tensions or conflicts with the members. Only the more "solid" producers are considered capable of combining models without putting the basket model in danger.

Before joining the system, many of the farmers produced vegetables (four or five varieties, and maybe only one season of vegetables) for wholesalers and mass distribution. The basket system forced them to change the mode of production: not only the agricultural methods (without fertilizer or pesticides) but also the organization of crops. To be able to provide a variety of vegetable baskets each week, they must plan the production of about forty-five or fifty different varieties of vegetables. This requires a precise planting schedule for the entire year, a model of production that is extremely difficult for farmers without prior experience of this type: "You can't afford to make mistakes [with the vegetables or the baskets], and not all the farmers are able to do that. It takes experience, you have to be consistent" (R. R. farmer PAMA, 2017).

When producers are seen as having difficulty for a long time—usually due to a prior economic situation, such as whether or not they are landowners—members are suspicious if the producer has other outlets, viewing it as cause of poor functioning of the system (reductions in quality or quantity in the baskets). In these cases, the market reinserts itself in a more obvious fashion. This was the case in the relationship between Cyril and the Marseilles group. The members began weighing their baskets and calculating the "real" prices of the basket each week: August 17, the basket "value" was €16.10; August 24, it was €14.65; August 31, it was €12.05; September 7, it was €10.45 and almost the same on

September 14. Not only was the "price" getting further and further away from the weekly subscription paid by the members (€14), but the "value" was no longer equivalent to the farmer's commitment: the number of varieties was reduced, the tomatoes were of poor quality during the peak growing season when the baskets should be particularly "beautiful," and there was no compensation between higher and lower periods of production. If the value of the basket decreases and the determined price is higher than the market price, when it should be lower, the level of confidence decreases. Since this level of trust is considered the basis of the contractual relationship, the relationship is put into danger. Some months later, at the time for renewal of the contract, Cyril decided to keep the other group near his farm along with a newly created one, and broke his relationship with the group from Marseille, who then with the help of the association found another farmer.

These "alternative food spaces" are imagined as islands outside of the market, where social interactions replace the impersonality of supermarkets, where quality and variety replace the lack of flavor and homologation, where solidarity and confidence replace the mistrust of largescale commerce. When that confidence falls, these islands can become, or be perceived as, spaces of constraint for the consumers and/or for the producers. The same elements that serve to construct this "alternative food space" become elements of conflict, and the market is seen as an external agent entering this privileged economic and social space to corrupt it.

Local versus ethical: The elasticity of the system

Solidarity and food sovereignty, a "fair" price for both consumers and producers, their living and working conditions, and, more generally, the defense of good food for everyone—the words representing this ensemble of ideas have become key words in a political engagement compelled to navigate through the economy. They challenge society to rethink the system of production and exchange in a way that accents a moral dimension combined with the concrete economic realities that ensure long-term viability for agricultural activities. Values refer to the political and moral dispositions that allow people to imagine economies as an alternative to capitalism even when these values must cohabitate with the values of exchange that are elaborated in different markets (work, land, production, etc.) and implicated in the determination of prices.

Some frameworks of interpretation such as the one described by Donald M. Nonini, on terrains in North Carolina (2013) do not help us understand of this type of contractual relationship. In his interpretation, Nonini criticizes and distinguishes the "local-food movement" and "food security activists." According to Nonini, mobilization is minimal in the strategies and ideologies of the "local-food movement." Responding to the mistrust of a global food system that is too complex and too vast, these movements find a response in the establishment of personal relationships with the producers. Nonini considers the phrase, "know your local farmer," to be a very individualist perspective that stands in opposition to one that advocates social justice and "access to food for the large number of poor" (2013: 272). But this dichotomy considers consumers exclusively and does not enable a view of what happens in-between the producers and consumers, or the porosity among diverse forms of food activism.

In general, basket systems like AMAP "also affect the indifferent and that's their strength," says Lamine (2008: 14). In fact, the values of the members change over time and new values are learned by participating. Sometimes these systems represent a place where consumers, participating for "individual motivations," become acquainted with "the rhetoric and expertise of activists that are challenging agricultural systems" (Dubuisson-Queiller 2009: 116).

Pratt and Luetchford use the distinction between "open" economies and "closed" economies as ideal types: open versus closed, market relationships versus autarky. They do not exist empirically in a pure form but they constitute models for/of economic activity that are able to orient the action. In this sense, they are political ideologies. The alternative and the "food movements" act against the market model and try "to create some measure of closure in economic circuits involving food" (2014: 16). In the case of the PAMA, the paradigms (local and proximity) appear to be ideal models more than models for action. Over time, the system has expanded from vegetable producers to other producers (flours, oils, cheese, meat, etc.). This can support other small local producers and help keep more consumers out from the mass market. The consumer-actors of the PAMA have increasingly accepted expanding the limits of what is considered "local" with complementary products. The citrus fruits may come from Corsica or from the south of Italy, and the cashew nuts, even if they are labeled as equitable trade, obviously come from far away. In this case, the ethical dimension appears to intervene and ease the consideration of imported production.

Among these alternative actions, the economic imaginations mingle with the political imaginations, highlighting the continuities and ruptures with the market system. The emerging tensions between "monetary value associated with market relations, and the search for other kinds of value in the production or consumption of food" (Pratt and Luetchford 2014: 7) reflect the tensions between the market dimension and those of the community that characterize all economic phenomena— the "economy's tensions" of Gudeman (2008). The "community" refers to the social relations that represent the "basis" of the production, distribution, and consumption, while the "market" reflects the impersonal logic of profit. Food activists value and use the dimension of community to affect the market system. But the tensions observed also express the difficulties of finding an equilibrium between value and values, between political paradigm and concrete economic actions.

Notes

1   Lamine (2008) presented one of the first deep ethnographic analyses of the AMAP system, from a sociological point of view, based on enquires conducted in the PACA Region. I have analyzed some aspects of this system in two other texts: one comparing Slow Food and AMAP as examples of Food Activism in Europe (Siniscalchi 2015), and a second one exploring the notion of "local" from an interdisciplinary perspective (Siniscalchi et al. forthcoming). Some parts of this chapter are a re-elaboration of Siniscalchi (2015). Translation by Ben Boswell.

2 Not all AMAPs in France belong to the network and belonging to it is not required to be considered AMAP. This model makes it possible to have a wide variety of typologies, while sharing some of the main principles.

3 I have been member of two local groups since 2006 and I started my fieldwork on the basket system in Marseille in 2010 as part of two interdisciplinary research projects (DEVAMAP and EQUALIM-Terr), funded by the PACA Region. Some of the producer interviews were carried out in 2013 by Nicoletta Stendardo, anthropologist and postgraduate student, in the framework of the research project EQUALIM-Terr.

4 The second network could not use the acronym AMAP—even though it had become a generic term—so they invented the acronym PAMA that is also an anagram of AMAP.

5 www.lespaniersmarseillais.org

6 Some of the groups, like *Fans de carottes*, add a specific name, used by the members of the local group and for internal communication (the French love word jokes, *fanes de carottes* are carrot greens, and *Fans de carottes* are of course avid supporters); but among the networks, the groups are usually identified by the neighborhood name.

7 The minimum is around twenty households and the maximum is 200 households for one of the oldest groups in Marseille (organized in two weekly subgroups). Today around 1500 families (representing roughly 5000 consumers) adhere to the PAMA in the town of Marseille. Another six local groups are member of the *AMAP de Provence*. Responding to increased demand in the last few years, other systems similar to these but more commercial have been developed in the area. The number of organic shops has also been growing in Marseille, and more generally in France (Willer and Schaack 2015).

8 This land tenure system was dominant in the South of France and in several Italian regions, taking various forms (cf. among others, Wallerstein 1974; Silverman 1975; Béaur and Arnoux 2003). See Narotzky (2016) for an overview of peasant transformation.

9 For other kinds of transactions imagined as out of the market, cf. Satta (2002).

References

Anderson, E. N. (2005). *Everyone Eats: Understanding Food and Culture*. New York and London: New York University Press.

Béaur, G., and M. Arnoux, eds. (2003). *Exploiter la terre: Les contrats agraires de l'Antiquité à nos jours*. Rennes: Association d'Histoire Rurale.

Counihan, C., and V. Siniscalchi, eds. (2014). *Food Activism: Agency, Democracy and Economy*. London: Bloomsbury.

Douglas M., and B. Isherwood (1979). *The World of Goods: Towards and Anthropology of Consumption*. New York: Basic Books.

Dubuisson-Quellier, S. (2009). *La consommation engagée*. Paris: Sciences Po, Les Presses.

Dubuisson-Quellier, S., and C. Lamine (2004). "Faire le marché autrement. L'abonnement à un panier de fruits et de légumes comme forme d'engagement politique des consommateurs." *Sciences de la société*, 62: 144–67.

DuPuis, E. M., and D. Goodman (2005). "Should We Go 'Home' to Eat? Toward a Reflexive Politics of Localism." *Journal of Rural Studies*, 21: 359–71.

Grasseni, C. (2013). *Beyond Alternative Food Networks: Italy's Solidarity Purchase Groups*. London: Bloomsbury.

Gudeman, S. (2008). *Economy's Tension: The Dialectics of Community and Market*. Oxford: Berghahn.

Lamine, C. (2008). *Les AMAP: Un nouveau pacte entre producteurs et consommateurs?* Gap: Yves Michel.

Lien, M. E. (2004). "The Politics of Food: An Introduction." In M. E. Lien and B. Nerlich (eds.), *The Politics of Food*, 1–17. Oxford: Berg.

Narotzky, S. (2012). "Provisioning." In J. Carrier (ed.), *A Handbook of Economic Anthropology* (2nd ed.), 77–94. Northampton: Edward Elgar Publishing Ltd.

Narotzky, S. (2016). "Where Have All the Peasants Gone?" *Annual Review of Anthropology*, 45: 301–18.

Nonini, D. M. (2013). "The Local-food Movement and the Anthropology of Global System." *American Ethnologist*, 40 (2): 267–75.

Poulot, M. (2014). "Histoires d'AMAP franciliennes: Quand manger met le local en tous ses états." *Territoire en Mouvement*, 22: 40–53.

Pratt, J. (2007). "Food Values: The Local and the Authentic." *Critique of Anthropology*, 27 (3): 285–300.

Pratt, J., and P. Luetchford (2014). *Food for Change: The Politics and Values of Social Movements*. London: Pluto Press.

Robertson, A. F. (1980). "On Sharecropping." *Man* n.s. 15 (3): 411–29.

Satta, G. (2002). "*Maiali per i turisti*. Turismo e attività agro-pastorali nel 'pranzo con i pastori' di Orgosolo." In V. Siniscalchi (ed.), *Frammenti di economie. Ricerche di antropologia economica in Italia*, 127–57. Cosenza: Luigi Pellegrini Editore.

Silverman, S. (1975). *Three Bells of Civilization: The Life of an Italian Hill Town*. New York: Columbia University Press.

Siniscalchi. V. (1995). "Simmetria e asimmetria nel legame tra 'parsenali': relazioni e contratto in un rapporto agrario (San Marco dei Cavoti)." *L'Uomo*, VIII n.s., 2: 239–71.

Siniscalchi, V. (2015). "'Food Activism' en Europe: changer de pratiques, changer de paradigms." *Anthropology of Food* [Online], S11, Available online: http://journals. openedition.org/aof/7920 (accessed November 20, 2018).

Siniscalchi, V. (2018). "Political Taste: Inclusion and Exclusion in the Slow Food Movement." In C. Counihan and S. Højlund (eds.), *Making Taste Public*, 185–97. London: Bloomsbury.

Siniscalchi, V., N. Giraud, and J. N. Consales (n.d.). "Les expériences du 'local'. Variations et tensions autour de l'alimentation 'locale' dans la région marseillaise." Unpublished manuscript.

Stuiver, M. (2006). "Highlighting the Retro Side of Innovation and Its Potential for Regime Change in Agriculture." In T. Marsden and J. Murdoch (eds.), *Between the Local and the Global*, 147–73. Bingley: Emerald Group Publishing.

Wallerstein, I. (1974). *The Modern World-System: Capitalist Agriculture and the Origins of the European World-Economy in the Sixteenth Century*. New York: Academic Press.

Wilk, R., ed. (2006). "From Wild Weeds to Artisanal Cheese." In *Fast Food/Slow Food: The Cultural Economy of the Global Food System*, 13–28. Lanham, MD: Altamira Press.

Willer, H., and D. Schaack (2015). "Organic Farming and Market Development in Europe." In *The World of Organic Agriculture: Statistics and Emerging Trends 2015*, 174–214. Research Institute of Organic Agriculture (FiBL) and International Federation of Organic Agriculture Movements (IFOAM).

9

Within and Beyond the Market System: Organic Food Cooperatives in Catalonia

Patricia Homs[1] and Susana Narotzky

Cooperation in the interstices

Market exchange and capitalist production have become hegemonic forms of cooperation in Western democracies, supported by a model of optimal allocation of resources through individual transactions. This assumes a disembedded model of social action where social and cultural meaning operate only through the psychological drive of utility maximization. The ongoing environmental and economic crises have enhanced other forms of cooperation that thrive in the cracks of the system, sometimes as a result of an ideological positioning, at other times as a pragmatic practice to ensure livelihood resources. These forms are predicated in a strong re-embedding of cooperation within social and cultural discourses.

With the crisis in Southern Europe, as de-commodification becomes a necessity and state provisioning shrinks, personal ties and obligations are redefined in order to involve material expressions of care that are tangential to the market. These include giving shelter to kin, re-circulating second-hand objects through solidarity networks, providing food (often cooked), taking care of children, making small loans, allowing energy borrowing, caring for the old or the sick, etc. Morally framed obligations (such as between kin, neighbors or friends) are spontaneously reviving and being steered into the provision of needed goods and services in the interstices of the market system.

Simultaneously, some groups of people attempt to organize mutual-help networks through associations, cooperatives, and other kinds of collectives. Those we describe in this chapter try to coordinate food provisioning processes. Awareness of environmental issues added to a critique of "growth" models of the economy have motivated the emergence of proximity food provisioning networks, often organized as production-consumption cooperative projects seeking to enhance ordinary people's well-being (Grasseni 2013; Counihan and Siniscalchi 2014). In conjunctures of crisis, municipalities and other regional administration bodies are often key players in framing, legitimizing, and institutionalizing these options as substitutes to conventional market and state provisioning routes. Somewhat paradoxically, the autonomous mutual-help model of a solidarity "alternative" organization grounded in local communities is often underpinned by the neoliberal state's disengagement from its responsibilities for the welfare of citizens. At the same time, scholars and activists of the new social movements are strong supporters of livelihood practices that thrive between state and market which they define as "commoning": practices that expand and recreate the commons as a central aspect of social life (Harvey 2012).

Whether these practices are used as a political experiment or statement, or whether they appear as a result of necessity or as a mismatch between livelihood expectations and real everyday resources, all participants in these solidarity networks agree that the aim is not to depend on the market (or the state). Market provisioning is mistrusted. Participants in the proximity food networks described here perceive the market as predatory for producers and consumers alike as a result of relations of exploitation and intermediation. It is also deemed unreliable as to the quality of food provided and described as an unfair system of value assessment resulting in unjust prices. Indeed, the market is defined as an inefficient system of allocation of resources geared mostly to skimming rent returns through speculative practices.

Ambiguities emerge, however, when people engage in alternative provisioning routes whether out of necessity or as a political project that will open spaces beyond the market. The objectives of participants are mixed: sometimes they aim at "going off the grid" toward a utopian version of self-provisioning projects, at other times they envision a more moderate "de-growth" approach within the framework of plural economies (Gibson-Graham 2005, 2008; Escobar 2008; Laville 2000). Indeed, most of these practices are still predicated on the existence of a functioning market and a structured state that provide some of the inputs entering into food production and most of the infrastructure needed to support and maintain the alternative projects and networks (e.g., energy grids, water system, roads, satellites, IT server farms, etc.). The apparent contradiction of being beyond and simultaneously within market structures is superseded in the discourse of participants by the beneficial effects of regaining "dignity" and "respect" through collaboration with others, and regaining a sense of autonomy while remaking society around the humane objective of making a life worth living (Ploeg 2008; Narotzky 2016).

Activist discourses highlight the value of relationships entangled with material circulation, the centrality of making people valuable again in social terms, turning their mutual dependency into an expression of individual worth and even of regained autonomy. They also stress the value of remaking society through solidarity. The expansion of de-commodification in Southern Europe as a result of the economic and environmental crises indicates that peoples' sense of worth is entangled with the different meanings that pervade particular provisioning routes and their blockages (Narotzky 2012). This reframes value as emerging from social relations produced along diverse provisioning paths and understood as part of the process of making a life that is worth living (Narotzky and Besnier 2014). The main political argument that activists present for these forms of mobilization rests on their support for a kind of mutual obligation that is not predicated on social or individual contract (backed by the "rule of Law" or the "rule of the Market"), but rather on shared humanity and on an often vague and allegedly self-evident definition of the "common good." This becomes a moral justification for everyday activism and responds to a moral critique of the collusion of state and capital in depriving people from their dignity through dispossession of their basic needs, including food and a sustainable environment (Narotzky 2016).

We address these issues through an ethnographic case in the politically autonomous region of Catalonia, Spain. The case analyzes discourses and practices that emerge in proximity food provisioning networks that link consumer food coops and small organic producers where different forms of cooperation and reciprocity articulate socioeconomic exchanges. In a first section we present the socioeconomic and historical context and the general ethnographic case. We then address the position of these local agroecological provisioning projects within the framework of a capitalist hegemony. The next section focuses on the kinds of calculative reason that participants in these projects use. We then consider political and moral economy issues that contextualize the analysis. Finally, we debate the category of "alternative" that these organic food provisioning projects purport to represent. All along, we point to how reciprocity and cooperation networks are reconfigured in the present conjuncture while, at the same time, we underline the articulation of these embedded forms of cooperation with the allegedly disembedded system of market allocation.

Organic food provisioning networks

Different kinds of organic food provisioning networks have expanded in the last decade across Catalonia. The growing presence of organic products in conventional supermarkets and in distribution companies expresses the wide range of organic food supply chains. Namely, in Catalonia the global sales revenue of organic products was €34.5 million in 2003, while nine years later it reached €152 million.[2] On another scale, the number of food coops increased from a dozen to at least 130 between 2000 and 2010 (Badal et al. 2011).[3] The larger increase followed the financial crisis of 2008 (Federació 2010). Many of the region's crisis counter-movements[4] were disappointed with the hegemonic socioeconomic system and strived to self-manage many aspects of daily life such as housing, food, health, and education. Hence, food cooperatives became a possible model for alternative urban food provisioning, as part of the reconfiguration of new political values (Martín et al. 2017). Catalonia has a long history of agrarian and consumption cooperatives since 1865, a tradition that has continued to the present with its ups and downs and served as a reference point for contemporary activists in the food coop projects (Pérez Baró 1989). Nevertheless, many people also joined food coops motivated by environmental and health issues rather than as a political project, and only after participating in the collective for a time did they include other socioeconomic and political aims.

This ethnographic case analyzes proximity food provisioning networks formed by consumers' food cooperatives allied to small organic food producers. Although there is a wide variety of consumer food coops, this study refers to relatively small collectives of approximately fifteen to thirty consumer units. Each unit can be a family, a group of friends or of unrelated people, and they include about three individuals. These are urban food coops, they are self-managed and everyone may participate in decision-making through assemblies. The study also examines organic farmers who grow vegetables in peripheral urban areas and organic artisan bakers. These producer projects are horizontally organized in teams of three to six people, approximately, and are quite independent from food coops.

Farmers cultivate small amounts of land[5]—some two to three hectares—and directly distribute their production in vegetable boxes, what they often call "closed boxes." With this strategy, consumers can't decide what they want to acquire weekly; instead, farmers decide the quantity and diversity of vegetables in the boxes. Moreover, "closed boxes" have a fixed and stable price over time. This is a way to ensure that there are no surpluses in production and that farmers receive a fair amount of money throughout the year independently of possible seasonal or unforeseen variations in the quantity and quality of food. This method also guarantees price stability against fluctuations in the capitalist market system. Most of these farmers belong to agroecological[6] producer networks where they exchange knowledge, tools, and products in order to offer a greater diversity in their boxes.

These projects do not consider production, distribution, and consumption as separate activities; instead, they view them as interrelated areas that give shape to articulated economies. Hence, a specific kind of food production implies a specific kind of food consumption, and the opposite is also true. Organic food in these provisioning systems not only is food that has followed some organic productive techniques but also includes socioeconomic and political values all along the production-distribution-consumption cycle. In fact, the multiple food values embedded in the produce underscore tensions between these provisioning systems and the capitalist market. Indeed, these systems are neither inside nor outside the market, but intimately articulated with it. Here we seek to analyze the conflictive dimensions that embed these projects in a complex arena—"within and beyond the capitalist market."

Food resistances in a capitalist hegemony

Within these producer-consumer food networks, consumers and producers maintain close relationships—that is, excluding intermediaries—which are based on commitment and trust. The farmers and bakers we interacted with distribute their products to food coops directly and decisions are made jointly between producers and consumers. Economic aspects are here intimately and deliberately linked to participants' social relationships. As a result, this conscious process of embedding aims at subverting the neoliberal fallacy that economy and society are separate spheres (Booth 1994: 661). A concrete example of embedded practice is the codetermination of prices through member assemblies. In the establishment of prices, the various agents take into account different factors: producer's incomes, number of people working in the farms, surface of land cultivated, number of boxes distributed, investments made on the land, tools or other inputs such as fuel, crop rotation, and the economic situation of consumers (see Grasseni 2013). All these factors can be understood as environmental, social, or economic values, and each of them contributes to the global "viability" of these socioeconomics networks. Viability, as informants define it, is a wide and dynamic concept that is constantly being redefined among participants. Thus, it includes more items than just mere market economic factors, although these are not totally absent.

For the participants in these networks prices have to be considered fair both by producers and consumers and have to be maintained during a full year unless specific situations justify that they be redefined. With a similar aim, bakers propose equal prices for different kinds of breads to promote the consumption of ancient varieties of wheat. These breads should be more expensive due to the laboriousness involved in sustaining ancient varieties of wheat in a low biodiversity agricultural landscape and to the lesser productivity of these varieties, but their price is equated to the rest. In addition, bakers pay a fixed price for flour all year round ensuring a stable income to cereal producers.[7] These kinds of strategies guarantee that there are no surpluses and capitalist accumulation is restrained.

Furthermore, relations of production are taken into account in these provisioning networks. Thus, contrary to what generally occurs in a capitalist market where commodities seem to have value in and of themselves and production relations are hidden, in these experiences, products are meant to express the labor of farmers and all those involved, and value emerges from their mutual relationships. We can appreciate this in the following quote from a consumer member of a food coop: "Do we want to know what has happened with this product or not? I do want to know it. *I want to know all the steps [of production]*." Or in the words of a consumer who explains her reasons for participating in a food coop: "[I participate] because of people, of talking to people with ideals that I like, a way of living that I like, and *products as people*, because *you see what there is behind them* [products], and then, everything that you eat acquires a very important value" (Food coop member, thirty-one years old, 2010; emphasis added). Moreover, relationships with nature are also considered all along the production-distribution-consumption cycle (Garrido Peña 2007: 36).

In Marx's definition of commodity fetishism social relationships of production are perceived as exchange relationships between things, between commodities, rather than as relationships between people (owners of the means of production and laborers) (Marx 1999 [1867]: 36–47). It would appear that, in a conscious manner, participants in these food networks aim at subverting commodity fetishism. Here, the relationships between consumers and producers are placed at the core of the economy: "Bread, for us, is a produce that we want to make with high quality but it's also a mediator of relationships. It is a thing that allows us to establish a link, a network, to create the possibility of acting, of changing things. It is connected to the creation of an economy of our own" (Organic baker, female, twenty-eight years old, 2013). This process of relative de-commodification stresses the shift from maximizing individual benefit to enhancing social relationships. It attempts to subvert an ideology where economic motivation is based on the individual pursuit of personal interest and profit. Moreover, participants in these consumer-producer networks, through their collective price setting mechanisms, challenge the allocation power of the market system which allegedly tends toward the optimal distribution of goods.

These emerging socioeconomic practices also reveal the diversity of exchanges involved. While some exchanges belong to the so-called "formal" economy, most of them occur in the realm of "informal" economies. In some exchanges, money is used as the token equivalent, for instance, when trading vegetables for money (legal tender). But there are also plenty of cases where money does not intervene: for example, when labor is exchanged for vegetables between producers and consumers going through economic hardship; or when participants use swapping practices in free shops or in local exchange markets organized by food coops. We may understand these informal exchanges as forms of barter or as generalized or balanced reciprocity and hence different from ordinary capitalist market practices.

If we shift our attention to the political aspects of these socioeconomic networks, there is no uniform political positioning. Often, however, politicization processes emerge organically from collective practices rather than as an *a priori* ideological abstract framework. Therefore, these groups do not present an "alternative" *model* for social change. Instead, they present a performative *alternative*: practices change people and transform their values through daily activities such as eating, buying, decision-making, and so on. One of the most relevant changes among consumers participating in food coops is the modification of their motivation to take part in them: Most people get involved in a food coop in search of cheaper and healthier food; yet, after some time as members of the group, they redefine their motivations and interests in political terms, valuing aspects such as the kind of relations of production existing among farmers, or the social significance of collective self-provisioning of food.

The political dimensions of these collectives include specific strategies for "growing," that is, for expanding the scope of their practices. These collectives "grow" through the multiplication of groups rather than through enlargement. Every project we studied has a maximum number of participants that is agreed upon depending on multiple factors: room size, costs of the rent, people interested, and so on. Therefore, the "growth model" is based on supporting the creation of additional autonomous groups in order to resist "economies of scale" and capitalist accumulation. Furthermore, once they become established, many of these groups actively try to extend their cooperative relations beyond their own membership by getting involved in wider local social networks. Finally, the majority of food coops has an a-legal status and rejects official certification for their organic farming, an attitude that we interpret as opposition and resistance to processes of co-optation, bureaucratization and standardization of their projects. Often, formalization processes such as certification are perceived as specific strategies to ensure integration of these groups into the dominant agrofood system.

In these provisioning systems, trust is achieved by means of direct relationships between consumers and small producers; therefore third-party certification is avoided. Most small agroecological producers reject legal certification for various reasons. First, they report that producing in a more respectful way should not be made more expensive by including certification costs. Second, some farmers who process products do not want to register in the formal certification system because then they would not be able to endorse projects upstream that lack certification. Third, official certification is perceived as a form of top-down control and does not fit with small projects' expectations. In addition, agroecological producers claim that official certification does not guarantee fair social and working conditions of workers and transparent relations with consumers (Garriga 2006). Clearly, these socioeconomic and political dimensions are crucial to the projects we studied yet they are completely absent in formal regulation. This argument is shared by many consumers from food coops: "I do not value the [certification] label, it is marketing. What's important is to have links with the producer, without intermediaries, so that you know there is no exploitation" (Organic consumer, female, twenty-six years old, 2010). These political discourses and practices may be understood as different "ways of doing" that try to exist/resist in the interstices of a hegemonic food regime (McMichael 2009).

Prices come back!

Many facts resituate these agrofood coop projects as networks that are intimately articulated to the capitalist market economy rather than at its margins, however. For example, some inputs in farmers' projects and food coops still come from conventional product, financial, and labor markets (e.g. credit, petrol, tools, seeds, salaries, etc.). Scholars such as Ploeg (2008) have pointed to a process of "distanciation" from the market (de-commodification of inputs) that many peasant-farmers attempt in order to reduce their dependency on credit. Although these practices can also be found in our ethnographic cases, dependency on the market remains significant.

Furthermore, these provisioning networks also reproduce some of the axioms and values of neoliberal discourses and practices. For instance, many of the farmers' attempts at cooperation have failed because competitive attitudes appear in actual everyday practices. There are few extended networks of agroecological producers that operate smoothly in Catalonia. *La Xarxeta* is one such network. Set up in 2007 it comprises twelve farmers' projects organized in three local nodes defined according to geographical criteria. A node is described by participants as a localized group of members with weekly active face-to-face interaction. Farmers from *La Xarxeta* assert that they work together in order "to improve our experiences, the programming of crops, and to agree about prices among us, learning from each other and sharing knowledge" (Organic farmer, female, 2010). Further, since 2008, this network has been trying to develop a Participatory Guarantee System (PGS) of certification that would bypass official regulatory institutions. Even in successful cases such as this one, some farmers say that "we get along much better with colleagues that are farther away from us than with those who are closer to us, in the same node" (fieldwork notes). We found some farmers who modified their prices in relation to those of others in order to become, in their own words, a "good option for consumers," that is, more competitive. Moreover, most of the efforts to unify prices among farmers so as to avoid competition or even to share the stall in marketplaces have failed.

Consumers, for their part, compare the price of products in different distribution channels—food coops, supermarkets, marketplace, etc.—before making a decision on what and where to buy. The comparison is eventually used to argue for lower prices from farmers. These kinds of consumer attitudes are categorically rejected by farmers and increase mutual mistrust. Thus, the values taken into account when collectively deciding on the viability of the cooperative producer-consumer projects and on fair prices (values that include, among other aspects, caring for the environment, health, quality, relations of production, and trust) may be sidelined when making certain economic decisions.

When calculating the price of food, all these different arguments tend to enhance antagonistic interests between the various stakeholders in the food provisioning chain, namely between consumers and producers. Neoliberal ideology would interpret these conflicts as a result of obstructing the operation of free market through the intervention of agents that try to regulate prices according to "other" criteria in members' assemblies. Yet, what we observe are the tensions of a system that is either unregulated or regulated by the market. Then, although producers and consumers take into consideration the environmental and social values entangled in products, in practice these are often quantified and assessed through the dominant value of a market price. When this happens, values stop being relational and become reified values that tend to standardization, normalization, and institutionalization. These processes result in a complete integration of organic farming with capitalist hegemony.

In their attempt to include embedded relations of production and consumption in the calculation of food value these projects often replace actual participation with a mystified idea of personal contact and proximity that act as surrogates of real involvement. In addition, this imaginary disclosure of the complex social relations involved in the process becomes an argument that justifies higher prices for these products rather than resulting in a critical approach to relations of exploitation. This kind of commodity re-fetishization through symbolic discourses has been extensively analyzed in relation to Fair Trade (Goodman 2004) where it can contribute to the depolitization of some projects that aim at forwarding social change through the food provisioning chain (Heller 2007; Watts et al. 2005).

Each of these conflictive aspects, finally, shows how difficult it is to effectively resist in a capitalist world that tries to dominate and subsume all spheres of life. In this particular case, we do not find a coexistence of different possible organic food provisioning systems. Instead, there is a hegemonic agrofood system and the remaining systems of provision try to resist in the interstices of the capitalist food regime.

Dilemmas of organic farmers and food coops

The political and moral economies of the farmers and food coops in our study underscore paradoxes and ambiguities. We seek to address them here by engaging them within the larger scales in which they operate. First, we need to evaluate the articulation of the organic cooperative food provisioning circuit to capitalist farming and the relative weight of these cooperative practices in a region's total food provisioning. Do these new practices substitute capitalist market modes of provisioning or rather supplement them? Are they developing new institutional frameworks that will structure expansion and enable long-term sustainability outside capitalist pressures? Are they, on the contrary, the expression of local entrepreneurial coalitions of producers and consumers responding to a particular conjuncture and targeting niche markets? Our ethnographic evidence is ambiguous and we want to distance ourselves from the well-meaning discourses of participants that make it easy to lose perspective about the real social, political, and economic implications of these new practices in the overall structure of the economy.

During the last decade, organic products increased in both short food supply networks, such as the ethnographic case we have presented, and conventional supermarkets and large distribution companies. In Catalonia, the global sales revenue of organic products jumped from €34.5 million s in 2003 to €152 million in 2012 with gross sales in organic food increasing annually between 10 and 25 percent.[8] People acquire organic products via food coops as well as through conventional market circuits. Nowadays, organic agriculture is a growing sector of the agro-industrial regime which pushes for the development of institutional frameworks—such as certification—that benefit large firms seeking new market niches. Indeed, certification is the main tool regulating the organic food sector and this has important consequences for small agroecological producers because it implies accepting the imposition of regulatory standards that may be incongruent with their values regarding quality, direct involvement between consumers and producers, and social projects of economic transformation (Renard 2003; Sylvander 1997). The official evaluation of formal certification interferes with other mechanisms of assessing the value of organic food such as PGS rendering them liable to being identified as illegal and consequently penalized (Isaguirre and Stassart 2012; Minvielle et al. 2011). As our ethnographic cases underline, this situation creates a difficult competitive context for small organic coops that are trapped between value (in terms of the market) and values (the relational, embedded, transformative aspects present in, and mediated by, food). This situation is expressed in the anxiety that participants of small organic food networks feel when addressing the possible effects of the scaling-up of their alternative projects.

In Catalonia, the Gross Value Added (GVA) of the agro-industry represented 14.8 percent of the total industrial GVA of the region in 2010. Agricultural exports went up 12.7 percent between 2010 and 2011, especially in the unsustainable sector of pork meat. Agro-industry is considered a "strategic sector" and its resilience during the present crisis is underscored[9] while Catalonia has been defined as the first agro-industrial regional cluster of Europe in terms of people employed and competitive advantage (Peix i Massip 2008). In this conjuncture, policy makers support concentration of productive units because smaller farms cannot invest in new technologies or compete with food imports and multinational industries. At the same time, they point at the growing interest for "short-circuit" food provisioning and direct producer-consumer market transactions (Barcelona Treball 2013: 24). These new locavore, organic, and short-circuit practices of food production-consumption and the food values attached to them have become part of the agro-industrial sector and represent an additional provisioning path rather than an alternative one. In policy reports these practices are presented as part of the agro-industrial cluster of Catalonia, potentially one of the most competitive sectors of the economy: they are seen as catering to a particular niche of environmentally and socially conscious consumers, with the added advantage that they can render smaller farms viable and provide employment. When we read the reports and compare them to our ethnography, the marketability of alternative food values becomes salient while those committed to make them a real force of change appear extremely vulnerable.

A political economy approach requires that we evaluate these processes in terms of social differentiation. We need to assess how people involved in these practices produce or reproduce differentiation within the larger social environment. Three aspects are underscored in the practices and discourses of social actors in our ethnography. First, their activism: the intent that a different mode of food provisioning becomes hegemonic. Second, their weakness: the impinging forces of the capitalist system that tend to co-opt actual practices. Finally, their moral righteousness: the feeling that through these practices they contribute to the common good and they become better persons. In the tensions between these forces, differences among the participants in these projects emerge, as their activism, their weakness, and their moral righteousness struggle to produce value and sustain values, to provide people with means of supporting life, and to give meaning and worth to their life.

Relations in these processes recall practices described for market *places* as different from market *systems* (Bohannan and Dalton 1971 [1962]): market sites not fully integrated by the market principle which entails the determination of all prices through supply and demand. The market principle, however, is not as efficient as it is presented in ordinary mainstream definitions and we know that cultural and social aspects are present and create friction. Between marketplace and market system, the food coop experiences we have observed tend to define circulation, rather than production, as the site of the core conflict in the economy. They highlight the tension between value and values in exchange which explains the frictions around price determination that we have described above, while differentiation at the site of production (e.g. along gender or age lines, access to land, etc.) is obscured. Here, paradoxically, price becomes the final measure of value, whether it encompasses alternative values or not. Differentiation and struggle, then, are located between producers and consumers and tentatively challenged through the producer-consumer coop form.

Political economy also concerns the role of the state in these processes and the reconfiguration of the "social contract" in the wake of the 2008 crisis and austerity policies. As it appears in the ethnographic cases it merges with the issue of moral economy. The state's institutions and agents are depicted by participants in these new provisioning networks in an ambiguous manner. Basically, the state appears as "a failing state" and a "corrupt state," meaning it is perceived as colluding with capital instead of caring for citizens through redistributive policies. At the same time, its increased support of the "social and solidarity economy" is welcomed and positively valued. The harsh critique of governments for having promoted a consumerist lifestyle that led to the crisis and then responding to it with austerity cuts, does not generally involve a claim to take on the state's responsibilities. Nevertheless, these projects propose the empowerment of communities that will enable individuals to make life choices through self-managed systems. While not aiming at the substitution of the state, these systems are sometimes perceived as a viable option to address the negative effects of the crisis by strengthening solidarity networks. Likewise, the state appears to be actively involved in these food coop projects in a contradictory way, either by trying to co-opt them into agro-industry channels through certification, or by trying to shift responsibility for basic well-being away from the state and into self-organized civil society network structures by supporting them.

Alternatives to precarity or alternative economies?

This brings us to reflect on the relations between these new practices and what can be defined as "precarity," meaning the mismatch between livelihood expectations and identity building through work (or through consumption practices) and the actual ability to access the resources needed to attain them (Allison 2013; Neilson and Rossiter 2008; Standing 2011; for a critique of its political purchase, see Bailey and Brown 2012). In the ethnographic cases we studied, participants' practices seem to produce a shield against precarity. On the one hand, they redefine consumption practices that reframe expectations according to values ingrained in food, such as environmental sustainability, solidarity practices, producer-consumer cooperation, and autonomy from state and market forces. On the other hand, they provide alternative paths to material provisioning that are largely independent of monetary income. Showcasing these new values against the "old" values of wealth accumulation, conspicuous consumption, and reliance on state protection enables a reframing of the moral economy in terms of social and environmental sustainability linked to the remaking of community responsibilities that are closer at hand. It reconfigures expectations and channels of access to food by stressing relational and social values, caring practices, and reciprocity networks. As a result, it creates a dissident space where "precarity" loses its meaning.

These new commitments appear often as a bulwark against the drift toward social exclusion or total dependency on state or private forms of charity[10] (Ferguson 2013). If precarity points to the breakdown of a strongly institutionalized (Fordist-Keynesian) moral economy tying capitalism, the state, and the working class, and predicated on the expansion of an inclusive "middle" class through consumption practices (and credit), the new moral economy points to a withdrawal into direct, personalized trust relationships in what can be termed a "communal" moral economy of reciprocity. In these food coops, the material circulation of food values in food produce becomes the instrument for producing relations, creating a future, hedging against precarity, and making a life worth living.

Finally, we ask: To what extent are these new practices part of an "alternative" economy? The answer depends on how we define "alternative" and what aims guide these practices (Watts et al. 2005). The fact that those involved in these new provisioning practices are invested in re-localizing and re-embedding the economy in meaningful webs of relationships makes their objective different from that of capitalist accumulation. It also attempts to de-alienate labor. We see this as the main aspect of their positioning as "other" in regard to capitalist market practices but also to neoliberal transformations of the welfare state. Compared to so-called "informal economy" practices, with which they share much in common, appear as domesticated albeit politicized forms of it. They seem to be more institutionally daring in their attempt to produce a different form of food provisioning. In practice, however, they remain linked to capitalism and to the regulatory framework of state and supra-state institutions, and do not seem to pose a serious challenge to either. Their activist potential is questionable, often drifting toward an "identity politics" of solidarity where the individual autonomous choice to cooperate supersedes collective engagements. These new practices are often explained as a "lifestyle" that one might choose to enter freely, although they might be the consequence of hardship resulting from a particular vulnerable position in the structure of capital accumulation.

Consumer participants in these provisioning networks tend to define their projects in a pluralist economy framework similar to that proposed by scholars of "post-capitalist" theories (Gibson-Graham 2005, 2008; Laville 2000; Hart et al. 2010). Producer participants for their part describe the projects as a form of struggle and resistance to full capitalist integration thereby showing the difficult coexistence of "diverse economies" (Gibson-Graham 2008) and the underlying hegemony of the capitalist food regime. It is difficult to foresee in the present conjuncture the potential of these food coops for transforming the structures of the dominant food provisioning regime in the long run. Practice highlights the ambivalence of these projects and the different, often ambiguous, positions of their participants in the larger political economic context. These schemes are often simultaneous expressions of strategies treading unstable paths between "value" and "values": they target a niche market of food-conscious urban consumers, create a bulwark against growing precarity, and produce a better world. Being "in between" makes these projects viable, but it also makes them vulnerable.

Acknowledgments

This research was made possible thanks to the funding of the following projects "Addressing the Multiple Aspects of Sustainability: Policy Programmes and Livelihood Projects" [AMAS], PI Narotzky, Ministerio de Economía y Competitividad CSO2011-26843, 2012–2015 and "Grassroots Economics: Meaning, Project and Practice in the Pursuit of Livelihood" [GRECO], PI Narotzky, European Research Council Advanced Grant 2012, IDEAS-ERC FP7, Project Number: 323743, 2013–2018.

Notes

1   Corresponding author: patihoms@gmail.com
2   Data is from the Consell Català de Producció Agrària Ecològica (CCPAE), the public organization responsible for organic certification in Catalonia.

3 In 2013, the estimated number of food coops reached 150. The exact number is
   difficult to assess because many are a-legal and do not appear in official censuses.
   Only 9 out of these 150 cooperatives are legalized as consumer's cooperatives in the
   Catalan region.
4 Among these counter-movements we include Col·lectiu Crisi, Entesa pel
   decreixement, Aliança per la Sobirania Alimentaria a Catalunya (ASAC), 15M, etc.
5 Agroecological farmers usually rent their land or have assignment agreements with
   land owners. In our study only one farmer was the owner of the land he cultivated.
6 Agroecology is a theoretical framework developed by heterodox academics and
   organic farmers in the 1970s. This approach enhances a change in food production
   techniques but also changes in socioeconomic and political aspects of agriculture
   (Guzmán et al. 2000; Ploeg 2008).
7 Fluctuations of grain prices in the market range widely often subject to speculative
   hoarding practices.
8 Data extracted from the annual statistics of the Consell Català de Producció Agrària
   Ecològica (CCPAE).
9 Data extracted from the annual statistics of the Consell Català de Producció Agrària
   Ecològica (CCPAE).
10 The category of "social exclusion" points to this situation and has become more
   negatively tainted than the category of "poor" which refers only to material deprivation.

References

Allison, A. (2013). *Precarious Japan*. Durham, NC: Duke University Press.
Badal, M., R. Binimelis, G. Gamboa, M. Heras, and G. Tendero (2011). *Arran de terra: indicadors participatius de sobirania alimentària a Catalunya*. *Associació Entrepobles i Institut d'Economia Ecològica i Ecologia Política*. Associació Entrepobles and Institut d'Economia Ecològica i Ecologia Política. Barcelona: El Tinter.
Bailey, G., and K. Brown (2012). "The Rise of the 'Precariat'" http://socialistworker. org/2012/03/01/rise-of-the-precariat (accessed October 30, 2014).
Barcelona, T. (2013). *Indústria agroalimentaria: Informe sectorial*. Ajuntament de Barcelona, Barcelona Activa, Barcelona.
Bohannan, P., and G. Dalton (1971 [1962]). "Markets in Africa: Introduction." In G. Dalton (ed.), *Economic Anthropology and Development*. New York: Basic Books.
Booth, J. W. (1994). "On the Idea of the Moral Economy." *The American Political Science Review*, 88 (3): 653–67.
Counihan, C., and V. Siniscalchi (2014). *Food Activism: Agency, Democracy and Economy*. London: Bloomsbury.
Escobar, A. (2008). *Territories of Difference: Place, Movements, Life, Redes*. Durham, NC: Duke University Press.
Federació de cooperatives de consumidors i usuaris de Catalunya (2010). "Els grups i les cooperatives de consum ecològic a Catalunya Diagnòstic de la situació i promoció del cooperativisme. Novembre 2010." http://xarxanet.org/sites/default/files/Diagnosi_g rups_de_consum_Catalunya.pdf (accessed October 30, 2014).
Ferguson, J. (2013). "Declarations of Dependence: Labour, Personhood, and Welfare in Southern Africa." *Journal of the Royal Anthropological Institute*, 19: 223–42.

Garrido Peña, F. (2007). "Sobre la epistemología ecológica." In F. Garrido, M. González de Molina, J. L. Serrano, and J. L. Solana (eds.), *El paradigma ecológico en las ciencias sociales*, 31–54. Barcelona: Icaria.

Garriga, A. (2006). "Cistelles de verdura. Una xerrada amb la Kosturica." *Agro-cultura*, 27: 31–33.

Gibson-Graham, J. K. (2005). *A Postcapitalist Politics*. Minneapolis: University of Minnesota Press.

Gibson-Graham, J. K. (2008). "Diverse Economies: Performative Practices for 'Other Worlds'." *Progress in Human Geography*, 32 (5): 613–32.

Goodman, M. (2004). "Reading Fair Trade: Political Ecological Imaginary and the Moral Economy of Fair Trade Foods." *Political Geography*, 23 (7): 891–915.

Grasseni, C. (2013). *Beyond Alternative Food Networks: Italy's Solidarity Purchase Groups*. London: Bloomsbury.

Guzmán, G., M. González de Molina, and E. Sevilla (2000). *Introducción a la Agroecología como desarrollo rural sostenible*. Madrid: Mundi-Prensa.

Hart, K., J. L. Laville, and A. D. Cattani, eds. (2010). *The Human Economy*. Cambridge: Polity Press.

Harvey, D. (2012). *Rebel Cities: From the Right to the City to the Urban Revolution*. London: Verso.

Heller, C. (2007). "Techne versus Technoscience: Divergent (and Ambiguous) Notions of Food 'Quality' in the French Debate over GM Crops." *American Anthropologist*, 109 (4): 603–15.

Isaguirre, K. R., and P. M. Stassart (2012). "Certification participative pour une ruralité plus durable: le réseau ecovida au brésil." In D. Van Dam, M. Streith, J. Nizet, and P. M. Strassart. *Agroécologie. Entre pratiques et sciences sociales*, 79–95. Dijon: Éducagri Éditions.

Laville, J. L. (2000). *L'économie solidaire: Une perspective international*. Paris: Desclée de Bouwer.

Martín, A., P. Homs, and G. Flores-Pons (2017). *El canvi d'escala: un revulsiu per a la sostenibilitat del cooperativisme agroecològic?* Santa Coloma de Queralt: L'Aresta Cooperativa.

Marx, K. (1999 [1867]). *El Capital: Crítica de la economía política*. México: Fondo de Cultura Económica.

McMichael, Ph. (2009). "A Food Regime Genealogy." *The Journal of Peasant Studies* 36 (1): 139–69.

Minvielle, P., J. N. Consales, and J. Daligaux (2011). "Région PACA: le système AMAP, l'émergence d'un SYAL métropolitain." *Économie rurale*, 322: 50–63.

Narotzky, S. (2012). "Provisioning" (revised chapter)." In J. Carrier (ed.), *A Handbook of Economic Anthropology* (2nd ed., revised), 77–94. Northampton, MA: Edward Elgar Publishing Ltd.

Narotzky, S. (2016). "Between Inequality and Injustice: Dignity as a Motive for Mobilization during the Crisis." *History and Anthropology*, 27 (1): 74–92.

Narotzky, S., and N. Besnier (2014). "Crisis, Value, Hope: Rethinking the Economy." *Current Anthropology*, 55 (S9): 4–16.

Neilson, B., and N. Rossiter (2008). "Precarity as a Political Concept, or, Fordism as Exception." *Theory, Culture & Society*, 25 (7–8): 51–72.

Peix i Massip, J. (2008). "Catalunya, primer clúster regional Agroalimentari d'Europa." In *Documents de Treball n.5. Departament d'Agricultura, Alimentació i Acció Rural*. Generalitat de Catalunya.

Pérez Baro, A. (1989). *Història de les cooperatives a Catalunya*. Barcelona: Crítica.

Ploeg, J. D. van der. (2008). *The New Peasantries: Struggles for Autonomy and Sustainability in an Era of Empire and Globalization*. London: Earthscan.

Renard, M. C. (2003). "Fair Trade: Quality, Market and Conventions." *Journal of Rural Studies*, 19: 87–96.

Standing, G. (2011). *The Precariat: The New Dangerous Class*. London: Bloomsbury.

Sylvander, B. (1997). "Le rôle de la certification dans les changements de régime de coordination: l'agriculture biologique, du réseau à l'industrie." *Revue d'économie industrielle*, 80: 47–66.

Watts, D. C. H., B. Ilberya, and D. Maye (2005). "Making Reconnections in Agro-food Geography: Alternative Systems of Food Provision." *Progress in Human Geography*, 29 (1): 22–40.

10

Seventy Percent Zapatista? Solidarity "Ecosystems" and the Troubles of Valuing Labor in Food Cooperatives

Theodoros Rakopoulos

This contribution reflects on the position of labor in food values, as a means of creating value, as a value in itself, and as an aim of food-related value processes. The vicissitudes of the Greek "solidarity economy" include a movement of food networks that has developed and spread during the country's financial crisis. These mobilizations around food extend in a variety of forms and have included agrarian produce's distribution against market middlemen and the establishment of consumer cooperatives. It is these arrays of food activism (Siniscalchi and Counihan 2014) that I explore in this chapter, examining their point of convergence, which, as I show, is a concern with labor. My aim is to underscore how, in the field of solidarity economies, *labor* is a constant force ascribing meaning and content, as well as a stake around which struggles and fissures take place.

My main argument is that an ongoing evaluation and valuation process (of people and their actions) is taking place in the convergence of informal food-distribution activity and in the making of food cooperatives. I argue that labor, in terms of work, emerges as the paramount value in processes of cooperativization; however, it is a value that is rooted in the very microhistory of struggles of value and against austerity, currently taking place amid the Greek crisis (Rakopoulos 2015a). For instance, the measure of food activism's worth is done in labor hours in the context of Lykaon, a food-distribution cooperative with 430 members based in Thessaloniki, Greece's second-largest city. At the same time, within the context of the coop, labor is an enduring anxiety for everyone involved and emerges as a field of contestation and internal conflict.

As imaginaries of labor performed in activist, yet exoticized sites (like Mexico's Chiapas) suggest, no labor environment is fully agreeable. Just as a Chiapas-provenance coffee might not be "100 percent Zapatista," as solidarity activist informants point out, so too the labor of some might be seen as more valued than the labor of others. While some Lykaon informants are pointing in a direction of global connectedness, where solidarity seems a concept bridging (Rakopoulos 2016) different scopes, scales, and places, the rootedness of labor to the specifics of everyday life redirects us to more material, mundane anxieties. These include working toward the establishment of solidarity institutions and work positions for themselves, in the sense of creating livelihoods as an anti-austerity and anti-crisis prospect.

The chapter focuses on Lykaon, an outcome of urban mobilizations associated with the anti-middleman movement (see Rakopoulos 2015a), as well as on food activist cases that preceded it. The narrative places Lykaon in the broader setting of the folk, political concept of a "solidarity ecosystem," salient in Greece's cooperativism. This process is mainly done through using labor as a measure of value (cf Graeber 2001), but also through ascribing value to labor. In the labor recruitment to a food activist coop, an applicant is evaluated on a number of themes, including their political activity, while members of nascent coops count and measure their participation in labor hours. In an economy of reciprocity, labor arises as a common denominator to evaluate one's contribution in the field.

The chapter looks at ethnographic data over a period of time (from 2013 to 2016), reflecting transitions and continuums in my main informants' concerns. I start by presenting informal groups aiming to establish direct food distribution from farmers to urban consumers, while also concerned with direct democracy and with creating jobs in order to value and valorize the labor they do. This provides a backdrop to the main ethnographic discussion, two years later, where many of these solidarity economy participants have formed Lykaon, the largest food consumer's cooperative in the country, which does secure jobs. However, with labor valuations come internal tensions: in the coop, labor becomes a point of fissure and conflict. Scrutinizing such vested contradictions and commitments within the food solidarity movement, the chapter shows how the stakes of labor are the source of continuous concern, both before and after they become formally achieved.

Following recent takes on Polanyi's double movements (Hann 2007; Hann and Hart 2009: 5) or counter-movements (Burawoy 2013: 534), we might benefit from looking at the grounded, popular responses to capitalist crises. The social field of economic solidarity is one expression of "society's protection," in a Polanyian fashion (1957: 150), but no such response to crisis comes without contradictions. The term "solidarity economy" implies economic activity put to social use in a perspective critical of the conventional economy (Miller 2010; Hart et al. 2010). Debating solidarity economies in the context of crisis is still wanting: research shies away from accounting for how labor articulates with the ways people value their actions (for Greece, Vathakou 2016; Vaiou and Kalandides 2017). In this configuration, an acute prism is that of paying attention to the valuing processes and the value struggles that go into food activism.

"Food values" in the Lykaon food cooperative are those associated to having a non-mediated relation with the food we consume, which reflects a non-mediated relation to politics. Deciding collective matters through direct democracy is done in tandem with the maxim "we take food into our own hands." This central slogan, vital to the livelihoods and practices of the coop members, was a tangible case of an attempt to fuse food values with labor and politics. What links this twofold concern (democracy and labor) regarding food values is the need to establish a viable way to have unmediated access to resources of food and democratic participation through establishing stable and tenable labor lives for food activism's participants. In this way, labor security is an *end* of food activism; however, in the process of achieving this end, labor also becomes a *means* to measure the authenticity and vibrancy of food activist movements (Pratt 2010).

"Gefira": An anti-middleman action that would "take over the world"

The ethnographic field research on which this chapter is based has taken place in two different chunks, importantly arranged in two different stages of what is conventionally called the Greek crisis. I carried out nine months of fieldwork, mainly around informal food anti-middleman groups in 2013–14, followed by eighteen more months of fieldwork around a formalized food cooperative in 2015–16. Participant observation meant that I became a *member* in both groups, due to the centrality of membership in coop-related research. On the first occasion, I worked with groups that aimed to establish basic valuation of the labor provided by volunteers. In the latter occasion, I pursued participant observation with a group that had achieved some labor security, but continued to use labor as a form of measurement of their members' commitment.

The structural difference between these two periods has been mainly that they belong to a diverse modality of sociopolitical configuration vis-à-vis the state. In the first period, a right-wing government imposed austerity and was counteracted by activists generally hopeful that a political solution would come from the Left. In the second, a left-wing government first opposed and then (from the summer of 2015 onward) imposed similarly harsh austerity measures, leaving an array of movements that, by and large, helped it to gain power in a state of disappointment. In both cases, the research site was the eastern districts of Thessaloniki (also known as Salonica), in areas whose residents are usually classified as lower middle class, petty-bourgeois, and working class.

During the first period, social movements were plentiful and hopeful; indeed, some of the most successful and radicalized elements of the crisis' solidarity economy were located precisely in food distribution. The distribution of foodstuff in alternative circuits to those of the conventional market, already attached to the "immediacy" of household cooking (Sutton 2016), had become the locus of a vivid social movement that aimed to "cut out" market brokers altogether, to make sure agrarian produce is sold directly from farmers to urban folk. In Thessaloniki, I came in long-term contact with "The Gefira Commission" (hereafter Gefira[1]), an informal network group engaging this non-mediated practice that comprises people living in the district immediately to the east of the city center. The area is a dense district, heavily hit by the crisis.

Gefira is a group comprised primarily of young, unemployed people who organize the distribution of agricultural products in their communities directly from farmers. This is done without the mediation of market middlemen; those organizing distribution gain no profit for themselves. Gefira belonged to a (now defunct) coalition of anti-middleman groups in Thessaloniki, called "Open Network" and had loose relations with other such organizations around Greece.[2] The association operates like an informal network, organizing the collection and distribution of agrarian produce directly from producers to consumers. These commodities are then sold to community members at prices far below retail cost. Gefira is one of many informal associations that cater for the distribution of agrarian produce this way. Its members aimed to make it a cooperative in order to precisely ensure the main food value of their struggles, labor, is valorized. The goal was, in other words, to not continue their activity on a volunteer basis but to find paid work for some of the food activism contributors in a formal group of cooperative labor. The constant concern that underpinned their commitment to shaping alternative food networks focuses on the ways they thought of their activities as labor.

I took residence in the Anatoli district of the city and joined the activities of Gefira as a participant. The decision to inhabit that area proved useful in the long run, as Lykaon, the formal cooperative that arose from initiatives like Gefira was also based in the vicinity, suggesting a geographical continuity in urban food value struggles. Participating in their "anti-middleman" activities entailed meeting farmers, helping with setting up the informal farmer markets, and getting to know in person what the value of "cutting out the middleman" was for these food activists. The value of non-mediated practice has a directedness that articulates, according to informants, with the value of direct democracy. As a Gefira member told me, "We take food into our hands—we take politics into our hands." This key maxim described the importance of grassroots decision-making as a food value.

I followed several meetings of the group. On one of the first occasions, I spoke with Anna, who had been involved with the commission for almost three years. Her analysis of the social situation of solidarity economy participants was an important introduction to the politics of the organization. "We are doing all this and invest a lot of our time in managing this flow of people, and things, and ideas . . . it is not easy. There is a moral pay, if you will, yes. But people benefiting from this should understand we are not doing this for a living." Giorgos, a forty-year-old mechanic also told me that "our work is to mobilize people; they ask us when the next distribution will be, and we respond, *when you will be a part of it.*"

On one of the last occasions, things had evolved, as this was taking place before fieldwork was wrapped up and before Gefira started actively working with lawyers to create a food cooperative out of their group. In that case, I encountered Anna and several people involved (including farmers) in their usual meeting place, a small piazza in their district, pondering over a map of the world, with continents stretching in front of their eyes. Anna had laid the quite sizable paper map on the ground and would point to the possible flows linking localities that emanate from human cooperation. At one point, she forcefully claimed to the impressed farmers: "See this? Alone we achieve nothing. There are coops everywhere, from India to Brazil. With a coop we can take over the world."

Many Gefira members expressed sympathy toward or outright allegiance with parties of the Left, while those more senior in age derived their "activist experience," in their "years of struggles in unions." The phenomenal rise of Syriza, the left-wing party eventually voted to power in early 2015, was seen as a hopeful development to establish a viable food solidarity economy in the country. In their assemblies, the Gefira activists directed their everyday activities toward the prospect of organizing their work further. Their plan was to establish a cluster of cooperativist initiatives in order to find a way to sustain their project and even value the labor they invest into it. *"We don't believe in volunteering*, it's an idea that does not apply to our principles," as Maria stressed to me once. In the words of Mr. Stefanos, a sixty-five-year-old pensioned railroad worker with a unionist past, "in order to reshape the current, let's admit it, misery of our solidarity economy, where people work to organize stuff but never get paid for it, we might benefit immensely from a shift in government." The idea was that a progressive political establishment would embrace the solidarity economy (see also Rakopoulos 2015b: 170–72). The "misery" of the solidarity economy is a powerful notion that requires attention. In fact, it points to the direction of solidifying what is essentially a series of volunteering practices into a way of securing livelihoods and a future (see also Rakopoulos 2018).

The Gefira's members reject neither the state nor the market—and in fact the ambitions to "take over the world" implied an organized solidarity economy that would encompass both market transactions and state protection of their labor. They strove to link with similar activist initiatives around Greece to "get rid of middlemen in the wide sense of the word." With the idea of the middleman Gefira's activists often find an allegory for their broader political claims. A younger activist, Elena, pointed out to me that the Greek government "is, in a way, a kind of middleman itself, as it lets the troika's Memoranda speak through it." Here, there is an evident association between the directedness of the distribution of foodstuff, products that are of immediate concern to households, and the need to organize the polity in ways in which the voices of people may be heard directly in the political sphere. The sense of mediation in both food consumption and political organization is frowned upon. The idea of "taking food into our own hands" kickstarts broader ambitions over how "the economy" should be organized—ambitions premised on practices of directedness, shaping an unmediated sphere between food and politics.

"Ecosystem of the like-minded"

I was reminded of Mr. Stefanos words and reference to the "economy" a few months after that event, in 2015, when I went to Athens for the annual Social and Solidarity Economy Meeting at Plato Park. After spending time in negotiations and debates in forums like the "Open Network" of Thessaloniki over how to go about formalizing the nascent solidarity economy of food in Greece, the Solidarity Economy Meeting was established as a yearly event. The festival lasts for three days and takes place in the same month in two different cities (Athens and Thessaloniki); it has become the main vehicle of organization, discussion, and collective arrangements in the movement. The formation of many coops and collectives that acquired legal form across the country in the years following the massive development of an informal solidarity economy up to

2014 were now giving way to a network of small, but intensely working, cooperatives. Their members were mostly participants earning a wage from the shared profits of these non-for-profit new organizations. Such coops included mainly shops and retail spaces where farmers' produce was sold with no middleman mediation, as well as coffee shops and taverns, where such food was cooked and prepared to be sold.

Plato Park is one of the biggest parks in the city. I arrived way too early on the first day of the 2015 meeting, it seems. There were forlorn spaces of thin grass, with a sign or two scattered around tied to trees, where thematic meetings were meant to take place in a few hours. One of the signs read a lonely and semiotically tragic "ECONOMY," with no one around the tree attending to it. Minutes later, I was sitting in the cooperative café "Together" waiting for Mr. Stefanos, who was also visiting from Thessaloniki. As I waited, I spent some time with Eva, a thirty-year-old woman who worked at another coop café, LaCiudad, at the center of the city. She pointed out with some fervor that "we are part of an ecosystem. Solidarity is the ecosystem in which we move in." This resonates with the thoughts that Mr. Stefanos also shared: "Shaping an ecosystem of solidarity implied that some of these young people found a remunerative way to make a living by cutting the middleman." Soon, we all headed to the thematic meetings that would hold us together for the following three days.

Just like the equivalent festival in Thessaloniki, we spent these days in endless conversation, navigating across theme groups like "labor" and "ecology," carefully maintaining distance from other workshops that focused on Falun Gong, Reiki, Ayurveda, and making your own compost in your garden. "We feel closer to the workers of a commercial supermarket, that work as dependent labor for a capitalist enterprise, than we would ever feel for those people," Elli, another LaCiudad member, told me. The choice of a Spanish name for their small cooperative café—where four women members worked—is indicative of their choice to have "an international outlook" as she said. It resonates with the informants' concerns, as with the example of Anna and her map of the world.

A few days later, I was invited to LaCiudad café to continue the conversation. There, just like in Thessaloniki's informal or formal coop initiatives, I came across two types of coffee, which Elli suggested I buy. One had a name that confirmed its internationalist pretense. I had come across this same brand of coffee in other shops and cafes belonging to the "ecosystem," although I could not recall exactly where. Just like coop members in Thessaloniki did some time ago and throughout my fieldwork, Anna and Elli argued that this was a different type of coffee, one that needed support. It was a *Zapatístikos kafés*, that is, a Zapatista coffee.[3] Its name was, tellingly, *Compañero* ("Comrade") coffee.

On the cover of one of the three *Compañero* coffee labels though, there was an ambiguous bit of information. The cover suggested that the coffee was only 70 percent *Zapatístikos*, while the rest was sourced from elsewhere—presumably outside Chiapas. The price also seemed to echo that slight impurity: at €3.60, it was 40 cents cheaper than the 100 percent *Zapatístikos kafés*.[4] For 250 grams of "Greek" coffee, the Arabica blend roasted and ground to be served in the typical *bríki* Balkan preparation of coffee brewing, this was considerably more expensive than the conventional Greek coffees out there. Its hybrid content encapsulated much about the solidarity economy of the ecosystem.

A global commodity was taking local forms and was endowed with a politicized— and exoticizing—rhetoric. The exotic revolutionary labor that took place far away endowed the imported commodity with particular meaning (and high exchange value). Elli explained that the rest 30 percent was sourced from "other realities, outside Chiapas, but surely somehow close to it as an ideology. It is hard to find anything pure anyway, *anything you agree 100% with*" (my emphasis). Here, the material food value seems to be measured according to local, ideological values: valuation travels according to agreement, and can metaphorically or literally be deemed not pure. This was an item sourced from exoticized labor and marketed not as Mexican but as a radical commodity, one with a strong political note; at the same time, it was a coffee designed to be consumed in a Greek traditional(ist) fashion, in a way strictly localized, culturally ingrained in local specifics. The *Compañero* coffee, 70 percent or 100 percent Zapatista, was a point of conversion of labor and (alter- or anti-) globalization idiom to a consuming language of radicality, as well as a point of convergence for the global concerns and the local identities pertaining to Greek solidarity economy's food values. It was at once flamboyantly ambitious and solidary with global trepidations while rooted in the realities of a place with a particular history, currently undergoing an enduring crisis, one that imaginatively brought it "closer to the realities of Chiapas," as Eva suggested.

That same 70 percent purely Zapatistic coffee was sold and promoted in Lykaon, the largest consumer cooperative of the Greek solidarity economy, as I recalled and was told by Eva and Elli. Workers at LaCiudad asked me to convey their greetings to my informants in Lykaon—parts and members of LaCiudad's "ecosystem." Like most people in the solidarity economy festival, they spoke to me very fondly of the Thessaloniki coop where I had commenced fieldwork. The idea was to follow the one case of a coop that interlocutors suggested was "about more than just a couple of people finding work." Interestingly, the main issue with the coop's development proved to be labor, again.

Lykaon: Troubles with labor

Lykaon is the biggest consumer cooperative in Greece. It maintains a shop east of Thessaloniki's center (around the same area that my informants from the anti-middleman movement come from). The shop is visible from the main avenue of the city, Egnatia, with a large banner to recall "an eco-friendly aesthetics," as a Lykaon member told me. The banner, displaying large green letters and ornamented with a progressivist arrow pointing to an optimistic future, reads "we are taking food in our own hands."

In the shop, there are seven paid workers, all of them members of the coop. Apart from the shop, there is what most members of Lykaon call "the real institution" or "the actual coop"—that is, the various meetings of the collective of Lykaon, held weekly, monthly, or triannually. All members are allowed and indeed encouraged to participate in the meetings and assemblies of the coop, as well as partake in its everyday, ongoing logistics. This condition is a prerequisite and is understood *as labor*. In fact, labor creates a value system that has become the conversion rate of all contributions to the coop. One can understand the emic exegeses of membership within the coop, as well how it ties with labor, across two broad sociological axes.

The first axis can be seen as a social configuration of concentric circles. There are 430 members overall, but most do not do much for or with the coop; indeed, some live outside Thessaloniki and are thus unable to contribute much.[5] Among these members, there are "the 120," a numeric category popular with all members, which stands for a specific understanding of participation, based on labor. "The 120" are those members who manage to commit some of their time and energy laboring for the coop, mostly on a volunteer basis, and are indeed those closest to the views and practices of the coop. "The 120" receive emails with the weekly assemblies' proceedings, and are invited through emails to all the events and happenings of the coop. While "the 430" would receive a notification of a coming general assembly, it is only "the 120" that would be notified of current events, from simple issues such as a mass order of meat to politically intricate themes such as workers' recruitment and how to go about it. "The 120" group's informal name interestingly resonates with "the movement of the 136," a social mobilization against the privatization of water in Thessaloniki from 2011 to 2013, in which many of the Lykaon coop's most active members met and through which the idea of a coop solidified and was eventually consolidated in late 2013.

After that, there is the group of about fifty, who constitute the core membership of the coop. Almost all of these people would be present at the general assembly every three months; most would come to the weekly assemblies every Wednesday evening, and some, around twenty, would actually be there every single week. In fact, in the twelve general assemblies conducted so far, there have been 250 members taking part, while up until today at least 70 have participated in all of the weekly assemblies. What all members have in common (apart from ostensibly abiding by the direct democracy idea of "taking food in our hands") is the one-time contribution of €150 that they offered when they joined the coop, a considerable amount for most Greeks. When I first paid it and became a member, I asked the shop the provocative, tongue-in-cheek question, "What's in it for me?" only to receive the equally teasing answer, "a place in Heaven."

Membership is also negotiated on the grounds of labor contribution; in fact, members who do not at least show up in assemblies are often critiqued for their inactiveness. Therefore, the second axis to differentiate among members concerns a more specific and detailed analysis of the inner workings of the core group, and concerns with whether one's labor is valorized. On these grounds there are the aforementioned seven members on a paid labor basis, around twenty-eight on an everyday voluntary labor basis. Both these subgroups belong to the all-encompassing "the 120" group. There are, therefore, members who are paid workers, and—many more—members who offer voluntary labor. Some of the latter are pensioners, all of the former are people between the ages of thirty and forty; overwhelmingly, the younger members are working class, coming from the poorer areas of the city, while most of the pensioners have or had jobs in the public sector or are small entrepreneurs themselves. Most of the paid worker-members and many volunteer-members have a history and presence in the social movements of Thessaloniki.

This differentiation in wage-earning worker-members and volunteering worker-members arose as an emic distinction from numerous discussions with members of both groups and also from the assemblies themselves. However, there was resistance to the idea that these were two fully distinct groups, as many in Lykaon argued that "in fact, there is no employee status in a coop, and we are all, paid or not, labor-based members." Core voluntary members, especially those elected annually in the administrative council would show up each and every week for the coop's open assembly in the damp and unceremonious, but spacious, warehouse of the coop where a huge oval table with many chairs hosted these meetings. Among the paid working members, all would show up in the Wednesday meetings only when there were "work issues" to be discussed.

No other issue attracted so much attention as labor did, and the assemblies with the most heated and spirited conversations were those around "issues of labor" as members put it. Such issues concerned the treatment of the "working members" and turned out to be the most subtle, but also the most ambivalent. These were the meetings with the longest duration and the highest attendance, typically starting at 8.00 p.m. and ending at midnight. On a few occasions, such meetings would end in colorful language, tears, yells, and accusations hurled at the administrative council against Stalinism or corruption.

All such processes were concurrently operating on a direct democratic basis while remaining fully bureaucratized, with committees voted by the assemblies to operate on ten different subjects, from ecology and hygiene to social impact. But the meticulous, and often optimistic, atmosphere of the 2015 assemblies, now that labor was arising as a tense concern, had been jeopardized. This process was the gradual culmination of a five-month period that was slowly building up as work-related tensions were piling up. Between May and June 2016, there were routinely four hours spent discussing the results of the recruitment report of the "Committee for Work" over the hiring of new paid members and the discontinuance of one paid member's contract. The buildup of resentment was evident from the way active members of Lykaon were chatting to each other before the meetings, or were exchanging glances during them, as the ambience in the coop's warehouse became stiff and embittered. As Dimitris told me, "from January to June, we have a different coop."

Dimitris, a 43-year-old member-worker, a tall man with a beard with an austere look and a political commitment to left-leaning anarchism, had been recruited as a working member via a state program for twelve months. His post was prolonged on a month-to-month basis while a system of audit for all *paid* working members was established by the work committee. Dimitris and his other paid member-worker friends and συνεταιριστές (*syneteristés*, cooperativists) were unhappy with this system that was supposed to audit paid workers only and was indeed set up to investigate the opening of a position for another paid worker-member. Indeed, the administrative council of the coop, composed of volunteer-members, was screening the working members. Administrative council members argued that they had the right to do so not only as coop managers but also because they worked for the coop, albeit voluntarily, and "knew what labor meant."

The position was opened up and was publicly advertised. Dimitris applied internally; there were forty-five applications overall. The audit list, which had been discussed in seven more assemblies in those last months, was shaped in seven columns. They were arranged in the following way: "Movementality"[6] was awarded 20 points, "Education" 10 points, "Computing" 10 points, "Languages" 10 points, "Experience" 15 points, "Team-work" 15 points, "Organizational skills" 10 points.

These would all sum up to a 100 top grade. The result of the eight shortlisted candidates was shared with attendant members of the previous week's assembly. As revealed, Dimitris came third in the ranking. This came as a shock to 45-year-old Alina, a founding member of the council, who was a friend and long-time comrade of Dimitris whom she had met in a similar food activism attempt in an anarchist squat. She started crying during the meeting and, in a monologue, asserted that Lykaon' democracy was in shambles. She was joined by Eleni, a forty-year-old paid worker-member, who became tearful while stating that Dimitris was a committed unionist all his life and a fiery cooperativist, so that marking his "movementality" with a grade 11 out of 20 was "literally shameful."

Virtually all other paid member-workers agreed in long monologues with spite and anger. Another founding member of Lykaon, Nikos (56), asserted that this was the end of the coop. The cooperative, he noted, was supposed to "rise to the occasion for labor" (meaning laborers), "despite the crisis." The eventual layoff of Dimitris thus signaled the ethical end of the coop. Needless to say, as in a few previous assemblies, Dimitris was enraged, yelling his way throughout the assembly. The end of the assembly found him shouting, swearing, and even, by accident, forcefully throwing the keys of the warehouse on the table. The keys landed on an elderly woman who was a committee member. His behavior made some committee members comment on how and why their decision was proved right: "We shouldn't have this kind of behavior around," was the phrase the administrative council agreed upon.

The case of labor tensions and rising hierarchies within Lykaon is not comparable to debates on how cooperativists become coopitalists (Errasti et al. 2016). Here, we do not encounter a devaluation of labor, but a valuation and, indeed, constant re-evaluation of members on account of their labor contributions in a food coop. The tensions arise not because the food coop is becoming capitalist—but because tensions related to labor have been at the forefront of food concerns. As the coop was established to partly serve such issues, the sense that many members had that it has not risen to the occasion but yielded to conflicts.

This is an area where, despite tensions and eventual diversion (see Rakopoulos 2015b), the Lykaon coop matches the futurity-related visions of labor among Gefira food activists. In their case, political planning encompasses a wider picture of political activism and is rooted in the future prospect of establishing anti-middleman activity *as work*, where solidarity can assume the frame of what Raymond Williams calls "resource of hope" (cf Williams 1989). In the case of Lykaon, where a coop that caters to the livelihoods of some (paid worker) members through wage pay, labor arises as an established, yet controversial, concern with related tensions arising thereof.

Local peripheral actors imagine themselves as part of a larger, international community of discontent and political authenticity (Pratt 2010). But their imaginative projections extend toward their own future, too: here, this imagination regarded the well-founded possibility of formalizing into coops which might pay the workers' shares. Importantly, their discontent is sometimes turned inward, not toward external, structural forces (such as "the market" or "the state") that corrupt or weaken the direct democracy of a coop, but toward their fellow cooperativists. The idea that labor is valued differently by different members in food activism has been a premise. It is structured across an axis of volunteer-paid work. Many members experience it as a disconcerting element for the coops' cohesion, while many others see it as a matter of fact.

Toward a conclusion: Labor troubles in food struggles

This chapter has sought to respond to two questions: Where is labor situated in the valuations of new food cooperative movements, and how is this configuration envisioning a future-oriented prospect for people hit by the crisis? My answer lies in assessing labor as precisely the bridge between food cooperatives and the solidarity economy. Labor arises as a major *food value*; indeed, it stands as a *measure of value* for contemporary food systems and a field of contestation within food activist groups. A metonym for valuation at large, labor is at the forefront of food struggles.

Food coops, often geared toward consumption, emerge, as they do in Greece and elsewhere, from struggles associated with neoliberal crises. The inspiration to engage with such grassroots organizations surely transgresses the narrow scope of a one-issue movement; in fact, such coops intersect with broader concerns in the crisis' predicament, dramatically associated with the loss of waged labor, within these struggles. For this reason, conceptualizing alternative food economies as protective enclaves for valuing foodstuff may not suffice; the social-movement features of Greek food activism imply that it is entangled with broader responses to the current anti-austerity climate in Southern Europe.

Raymond Williams has also talked of movements' "militant particularism" (1989). Sharryn Kasmir (2011), using this framework, asks whether cooperatives can move away from that particularism and embrace social movements more broadly. The case of the Greek anti-middleman cooperatives necessitates that we consider everyday practices as carrying with them the possibility for social change (tentatively, an economy of solidarity). Such food-associated practices are surely a response to a historical shift—what we conventionally call "the crisis" and the potential for moral economies that might ensue.

It might be worthwhile to take a step back to rethink Karl Polanyi's "double movement" concept, a historical economic anthropology suggesting societal response to protect labor from the market aggression (1957: 130). Not all double movements are "democratic," as Polanyi himself has suggested; they might be associated with populist workfare, for instance (Hann 2016). At any rate, such responses suggest that a solidarity economy strives for more autonomy from markets, an idea that, unlike autarky, brings coops at times into a relation of "closed" circuits of food production that protect local interests (Pratt and Luetchford 2014: 14–16). Different scholars have addressed the state and market as objects of food activism in different ways: David Hess (2005) writes about "alternative pathways" that fuse together market and social movement strategies, while Don Nonini (2013) marks a distinction between "local food movements" and food justice, which focuses on state-versus-market strategies.

Food justice, however, as Nonini himself notes, aligns with global systems—and their crises. The materiality of food activism relies not only on foodstuff itself but also on the "non-economic economies" built on the labor of activist participants; it is a food-related materiality answerable to political economy (Lee 2016; cf. Wilson 2013). My interlocutors view food cooperativism *as labor*, linked to sustaining the livelihoods of precisely those people organizing food distribution. They also scale up that critique toward the current configuration of Greece's recession and potentially the politics of austerity at large (Stuckler and Basu 2013). The democratic institutions they create, like Lykaon, are premised on this priority of the value of labor; however, they are not immune from conflict and crisis themselves, precisely because of the social weight labor caries as a material concern.

In Greece's food solidarity economy, participants envision the resilience of their project through fixating their activity into the category of "work," via projecting it to forms of cooperativism. The bridge from socially concerned labor into valorized work is a main factor in their political imagination and a signifier in their everyday lives. The case of Greece indicates that the horizon of food cooperativism offers the potential of labor valorization in the context of a loosely understood "ecosystem" of solidarity. This is particularly pressing in a regime of constant unemployment. Linking labor to food cooperatives elucidates how recognition of labor offers a work perspective that acts as a binding element among the different activities of those participating in the food solidarity economy. The strategic significance of doing away with middlemen in distributing food lies in the potential of the distribution sector where they locate their labor. It is within this interplay that they evoke what is known as "solidarity economies" where "taking food in our hands" means laboring hands.

Notes

1 All names and toponyms, except that of the city, are pseudonyms.
2 The vast majority of the anti-middleman initiatives across Greece was established after 2011, and at some point in late 2013; they number more than sixty.
3 My informal conversations with anthropologists who have worked in Chiapas suggest that the possibility of that commodity actually coming from "the Zapatistas" is actually small. This would make sense, as the revolutionary Chiapas areas have not managed an economy of scale that could reach export levels in terms of their coffee production. The *Compañero* coffee, distributed by the Italian Fair Trade multinational LiberoMondo

("Free World") is likely to have other sources. In LaCiudad, but not in Lykaon, one can also find a sketch in an amateurish style, depicting a masked Indios, allegedly members of EZLN, suggesting that some products come from that region.

4 The price at the time of publication is already €5.20.

5 Indeed, a few live abroad (there are a couple members in Canada, for instance).

6 The condition of being in mobilization, participating in social movements (see Rakopoulos 2015a). In Greek, *κινηματικότητα* (kinimatikotita) is a concept joining activist commitment with solidary agency.

References

Burawoy, M. (2013). "Ethnographic Fallacies: Reflections on Labor Studies in the Era of Market Fundamentalism." *Work, Employment and Society*, 27 (3): 526–36.

Errasti, A., B. Ignacio, and E. Etxezarreta (2016). "What Do Mondragon Coopitalist Multinationals Look Like? The Rise and Fall of Fagor Electrodomésticos S. Coop. and Its European Subsidiaries." *Annals of Public and Cooperative Economics*, 87: 433–56.

Graeber, D. (2001). *Toward an Anthropological Theory of Value: The False Coin of Our Own Dreams*. New York: Palgrave.

Hann, C. (2007). "A New Double Movement? Anthropological Perspectives on Property in the Age of Neoliberalism." *Socio-Economic Review*, 5: 287–318.

Hann, C. (2016). "Cucumbers and Courgettes: Rural Workfare and the New Double Movement in Hungary Intersections." *East European Journal of Society and Politics*, 2 (2): 38–56.

Hann, C., and K. Hart (2009). "Introduction: Learning from Polanyi." In C. Hann and K. Hart (eds.), *Market and Society: The Great Transformation Today*, 1–16. Cambridge: Cambridge University Press.

Hess, D. (2005). "Technology and Product-Oriented Movements: Approximating Social Movement Studies and Science and Technology Studies." *Science, Technology, & Human Values*, 30 (4): 515–35.

Hart, K., J. L. Laville, and A. D. Cattani, eds. (2010). *The Human Economy: A Citizen's Guide*. Cambridge: Polity Press.

Kasmir, S. (2011). "Alternatives to Capitalism and Working-Class Struggle: A Comment on Alice Bryer's 'the Politics of the Social Economy'." *Dialectical Anthropology*, 36 (1–2): 59–61.

Lee, R. (2016). "It's the Political Economic Geography!" *Dialogues in Human Geography*, 5 (2): 234–36.

Miller, E. (2010). "The Solidarity Economy: Key Concepts and Issues." In E. Kawano, T. Masterson, and J. Teller-Ellsberg (eds.), *Solidarity Economy I: Building Alternatives for People and Planet*, 25–41. Amherst, MA: Center for Popular Economics.

Nonini, D. (2013). "The Local-food Movement and the Anthropology of Global Systems." *American Ethnologist*, 40 (2): 267–75.

Rakopoulos, T. (2015a). "The Solidarity Economy in the Greek Crisis: Movementality, Economic Democracy and Social Reproduction." In K. Hart (ed.), *Economy for and against Democracy*, 161–81. London and New York: Berghahn.

Rakopoulos, T. (2015b). "Solidarity's Tensions: Informality and Sociality in the Greek Crisis." *Social Analysis*, 59 (3): 85–104.

Rakopoulos, T. (2016). "Solidarity: The Egalitarian Tensions of a Bridge-concept." *Social Anthropology*, 24 (2): 142–51.

Rakopoulos, T. (2018). "The Future of Solidarity: Food Cooperativism as Labour." In D. Dalakoglou and G. Agelopoulos (eds.), *Critical Times in Greece: Anthropological Engagements with the Crisis*, 202–17. London: Routledge.

Polanyi, K. (1957). *The Great Transformation: The Political and Economic Origins of Our Time*. Boston, MA: Beacon Press.

Pratt, J. (2010). "Food Values: The Local and the Authentic." *Critique of Anthropology*, 27 (3): 285–300.

Pratt, J., and P. Luetchford (2014). *Food for Change: The Politics and Values of Social Movements*. London: Pluto Press.

Siniscalchi, V., and C. Counihan (2014). "Ethnography of Food Activism." In C. Counihan and V. Siniscalchi (eds.), *Food Activism: Agency, Democracy and Economy*, 3–12. London: Bloomsbury.

Stuckler, D., and S. Basu (2013). *The Body Economic: Why Austerity Kills. Recession, Budget Battles, and the Politics of Life and Death*. New York: Basic Books.

Sutton, D. (2016). "The Anthropology of Cooking." In J. A. Klein and J. L. Watson (eds.), *The Handbook of Food and Anthropology*, 349–69. London: Bloomsbury Academic.

Vaiou, D., and A. Kalendides (2017). "Practices of Solidarity in Athens: Reconfigurations of Public Space and Urban Citizenship." *Citizenship Studies*, 21 (4): 440–54.

Vathakou, E. (2016). "Citizens' Solidarity Initiatives in Greece during the Financial Crisis." In J. Clarke, A. Huliaras, and D. Sotiropoulos (eds.), *Austerity and Third Sector in Greece: Civil Society at the European Frontline*, 167–93. New York: Routledge.

Williams, R. (1989). *Resources of Hope*. London: Verso.

Wilson, M. (2013). *Everyday Moral Economies: Food, Politics and Scale in Cuba*. London: Wiley-Blackwell.

Part Four

Consuming Values

11

Fairness Is Elsewhere: "Training" Fair Trade in Post-Socialist Contexts

Guntra Aistara

Introduction

Ethical food consumption means that consumers exhibit a "growing preference for objects that are produced in ways that are seen to be socially and environmentally good; or at least, better than the alternatives on offer" (Carrier 2012: 2). Concepts such as "fair" are context-dependent, however, their meanings determined in relation to both historical and contemporary political regimes and social circumstances.

A writer in Latvia posted the following Soviet childhood memory of the scarcity of exotic foods in a popular news weekly:

> Bananas were in a cartoon. . . . I guess the story wasn't exactly about bananas as edible objects, but about friendship and helping, but I remember that we all thought that all adventures and all terrors were ultimately about getting bananas. Because *getting* was the main thing. All mothers and fathers were constantly trying to *get* something, but bananas could not be *gotten* even with the hardest *getting*. (Dāboliņa 2011)[1]

Strikingly, in the cartoon, entitled "Three bananas," the child-hero outwits the evil queen by collaborating with friends to steal three of the magical bananas to which she has exclusive access. When the child returns the bananas to the magician who sent him to get them, the magician congratulates him and says, "Now you can eat them immediately." But the boy replies, "What do you mean, eat them? I thought they were magical bananas! I can help someone" and proceeds to share them with his new friends who helped him outwit the evil ruler.

The cooperation in the cartoon reaffirms the truly magical power of social connections in the Soviet era for obtaining scarce food items like bananas. Indeed, peoples' memories of bananas and coffee, in particular, as well as foreign-made chocolate, revolve around the special social networks through which they could be "gotten," and shared with others as part of an ethical food system embedded in the local socialist context.

I juxtapose here the ethics of these Soviet networks for procuring and sharing exotic foods through solidarity with other consumers with the prescribed solidarity with producers implicit in contemporary Fair Trade networks. Fair Trade cuts out middlemen in export commodity chains for coffee, tea, bananas, and chocolates by buying directly from farmers' cooperatives. Producers in the Global South are paid a supplement over market prices if they meet certain production standards; the system is "designed to address the imbalance of power in trading relationships, unstable markets and the injustices of conventional trade" (Fairtrade International 2016).

The European Union accounts for more than 60 percent of the market for Fair Trade food worldwide (Boonman et al. 2010) but mostly in older member states of Western Europe. Fair Trade has been slow to take off in new member states such as Latvia, which had the lowest level of Fair Trade consumption in 2010 and has fluctuated since (Boonman et al. 2010).[2] As a result, Fair Trade campaigns in new EU member states are pressuring consumers to support marginalized producers in the Global South by purchasing Fair Trade. The fact that this subjectivity must be "trained" in post-socialist contexts, rather than being a "natural" ethical choice for the discerning moral subject incentivized by the market, belies the fact that different assumptions regarding fairness undergird the Fair Trade model than have been historically produced in post-socialist contexts.

I analyze here differences between the moral economies of Soviet and Fair Trade networks. James Scott's (1976) theory of the moral economy of the peasant rests on the principles of subsistence and reciprocity. He emphasizes that an analysis of the moral economy should include "the relational or exchange quality of social relations; it must seek out the shared human needs that social actors expect from these relationships; and in context, it must work from the actual notions of 'fair value' that prevail" (165). He observes that if the subsistence possibilities of peasants are undermined, it is the responsibility of the elites to support them.

I show how Soviet and Fair Trade networks create different moral economies and geographies of ethical food, entailing a simultaneous narrowing of social networks but a widening of geographic scale. This necessitates a shift in subjectivity and in understandings of the causes and remedies for injustice, locating fairness at different points in the food chain. Furthermore, because the top three Fair Trade commodities of bananas, coffee, and chocolate coincide with the most exclusive food items available mostly to elites under socialism (but previous informal networks for "getting" such exotic goods are no longer effective), new pressure for Eastern European consumers to purchase Fair Trade products may replicate past forms of exclusion and foster new forms of resentment.

This chapter is based on ethnographic observations and interviews with rural small-scale producers, consumers, and NGOs promoting Fair Trade and global social justice from 2011 to 2016, building upon research with organic farmers since 2005. I first describe exchange relations embedded in Soviet versus Fair Trade networks, then discuss the shared values of solidarity that social actors seek from these systems, and finally analyze the notion of fairness that prevails in each, and the subjectivity required to achieve it.

Narrowing networks

In the Soviet Union, production was centralized, resulting in an "economy of shortage" (Kornai 1980, cited in Verdery 1991: 423), in turn promoting an informal economy and exchange relations (Verdery 1996). Informal networks and underground markets served various functions for obtaining both domestic and exotic food products, rendering consumption a political practice. Katherine Verdery (1996: 29) has noted that in socialist systems "acquiring objects became a way of constituting your selfhood against a deeply unpopular regime." Fehérváry (2009) has also demonstrated how consumption practices and critiques of state-produced products helped form a political subjectivity.

Consumption practices were not formative only, or even primarily, of individual identities, however, but inextricably bound up with social networks. Most workers on collective farms managed private gardens on the side for food items they could barter and exchange. Local products, like home-baked breads, could be obtained through underground networks, using social connections to stockpile scarce ingredients (sometimes pilfering from collective farms), transport equipment, and manage the timing and distribution of the product in exchange for other favors (Aistara 2015). Connections in both socialist and continuing post-socialist networks extended out from the household to include neighbors, extended family members, co-workers or higher-ups at state institutions (Smith and Stenning 2006).

If local products could often be procured through personal networks to avoid long lines for state-rationed goods, exotic ones were hardly ever available, and if so, only through extremely special connections. Significantly, three of the main deficit goods of the Soviet Union coincide with the current top Fair Trade products, which are thus highly symbolic in people's memories: bananas, coffee, and chocolate. In an online forum for Soviet memories, one person remembered that his mother could sometimes smuggle bananas because she worked in a cafeteria that catered to the army (klab.lv 2006). Another person recalled: "I still remember when I was little, during a break, someone's mother treated us with bananas, doing it so others couldn't see, because back then that was a highly exclusive product—even more elite than Western chewing gum" (klab.lv 2006). Bananas were thus transformed into a scarce, but social, good. Often such highly prized items were cut into extremely small pieces to be shared as widely as possible. Yet they were still only available to the select few. Melissa Caldwell has reported that in Russia, a professor lamented that "it was unfortunate that she liked bananas because 'they are unpatriotic,' meaning . . . that they were unavailable to the general Soviet public" (Caldwell 2002: 300). Indeed, most people I spoke to in Latvia only tasted bananas for the first time after Latvia's independence in 1991.

A retired couple told me they didn't remember ever having exotic fruits as children, but later when they had kids and the first mandarins and oranges became available around Christmas time, they were too expensive to buy. The man stacked crates in the port, however, and could occasionally sneak two mandarins home for his daughters. Another woman told of her childhood trauma, when her mother brought home a whole bag of mandarins from a trip to another Soviet republic. Because they were so exclusive, she only allowed the kids to eat them occasionally, but as a result half the bag rotted. "To this day I can't understand why I was so obedient and didn't just eat them all secretly!" she exclaimed.

Other exotic products, like coffee, were more widely available, but mostly a locally produced instant brand. Highly prized foreign coffees were primarily obtainable when relatives sent packages from abroad. Afterward, as a forum participant noted, "foreign coffee tins were proudly reused again or put on the living room bookcase so that others could admire them" (Odiņa n.d.) thus also proudly displaying the social connections embodied in the coffee. While such stories display pride in the objects and ability to "get" them, sometimes they were also seen as a reflection on one's own poverty. One woman wrote online that receiving chocolate and coffee sent from a Swedish acquaintance made her feel sad and ashamed about her country (klab.lv 2006). Another woman told me her sister worked in a café in town, so they had regular access to coffee. Sometimes they would even get green coffee beans and roast them at home or use them in exchange for other products. The local chocolate factory produced many sweets, which circulated as gifts on special occasions, but some suspected there was barely a trace of real chocolate in them.

Informal exchange networks were thus a necessary part of life and consumer subjectivity under socialism. One woman who worked in a shop during the socialist era explained that even shop managers needed connections to get exotic products to their stores, which usually disappeared under the table long before the shop opened. These informal exchanges thus formed a slippery border between favors, social relations, and rings of "corruption." Ledeneva (2009: 259) has argued that this system of favors for procuring scarce goods, known as *blat* in Russian (*blats* in Latvian) was not always considered illegal or criminal, however, since the regime itself was seen as corrupt: "If *blat* corrupted the corrupt regime, can we refer to it as corruption?"

How, then, do Fair Trade networks for the ethical procurement of exotic goods compare with previous socialist food networks? Fair Trade emerged in Western Europe in the 1950s as an effort to promote "more equitable exchange between the developing and developed worlds" (Fridell in Moberg and Lyon 2010: 2). Since the 1980s it is a certification program that pays higher prices for goods that meet social equity and environmental sustainability criteria (Moberg and Lyon 2010). Fair Trade aims to "deliberately work with marginalised producers and workers in order to help them move from a position of vulnerability to security and economic self-sufficiency" (Boonman et al. 2010: 4). Fair Trade has been imagined as "alternative globalization," a form of "decommodification," an expression of solidarity with producers, and as a means for consumers to reflect their political beliefs and personal identities through consumption choices (Moberg and Lyon 2010: 8).

Fair Trade campaigns aim to connect the consumer with a faraway, and otherwise invisible and unknowable, producer. The Fair Trade International website presents this as a "partnership between producers and consumers," where consumers can view pictures and read case studies about producers. The network is held together by the distribution of responsibility in a political and ethical imaginary of a moral economy (Goodman 2004). This moral economy is made up of the idea that consumers feel a responsibility to buy Fair Trade, preferably from the poorest producers, symbolically linking producers and consumers as laboring together to make trade more fair (Goodman 2004).

While Fair Trade products are often portrayed as building such relationships, this sense of connection is more possible for consumers who are expected to peruse webpages to gather information about where their food comes from, whereas producers who supply Fair Trade cooperatives may know little about the program, let alone about the consumers who purchase their products (Doane 2010; Lyon 2006).

This highlights important differences in the exchange relations involved in socialist informal food networks versus Fair Trade networks. On one hand, the move from informal socialist or post-socialist networks to certified Fair Trade implies a narrowing of social networks. In the Soviet era, neither networks for local goods nor exotic goods connected exclusively the consumer and the producer. In networks surrounding local homemade products, the network was much wider than just the producers and the consumer, including all other people from whom one had received favors in the past or from whom one might need them in the future, in a reciprocal exchange system (see Aistara 2015). Limiting the network to only consumers and producers narrows the scope of actors involved and the social capital beyond a commodity transaction that such food items represent.

On the other hand, focusing on relations exclusively between the producer and consumer seemingly replaces connections with a wider group of consumers. In Soviet networks for exotic products like bananas, the producer never entered the picture at all. Consumers generally knew nothing about who produced the exotic goods that would magically appear as rare treats. Two women seemed to remember stickers on citrus fruit indicating an origin in Morocco, but no other information was ever available. "It didn't interest us either," admitted one man, emphasizing that the sudden availability of such a product was more important than its origin. The types of social connections, and the leverage they possessed to "get" exclusive items, were related to the solidarity exhibited with family members or other consumers by sharing the products. These connections were largely lateral, while the producers were well-hidden behind the state that controlled supply. Any connections to producers in other socialist countries were managed through geopolitical connections among states, and production details almost never traveled down the food chain along with the products. This tight state supply thus paradoxically resulted in a twist on commodity fetishism, where the means of production were hidden not by capitalist enterprise but by the socialist state.

Yet there is a further crucial difference in that if in Soviet times, bananas, mandarins, or coffee could at least sometimes be "gotten" by mobilizing particular social networks and special connections, then these are no longer functional tools in the new market economy of today, in an example of what Caldwell (2004) has called the separation of social and economic capital. While previous social networks may still be mobilized for procuring local farm products, exotic products can now only be obtained with money. And Fair Trade products can only be procured with more money than conventional ones. Thus, if one has social connections, but not much money, as is true for many pensioners who lived through and remember socialist-era scarcity, these Fair Trade goods may be off-limits again. This resonates with Harper's (1999) observations in Hungary in the 1990s that boycotts against French products were ineffective because the average Hungarian consumer could not afford French imports anyhow. Such examples prompt us to rethink how consumer politics originating in Western Europe play out when transferred to new member states with different histories.

Expanding solidarities

After the collapse of the Soviet Union and entry into the global market economy, there was a huge banana boom, as if people were trying to eat all the bananas they had been unfairly denied throughout their Soviet childhood. One woman told me her shock when she had first traveled abroad during the last years of the Soviet Union and saw the mountains of exotic fruit and other products, which rendered her speechless and depressed for several days. "Why did I have to be born in this country?" she thought to herself. But suddenly after 1991, bananas were cheap and readily available. For many people in former socialist countries, the sheer abundance of these magical bananas was the ultimate symbol of having entered the West (Passmore and Passmore 2003).

This banana boom, and its eventual bust, as people became satiated, had a direct influence on deforestation and social welfare in Central America, unbeknownst to consumers in Eastern Europe. New areas of forest were cleared to supply the new wave of demand, and more workers got, and eventually lost again, jobs on banana plantations (Vandermeer and Perfecto 1995). These consequences were now well-hidden from Eastern European consumers through the long and oblique supply chains of capitalist agro-industry. Such market boom and bust cycles that produce price crashes and affect small farmer livelihoods, hidden from consumers, are exactly what Fair Trade attempts to remedy.

The historical moment of the post-socialist banana boom and subsequent bust reveals the difference in the causes and location of the perceived unfairness in these two types of ethical food networks. In the stories and memories consumers share of informal Soviet networks, particular products are tied up with stories of "getting" in the face of injustices suffered by both consumers and producers at the hands of the state. Meanwhile, Fair Trade attempts to establish social networks between producers and consumers, in order to remedy the unfairness experienced by producers in distant lands in the face of historical colonialism and contemporary injustices of the market.

These different foundations of unfairness also lead to divergent understandings of solidarity. Bacon explains that "solidarity—not market opportunity—motivated most pioneer fairtraders" working with coffee cooperatives in Mexico in the 1980s (2010: 124). Mardsen et al. (2000) call this the creation of a "transnational . . . short food supply chain," and Goodman (2004: 908) describes this as a way to create solidarity in difference and across distance. Nevertheless, this differs from the solidarity expressed with other consumers in Soviet networks through sharing scarce and difficult to obtain goods. Thus, while both Soviet informal food networks and Fair Trade networks are based on values of fairness and solidarity, the location of solidarity both within the food chain and geographically differs. The shift to Fair Trade necessitates an expansion of the geographic scope of solidarity to faraway producers. Because these producers were never visible in Soviet times, their inclusion now feels to some local consumers like a move away from solidarity with producers and consumers at home.

This shift in solidarity can sometimes be upsetting because producers at home have not yet achieved stability, causing feelings of resentment. Indeed, while many consumers in Latvia may still be unfamiliar with Fair Trade (only 12 percent recognized the logo in 2016, according to a survey carried out by an NGO promoting Fair Trade), early discussions about it led back to debates about farmers' conditions at home: "Peru, Taiwan, Philippines, Mexico . . . do Latvian farmers get enough for their work? How much do they get for a liter of milk, and how many times more expensive is the watered-down milk in the store?" (Zaļā zeme 2005) and "Fair trade? What is that? Does anyone have an idea how much the baker gets for the loaf of bread that costs 5 LVL/kilo in the supermarket?"(Vides vēstis 2012).

Thus, some consumers feel that Latvian workers' and farmers' conditions are also unjust and want to demonstrate solidarity for local producers. Because of these concerns, NGOs working to promote Fair Trade observed that it is important to show that there is no conflict with domestic products. In Estonia, for example, Fair Trade coffee was promoted by serving it together with local milk. Sugar, however, which used to be produced in Latvia from sugar beets, does elicit feelings of competition. In 2004 the WTO ruled that the European Union's sugar production was distorting the market and had to be reduced. The European Union offered compensation for inefficient producers to close down, resulting in the elimination of Latvia's entire sugar industry (Kārkliņa et al. 2011). While farmers and processors received compensation, beet sugar was replaced with cane sugar and prices went up for consumers, fostering resentment toward imported sugar and EU policies. One shopkeeper who stocks Fair Trade products told me that "people are still angry about the sugar."

Solidarity is borne out of particular historical understandings of injustice, which differ according to one's positionality. NGOs working to promote Fair Trade in Latvia link the lack of solidarity to a narrow understanding of one's place in the world. In a representative survey of Latvia's inhabitants commissioned by an NGO in 2016 as part of a global sustainable development awareness project, 68 percent of respondents estimated Latvia's place in global development rankings to be much lower than it actually is. Furthermore, when asked what they would be willing to do to facilitate development in poorer countries, 44 percent indicated that they "should not interfere, because we are poor here in Latvia." This response was more prevalent among older respondents and those with lower education and income levels, but lower among farmers as compared to other professions. Another 25 percent felt that they "should not interfere, because problems should be solved at the national level."[3] Meanwhile just over 14 percent expressed a willingness to pay more for products and services that guarantee fair labor and environmental practices, and only 10 percent of responses indicated that they pay attention to labels about fair labor and environmental practices when purchasing tropical fruits.

A representative of the NGO that commissioned the survey admitted that Fair Trade products are expensive for Latvia, as the third poorest country in the European Union. Another NGO official working on promoting social justice and development in Latvia noted that the idea of sharing resources seemed threatening to people who felt they can barely make ends meet themselves. He lamented that this feeling of poverty, regardless of the actual relative level of development, can also lead to an assumption that, "if you are with them, you are against us," and result in a lack of human solidarity in society. Other observers have made similar reflections in relation to East Europeans' seemingly callous response to the refugee crisis, invoking a "compassion deficit" (Krastev 2017). Indeed, these attitudes in Latvia have only been compounded by xenophobia surrounding debates over migration: one caller on a radio program about Fair Trade expressed his support for the idea of buying Fair Trade products from less developed countries "so that they don't have to come here."

These attitudes may shock promoters of Fair Trade and consumers in Western Europe. Such comments exhibit a lack of compassion for those far away in "less developed" countries, simultaneously with a solidarity with workers and farmers at home. This stems in part from the fact that while EU accession made development funding more readily available to medium and large-scale farms, encouraging them to develop into commercial enterprises, it often left behind precisely the smallest home producers who are most similar to the ones targeted by Fair Trade programs abroad. Focus on supporting producers in the Global South through programs like Fair Trade may thus detract attention from these internal inequalities in Europe that remain unresolved over a decade after the first round of EU expansion.

There are further ironies in this, as Goodman (2009) has observed that the "quality turn" in Fair Trade is excluding more of the smallest producers in the Global South from Fair Trade networks, because they can't attain the standards required for larger mainstream markets. This should be even more cause for solidarity among producers in Eastern Europe and the Global South, who face similar barriers. Ideally, of course, fairness in trade should not be reserved only for poor producers at a distance. Jaffee, Kloppenburg et al. (2004: 171) have noted that Fair Trade as a set of principles guiding trade should equally apply within the Global North and Global South, not only between them, and that "fair trade . . . is not necessarily far trade."

Finally, solidarity may not even be so straightforward for consumers in Western European countries where the idea of Fair Trade originated. Goodman has noted that pictures of poor producers in Third World countries on Fair Trade packing may inspire pity and sympathy rather than true feelings of solidarity (Goodman 2009). An NGO worker in Latvia noted that to date Fair Trade products have become more of a stylish consumer item for hipsters. If this is so, then maybe Fair Trade networks are not so different than Soviet networks among friends and relatives, because they may do more to build connections with other consumers of Fair Trade products, who together feel "ethical," or "Western" (Dombos 2012), rather than necessarily building solidarity with actual faraway producers.

It is thus important to reflect on the causes and location of unfairness and solidarity in different food networks. Fair Trade relies on an idea of a consuming individual subject who cultivates his or her identity in relation to the market by the purchase of Fair Trade products in order to create ties of solidarity with producers in faraway places, yet this is the exact opposite of the ties of solidarity established among consumers in the socialist era. If in Soviet informal networks for exotic goods, solidarity was positioned at the end of the food chain among consumers to protest injustices by the state, in Fair Trade networks, solidarity is expected in the middle of the food chain as a means to link producers and consumers in order to help counter the injustices of the market. For consumers in post-socialist Latvia to move from one to the other thus requires an expansion of solidarity, but this sometimes feels jarring because producers at home have not yet achieved fair standards themselves. Further, it requires a shift in consumer subjectivity and historical positionality.

Shifting subjectivities

Even as funding for farmers and producers in new member states aimed at attaining EU standards is dwindling, Eastern European member states are becoming the target of a new type of assistance by the European Union: training to be supporters of European development policy abroad, including as consumers of Fair Trade products. Fair Trade campaigns are beginning to pressure consumers in new EU member states to take responsibility as rich Northern consumers and support marginalized producers in the Global South by participating in "official" ethical consumption practices, such as paying higher prices for Fair Trade products.

The European Commission has funded conferences in Warsaw and Prague encouraging Fair Trade in Central and Eastern European countries. The conference materials state: "The concept of Fair Trade enjoys increasing recognition in Central and Eastern Europe. As consumers get richer, they are gaining the freedom to be more conscious about their buying decisions" (Polish Fair Trade Coalition 2010). One Polish leader stated: "Central and Eastern Europe is not used to think[ing] of itself as belonging to 'the developed part of the world.' . . . So it is important to raise awareness that our region does now belong among the rich and ought to take responsibility for other regions of the world" (Ciobanu 2009).

Furthermore, efforts to encourage ethical consumption like Fair Trade are linked with programs training post-socialist countries to transition from being development aid recipients to being donors.[4] An NGO representative of one such project expressed the complexity and contradictions in these projects. He observed that on the one hand, Latvia has one of the highest rates of inequality in Europe and is one of the poorest countries in the European Union. Yet he lamented that, on the other hand, as residents acutely feel their own poverty, they lack information or perspective on the situation in other parts of the world, and the education system does not address this. This was corroborated by a farmer who told me she would need more personalized information about the conditions in which producers live, because she and other consumers did not really know enough to feel motivated to buy Fair Trade products. The NGO representative continued by saying that there is great policy incoherence at the European level, where large-scale trade and development policies create and perpetuate inequality and underdevelopment in other parts of the world, yet only small projects try to begin to address these inequalities.

Indeed, one of the critiques of Fair Trade has been its connection to free trade. Goodman (2009) has criticized Fair Trade for becoming part of a larger process of commoditizing "sustainable development" as a good that can be store-bought, in a neoliberal fashion putting responsibility on individual consumers, thereby detracting from the larger structural issues at hand. This takes pressure off of aid programs, as summed up in the slogan "trade, not aid," and links free trade and fair trade as two sides of one coin. Thus, along with the mainstreaming and growing popularity of Fair Trade, there has been an increasing questioning of how "fair" Fair Trade really is, and how much of a change it really produces in global markets (Bacon 2010; Moberg 2010; Raynolds et al. 2007). The emphasis on seemingly individualized connections between producer and consumer decontextualizes products from wider social networks of both production and consumption. For instance, because the main food products sold through Fair Trade networks are coffee, tea, chocolate, and bananas (Boonman et al. 2010: 63), Fair Trade reinforces the pattern that marginal producers in developing countries focus on a few key export commodities (Coronil 2000), rather than a more holistic agroecological farming system. This simultaneously allows EU consumers to feel good about themselves for making ethical food choices, without engaging in the broader politics of export dependencies and rural development. Moreover, the import of Fair Trade commodities like coffee and bananas is seemingly harmless for the European economy: since these are not produced in Europe, they pose no competition for European producers.

If the idea of fairness undergirding Fair Trade is based on responsibility taken by the Global North for historic injustices perpetrated against the Global South, this responsibility is largely transferred from the state to the individual consumer as a neoliberal governance mechanism. Goodman (2004: 908–09) has stated that "at a global scale, consumers are asked to place themselves in the current geopolitical and economic geographies of North and South as 'affluent,' yet, 'responsible' and 'caring.' . . . At the consumption end, being a reflexive consumer denotes a particular position in terms of class, education, and/or level of existing knowledge."

These new responsibilities and positionality in the world are ones to which "second world" consumers do not automatically relate. One NGO project promoting international solidarity in new EU member states identified the "lack of a colonial past" and "low awareness of the interdependencies between North and the South" as barriers for interest in European development cooperation in countries like Latvia and Poland (Kochanowicz 2007: 7). Indeed, bananas became controversial in the 1990s in relation to EU trade, because some member states were importing bananas from their former colonies in the Caribbean, but this was challenged in the WTO (Clegg 2005). The new member states had no relationship to uphold with the Caribbean countries, and also considered themselves poor, thus exhibited "little sympathy" (Clegg 2005: 38).

Projects that seek to educate the new post-socialist EU member states about their responsibility toward the Global South raise the question of where the "East" fits in the eternal battle between North and South. The perpetual "second world" gets shifted back and forth by necessity, depending on the issue, too developed to receive aid yet not developed enough to understand their responsibilities as part of the North. One of the stated goals of a global development training project in Latvia was "to inform and educate people about the fact that we all live *in a world*, not only in Latvia" (Kochanowicz 2007: 20 [emphasis added]). While this emphasis on broadening horizons may indeed be necessary to also successfully expand the geography of solidarity, it simultaneously seemingly blames consumers in new member states for their disorientation about their new position in the world. This pressure for Eastern Europeans to recognize their role as rich consumers and developed countries of the North positions solidarity as a stance to be exercised at a distance, simultaneously bringing into relief still unresolved inequalities at home. The new positionality as rich consumers requires that the East European consumers become part of the elite. Whereas they used to be in solidarity against the state, now they have to be in solidarity against old colonial inequalities exacerbated by the market, yet they feel neither as the elite nor as responsible for the inequalities[5]—rather they still feel poor, especially in relation to consumers in richer countries.

While promoting values of fairness, such projects simultaneously spread an expectation that East European consumers should stop narrowly reflecting on their problems, such as the conditions of producers at home, and prove their "Europeanness" by supporting Fair Trade products abroad. This translates as a presumption that Europeanness means support for the disadvantaged, but only in the faraway Global South, at the risk that those in the new EU member states—or old ones for that matter—become invisible. This is an example of what Carrier (2012) calls "nimbyism" in ethics, meaning morality regarding what is happening elsewhere, rather than in your own backyard. Böröcz (2006) and others have shown that by obscuring problems in the West, one perpetuates the discourse that "goodness is elsewhere," or, in this case: fairness is elsewhere. Consuming Fair Trade products thus becomes a way of performing that fairness abroad.

Moreover, the discourse of Eastern European responsibility to purchase Fair Trade goods in solidarity with the Global South unknowingly recreates past forms of inequality. While the East European countries may not have histories as colonizers, their past within a larger empire precluded access to certain goods. Now consumers' previous social networks are no longer effective for "getting" exotic Fair Trade items like bananas and coffee. It thus causes the re-elitization of certain faraway goods, in turn promoting a re-valorization of familiar informal networks. This may make producers from the Global South seem as remote as ever, despite their increasingly similar problems with producers at home.

Conclusion: Moral economies and geographies of fairness

While both socialist and Fair Trade networks have implied moral economies, the social categories and geographies of the exchange relations do not align. Fair Trade's appeal in post-socialist Europe has been slow because (1) Fair Trade entails a simultaneous narrowing of the scope of actors yet expansion of the geographic scale of social exchange networks; (2) Fair Trade stems from fundamentally different assumptions about the causes of and solutions for unfairness than those implied in Soviet social networks; and (3) Fair Trade networks locate the values of solidarity and fairness in a different place in the food chain and require a different consumer positionality and subjectivity than in socialist food networks. While Soviet networks operated in response to a presumed injustice of the state in restricting citizen access to both local and exotic goods, Fair Trade presumes an injustice of the market against formerly colonized territories in the Global South. This entails a reshuffling of social networks and geographic scales, and places emphasis on exercising solidarity with producers at a distance rather than those at home.

From a moral economy perspective, in the socialist era, producers and consumers both struggled to meet their subsistence needs, yet as a result were networked in a moral alliance against the resource-controlling state. Networks of reciprocity extended widely among citizens across consumption and production divides, working together to procure scarce ingredients and supplies. For exotic goods, whoever procured a highly prized item shared it as widely as possible, but the producer never entered the picture. Fair Trade thus represents a narrowing of social networks even as the geographical scale of solidarity widens. This means that fairness is differently located in both space and time, and in a different position in the food chain.

In Fair Trade networks consumers are imagined as part of the elite, who should express solidarity with poor, faraway producers in the face of inequalities stemming from colonial legacies and the resulting capitalist market. Consumers in post-socialist Europe are expected to shift their subjectivity to the position of the elites, even as some may still struggle to meet their own subsistence needs and remain aware of injustices perpetrated by the new market relations against producers at home. The shift in solidarity is therefore not automatic but is rather perceived as a breach in the moral economy of production and consumption and can even create a backlash of "empathy deficit" (Krastev 2017).

Post-socialist consumers' discomfort with their new position in the global economy has to do with required shift in their position in the moral food economy—from being aligned with the peasants in attempting to meet their subsistence needs to being part of the elite who should now subsidize the subsistence needs of producers, not even in their own economy, but elsewhere. Consumers' seeming resentment stems from the fact that local producers have seemingly been left out of the new moral food economy through the shift in attention to faraway places, as well as from a reluctance to take on responsibility for global inequalities which they do not feel they have perpetrated. This insight may be important not only in post-socialist contexts but also in other emerging economies where relations of production at home may still be experiencing similar inequalities, even as the role of the country in the global economy begins to shift.

If in Soviet times, everyone was supposed to be equal (if poor), but certain people still had access to exotic goods like bananas, now everyone, by virtue of being in the European Union, is supposed to be rich, but again, only certain people have access to exotic Fair Trade goods. If Fair Trade products get marked as elite products in the East, the possibility for solidarity with the South will be diminished. And if social justice gets constructed as something that should exist only for the disadvantaged abroad, rather than in one's local community, it will elicit a counter-reaction against those trying to "train" solidarity with faraway producers.

Acknowledgments

I thank Aleh Cherp, Zsuzsa Gille, Diana Mincyte, Karen Hebert, Kyle Piispanen, Vadim Vidichenko, and Hadley Renkin, as well as participants in the Foodscapes conference, the Max Planck Institute, and the EASA panel on Food Values in Europe for comments on previous drafts.

Notes

1   The Latvian verb is *dabūt* is related to the Russian verb "*dobyt*," which implies obtaining or procuring something through extremely difficult effort. In Soviet times it was often related to the invocation of *blat*, or special favors "*dobyt po blatu*," which could also provoke guilt. I thank Aleh Cherp for these observations on the subtle differences of various Russian verb forms.
2   By 2016 Fair Trade sales had fallen by 27 percent (Fair Trade International 2016), but an NGO representative explained this may be only for the FLO label, not others.
3   This response was more evenly distributed among age and income groups but more prevalent among respondents with higher education and higher positions.
4   See for instance Trialog (www.trialog.or.at) and GLEN (glen-europe.org).
5   Though see Dzenovska 2018 about the Latvians' complicated relationship to liberalism and colonialism in Latvia.

References

Aistara, G. (2015). "Good, Clean, Fair … and Illegal: Paradoxes of Food Ethics in Post-Socialist Latvia." *Journal of Baltic Studies*, 46 (3): 283–98.
Bacon, C. (2010). "Who Decides What Is Fair in Fair Trade? The Agri-Environmental Governance of Standards, Access, and Price." *Journal of Peasant Studies*, 37 (1): 111–47.
Boonman, M., W. Huisman, E. Sarrucco-Fedorovsjev, and T. Sirocco (2010). *Fair Trade Facts and Figures: A Success Story for Producers and Consumers*. Culemborg: Dutch Association of Worldshops.
Böröcz, J. (2006). "Goodness Is Elsewhere: The Rule of European Difference." *Comparative Studies in Society and History*, 48 (1): 110–38.
Caldwell, M. L. (2002). "The Taste of Nationalism: Food Politics in Postsocialist Moscow." *Ethnos*, 67(3): 295–319.
Caldwell, M. I. (2004). *Not by Bread Alone: Social Support in the New Russia*. Berkeley: University of California Press.

Carrier, J. G. (2012). "Introduction." In J. Carrier and P. Luetchford (eds.), *Ethical Consumption: Social Value and Economic Practice*, 1–36, New York: Berghahn Books.

Ciobanu, C. (2009). *Eastern Europe: Fair Trade Takes Off*. InterPress Service. http://www. globalissues.org/news/2009/09/29/2975 (accessed October 10, 2012).

Clegg, P. (2005). "Banana Splits and Policy Challenges: The ACP Caribbean and the Fragmentation of Interest Coalitions." *Revista Europea de Estudios Latinoamericanos y del Caribe*, 79: 27–45.

Coronil, F. (2000). "Towards a Critique of Globalcentrism: Speculations on Capitalism's Nature." *Public Culture*, 12 (2): 351–74.

Doane, M. (2010). "Relationship Coffees: Structure and Agency in the Fair Trade System." In M. Moberg (ed.), *Fair Trade and Social Justice: Global Ethnographies*, 229–57. New York: NYU Press.

Dāboliņa, I. (2011). "Trīs banāin" [Three bananas]. *Ir*, October 29.

Dombos, T. (2012). "Narratives of Concern: Beyond the 'Official' Discourse of Ethical Consumption in Hungary." In J. Carrier and P. Luetchford (eds.), *Ethical Consumption: Social Value and Economic Practice*, 125–41. New York: Berghahn Books.

Dzenovska, D. (2018). *School of Europeanness: Tolerance and Other Lessons in Political Liberalism in Latvia*. Ithaca, NY: Cornell University Press.

Fairtrade International (2016). "Driving Sales, Deepening Impact: Annual Report 2015–2016." https://annualreport15-16.fairtrade.net/en/power-in-partnership/ (accessed March 30, 2019).

Fehérváry, K. (2009). "Goods and States: The Political Logic of State-Socialist Material Culture." *Comparative Studies in Society and History*, 51 (2): 426–59.

Goodman, M. (2004). "Reading Fair Trade: Political Ecological Imaginary and the Moral Economy of Fair Trade Foods." *Political Geography*, 23 (7): 891–915.

Goodman, M. (2009). *The Mirror of Consumption: Celebritisation, Developmental Consumption and the Shifting Cultural Politics of Fair Trade*. Environment, Politics and Development Working Paper Series. London: Department of Geography, King's College London.

Harper, K. (1999). "Citizens or Consumers? Environmentalism and the Public Sphere in Postsocialist Hungary." *Anthropology Department Faculty Publication Series*, 74: 96–112.

Jaffee, D., J. Kloppenburg, and M. B. Monroe (2004). "Bringing the 'Moral Charge' Home: Fair Trade within the North and within the South." *Rural Sociology*, 69 (2): 169–96.

Kārkliņa, G., R. Maizītis, and A. Gulbe (2011). "Latvijas dīvainais pārtikas tirgus. Neizdarība vai Eiropas diktāts?" http://jauns.lv/raksts/zinas/180725-latvijas-divainais-partikas-tirgus-neizdariba-vai-eiropas-diktats (accessed October 10, 2012).

klab.lv. (2006). *Pārtikas veikali padomju savienībā*. http://klab.lv/community/pajautaa/1 320969.html (accessed October 10, 2012).

Kochanowicz, C. (2007). "Global Education Network of Young Europeans (GLEN) Managing Diversities. Linking individualities." Presentation at Promoting international volunteering in NMS of EU, Paris, May 4.

Kornai, J. (1980). *Economics of Shortage*. Amsterdam: NorthHolland Press.

Krastev, I. (2017). "The Refugee Crisis and the Return of the East-West Divide in Europe." *Slavic Review*, 76 (2): 291–96.

Ledeneva, A. (2009). "From Russia with Blat: Can Informal Networks Help Modernize Russia?" *Social Research*, 76 (1): 257–88.

Lyon, S. (2006). "Evaluating Fair Trade Consumption: Politics, Defetishization and Producer Participation." *International Journal of Consumer Studies*, 30 (5): 452–64.

Marsden, T., J. Jo Banks, and G. Bristol (2000). "Food Supply Chain Approaches: Exploring Their Role in Rural Development." *Sociologia Ruralis*, 40 (4): 424–38.

Moberg, M., ed. (2010). *Fair Trade and Social Justice: Global Ethnographies*. New York: New York University Press.

Moberg, M., and S. Lyon (2010). "What's Fair? The Paradox of Seeking Justice through Markets." In M. Moberg and S. Lyon (eds.), *Fair Trade and Social Justice: Global Ethnographies*, 1–24. New York: NYU Press.

Odiņa, I. (n.d). *Atpakaļ PSRS*. http://www.calis.lv/atputa/biblioteka/interesanti-zinat/atpa kal-psrs/ (accessed October 10, 2012).

Passmore, B., and S. Passmore (2003). "Taste and Transformation: Ethnographic Encounters with Food in the Czech Republic." *Anthropology of East Europe Review*, 21 (1): 37–41.

Polish Fair Trade Coalition (2010). *Strengthening Fair Trade in Central and Eastern Europe*. http://www.2010conference.fairtrade.org.pl/ (accessed October 10, 2012).

Raynolds, L., D. Murray, and J. Wilkinosn, eds. (2007). *Fair Trade: The Challenges of Transforming Globalization*. New York: Routledge.

Scott, J. C. (1976). *The Moral Economy of the Peasant: Rebellion and Subsistence in Southeast Asia*. New Haven, CT: Yale University Press.

Smith, A., and A. Stenning (2006). "Beyond Household Economies: Articulations and Spaces of Economic Practice in Postsocialism." *Progress in Human Geography*, 30 (2): 190–213.

Vandermeer, J., and I. Perfecto (1995). *Breakfast of Biodiversity: The Truth about Rain Forest Destruction*. Oaklnad, CA: Food First.

Verdery, K. (1991). "Theorizing Socialism: A Prologue to the 'Transition.'" *American Ethnologist*, 18 (3): 419–39.

Verdery, K. (1996). *What Was Socialism? What Comes Next?* Princeton, NJ: Princeton University Press.

Vides vēstis (2012). "Brazīlijas kafijas rūgtā netaisnības garša"- komentāri [Brazlian coffee's bitter taste of injustice-comments]. April 30. http://woman.delfi.lv/gimene/virtuve/bra zilijas-kafijas-rugta-netaisnibas-garsa.d?id=42319038&com=1&no=0&am p;s=1, *Vides vēstis* (accessed October 10, 2012).

Zaļā zeme (2005). "Godīgā tirdzniecība-" komentāri [Fair trade-comments]. January 26. http://www.tvnet.lv/zala_zeme/zala_dzive/173477-godiga_tirdznieciba/comments (accessed October 10, 2012).

12

The Changing Value of Food: Calculating Moldova's Poverty

Jennifer Cash

This chapter focuses on the use of "food" in the calculation, portrayal, and perception of poverty in Moldova. Since the early 2000s, Moldova has been dubbed "Europe's poorest country." Before the Soviet period it counted among both Europe's and Russia's poorest regions, but in the mid-twentieth century, it enjoyed the reputation of being a "flowering orchard" and "little piece of heaven." The country's changing reputation reflects empirical changes in living conditions and changing modes of measuring poverty. Current calculations of poverty compare individual income against a "basket" of key food items. Though informants agree that people are cash-poor, they insist that "no one is starving." Indeed, high levels of household food production, sharing within families and beyond, and strong rural-urban social networks render the official statistics paradoxical.

Food values

As other authors in this volume and elsewhere have made clear, the value of food cannot be easily equated with its market price. Indeed, various forms of food-distribution networks—some within the market (such as Fair Trade), and some more or less outside the market (such as cooperatives and gardening initiatives)—reveal the degree to which even the price of food is rarely calculated, by seller or buyer, as a brute calculation of inputs against desired profits (Pratt 2007). The "value of food," in the eyes of consumers especially, may also be calculated with concern for social relations near and far in terms of justice and equity; ecology; local employment opportunities; traditions, heritage, and culture; and, of course, taste (see Luetchford and Pratt 2011).

This chapter takes up the theme of food value from a slightly different perspective: how food has been used, and still is used, in brokering relations of social welfare in national and international arenas—that is, the use of food in calculations of poverty. As such, I seek to extend the discussion of food's capacity to mediate social relations into the domains of social policy. I am most specifically interested in how food is used to mediate social welfare within national boundaries, but national poverty lines (and with them food value) are shaped regionally and internationally, too. In Europe, there are tensions between national poverty lines that retain food as a major component of their calculation and newer "European" standards which increasingly emphasize the lack of access to or exercise of legal rights as the root cause of poverty. These new "European" standards, which remove food from direct considerations of poverty, have not yet been implemented in Moldova. There tensions over ascriptions of national poverty focus explicitly on food. I consider the food values that emerge from people's objections that "no one is starving."

Food and poverty in Europe's poorest country

This chapter is based on ethnographic fieldwork undertaken in 2009–10 on interrelated changes in economic and ritual practices, but it draws on fieldwork over the preceding decade as well. The main data comes from a study on "Wine and Saints" based in the village of Răscăieți in southeastern Moldova and conducted within the framework of the "Economy and Ritual" group at the Max Planck Institute for Social Anthropology. I devoted substantial attention to questions of household economy in terms of both ideal and actual levels of production.[1]

By the mid-2000s, it had become impossible to ignore the magnitude of economic reckoning in people's everyday lives. In Moldova, laws on privatization and decollectivization were passed in the early 1990s but little was implemented until the end of the decade. Thus, it was only on the eve of the twenty-first century that collective farms were fully dismantled, private plots of land distributed, and industrial complexes closed. Still, Moldova's economic situation worsened during the 1990s and was further weakened by the 1998 Russian financial crisis (International Bank for Reconstruction and Development 1999; Gorton and White 2003). With the profound disruptions to markets and employment caused by decollectivization and privatization at the end of the decade, the dislocating effects were immediate. In 1999/2000, 90 percent of Moldova's population was recorded as falling below the poverty line (Laur 2005), and Moldova was ranked among the poorer countries of the world. A map of world poverty produced in the year 2000, for example, placed Moldova in the third worst band out of 6, in which 28–50 percent of the population lived on less than $2/day. By 2004, news reports about Moldova in international media rarely failed to mention that it was Europe's poorest country. The percentage of Moldova's labor-based out-migration became one of the highest in the world. Through the mid-2000s, the rate of out-migration was sometimes said to be as high as one quarter of the population. Human trafficking, particularly of women, was of grave concern.

Yet I might still not have tackled the problem of poverty and the statistics used to document and control it, if it had not been for the evidence mounting in my fieldnotes that people in both rural and urban areas were concerned with the international image of their country as a "poor one." By the time I was investigating notions of household "self-sufficiency" in 2009–10, I had a backlog of anecdotes, jokes, ironic comments, and expressions of distress. It is this inventory, combined with later household-focused fieldwork, that I have brought to bear here.

Certainly, the available statistics reflect real economic change. Since 2004, statistics on poverty in Moldova have improved somewhat, such that in 2010, most urban households were considered to have sufficient income to meet their needs, while *only* rural households remained vulnerable (National Bureau of Statistics 2011, my emphasis). Yet these figures also indicate that poverty remains widespread: more than half of the population is rural. Moldova's status as the poorest country in Europe was reinforced when the UNDP placed the country's poverty in global terms as it calculated 8.1 percent of the population as living on less than $1.25/day in 2007.[2]

Yet at another level, the statistics are shot through with ambiguity about the balance of empirical representation against the political projects that they convey. For example, Moldovan intellectuals greeted the improved statistics of 2004 with skepticism—they thought that any "improvements" in the economic situation had been engineered (artificially and illegitimately) by the reelected Communist Party through calculated distributions of food and price adjustments. In subsequent years, analysts have attributed the improvement in poverty statistics to migrants' remittances (which as a ratio to GDP are now the fourth highest in the world [World Bank 2011]), blurring the assessment of improvement with the image of continued desperation.

Created in the interstices of national policies on social welfare, the multiple bids of government agencies and NGOs to secure international funding, and the efforts of the same to produce standardized metrics on economic and social growth, development, and welfare—none of these statistics are neutral. They should be assumed to have been developed in good faith, but nevertheless subjected to critical analysis. In my view, they reveal a rich discourse about the value of food, and about the relationship between rural communities and the state.

Poverty as lack of food

Food is at the center of poverty measurements in Moldova, and it reappears in extended discussions of remittances and their use. Poverty and food are connected too, albeit obliquely, in debates about "food security." Moldova has been identified as playing a potentially key role in averting regional and global food shortages; though households may be "poor" in food according to other statistics, the country nevertheless is more than "secure" (Cash 2015a; United Nations 2012). The use of food in poverty calculations might not be remarkable—after all, most countries and international agencies calculate levels of "minimum consumption" as an integral component of poverty lines—but for two other considerations. One consideration is that "European" agencies have, since 1975, and increasingly since 2000, pushed for new modes of calculating poverty that do not foreground basic subsistence (Betti et al. 2012; Bradshaw and Mayhew 2011). The second consideration is that Moldova's citizens, rural and urban alike, have been contesting the national image of poverty for quite some time. These two considerations prompt questions: Why does a food-based calculation of poverty persist so prominently in Moldova? And, why does the general population feel that official statistics thoroughly misrepresent "poverty" as stemming from a lack of food?

The national poverty line is calculated in terms of a "minimal basket of consumption." This basket is comprised from a set quantity of food providing adequate nutrition and sufficient calories, plus a few other necessities (such as electricity) (Laur 2005). The value of the basket's contents are then calculated in a monetary equivalent and compared against income. In its basic conception, the basket is based on the nutritional needs of an individual and scaled for gender and age. Adjustments in price are made for regional variations (particularly rural/urban). Composite baskets have to be made to address both the needs and incomes of households. The basic method is used widely in all world regions outside of Europe. With its focus on "basic subsistence," the basket is considered a method designed for identifying "absolute poverty" but inadequate for identifying "relative poverty." Its use presupposes food-related problems—populations in danger of starvation—rather than other forms of poverty or inequality.

The calculation of poverty thresholds by consumption baskets is commonly attributed, in English-language sources, to Mollie Orshansky who developed America's poverty thresholds in the 1960s. Considering only the history of baskets that have been most relevant to post-Soviet Moldova, however, we see earlier incarnations of the basket concept in the twentieth-century Soviet Union, which initiated a minimum consumer budget in the 1920s (Lokshin 2008: 2), but later severed the calculation from an application to "poverty." Until the 1980s, the Soviet Union had no official methods for calculating "poverty," but nevertheless tracked "normal" levels of nutritionally adequate consumption with baskets (McAuley 1979). The minimum Soviet budgets of the 1960s, in fact, were fairly generous in accounting for more than subsistence needs (Klugman and Braithwaite 1997: 11). By the 1970s, budgets were explicitly based on "baskets" (Lokshin 2008: 2). The Soviet baskets contained higher levels of protein and fat than the WHO recommended (Klugman and Braithwaite 1997: 13), and a higher proportion of potatoes to meat than the American version but were considered nutritionally comparable (McAuley 1979). Similar baskets were constructed throughout Eastern Europe, and indeed worldwide, throughout the 1970s (Hutton and Redmond 2000).

It is unlikely that Moldova's current use of a food-based poverty calculation reflects a concerted ideological or political motivation. Almost all of Moldova's post-Soviet legal and administrative reforms have been marked by compromise or balancing two strong and opposing political tendencies—one that favors alliance with Europe and its liberal social, political, and economic agendas, and another that favors the maintenance of Soviet forms under Russian protection. In many cases, these dueling agendas have co-existed even within the platforms of each political party (March 2004). Accordingly, the political value assigned to food through poverty calculations should be seen largely as the result of pragmatic decisions made between old (Soviet) and new ("European") models by professional researchers and administrators (compare Zenker and Hoehne forthcoming). In acknowledging poverty at all, however, the state shows clearly its own ideological transition from a Soviet to a post-Soviet state. And, as everywhere,

Moldova's poverty calculations remain "riddled with culturally embedded values and assumptions about needs" (Strader and Misra 2018: 393).

Though the basket method of calculating poverty is widespread, Moldova's use of it has spurred a unique social discourse. Concerns about adequate regional representation, dietary variations, and nutrition that have long appeared in relation to poverty and food in the American context are of little concern (see Orshansky 1965). Nor is there much concern to re-define what is in the basket to include, for example, childcare (another key issue in the American discourse on poverty calculations; see Roosa, Deng, Nair, and Burrell 2005). In Moldova, public discussion focuses on the price that is assigned to the food in the basket, and the subsequent comparison of this figure with income. The logical conclusion is that a person who lacks the requisite income also faces a lack of food. It is this conclusion that people in Moldova contest so strongly. They agree that they lack income—but they insist that they have food.

Contestation: "We are not starving"

Findings of food-based poverty are contested by Moldova's citizens, particularly those in rural areas, because the calculation implies that poor people have difficulty accessing food. Moreover, as most of the "poor" are in rural areas, the implication is that food is particularly difficult to access in rural areas. Yet in local context, this seems patently false. Most people are quick to acknowledge that the country is "poor" in terms of infrastructural development (unpaved and badly paved roads and the lack of public sanitation in rural areas are considered major problems). They also find themselves poor in terms of income. But, they resist any suggestion that the country lacks adequate food or that they themselves have difficulty accessing food. "We are not starving" and "No one dies of hunger" are frequent refrains that I have heard since 1999.

As will become clear, food—in its availability or its lack—is a morally charged topic. In rural areas, people work hard to produce food; they are proud to display the results of this work (undertaken in fields, household gardens, and kitchens); and they face multiple moral imperatives to provide or share food with social relations. Because they strive to meet these obligations to care and to provide, most of the time it would be patently false to claim that there is not enough food in the countryside. There is enough food because people produce it and redistribute it. But beyond this, the pride and obligations associated with the production of food, from field to feast, has a history that is part (at least) of the collective memory of Soviet life and strongly contributes to collective identity. To accept the national poverty statistics, as they have been constructed, would be to deny too much of what people know they do, have experienced, and take as important.

Visions of plenty

In July 1999, I made my first trip to Chişinău. As I climbed down the steps of the bus I had taken from Iaşi, Romania, my eyes were greeted by the sight of market stalls overflowing with eggplants, tomatoes, cucumbers—all the bounty of the summer. Within a week, I met with a young political scientist and two of his students. They were the first of many to point out the incongruities of material life in Moldova, and especially in the capital city: well-dressed women, shiny new cars, streets full of potholes. Nicu leaned toward me and asked, "Do you like jokes?" He continued, "Do you know what the difference between an American and a Moldovan is?" I shook my head no. "An American" he said, "gets his pay at the end of the month, and says: 'with this I pay $500 for rent, $200 for my car, a couple hundred for food and clothes, and with the $500 that is left, no one asks me what I do with it.'" He looked at me for confirmation, and I agreed. "The Moldovan" he continued, "gets his pay at the end of the month, and says: 'with this I pay the rent, and about the other $500 no one asks me where I get it.'" Nicu and his students laughed, and I along with them, but it was to be some time before I understood that the joke was serious. Faced with absolute shortages of money from their official salaries to meet the necessary costs of life, people across Moldova nevertheless managed, at the turn of the twenty-first century, to meet their basic needs and project a public image of some level of personal affluence.

The same show of personal pride that was expressed in ever-coiffed hair, immaculate clothes, and polished shoes that defied the dust and mud of the cracking and buckling asphalt in city streets, appeared too in the guise of feasts. In 2005, a retired school teacher described her preparations for her village's Patron Saint's Day (Hram). I had asked about the number of dishes and courses that she was preparing and discovered that the cost amounted to a few hundred dollars. Why not celebrate more simply, I wondered? Her answer: "It is our tradition to make rich feasts. Even if you have nothing, you go and borrow the money to put on a better feast." Women sometimes encouraged each other to make simpler celebratory tables, but they rarely succeeded. Often enough, they bowed to pressure within the household to follow "tradition" with at least three courses (various cold salads and meats piled high on the table from the start of the meal, a warm dish for the second course, and desserts). In 2009–10, I documented how feast menus became self-inflating too; while a woman might start with a modest menu, children and husband would make requests for favorite dishes, a colleague might mention a new salad that piqued the cook's interest, and the woman herself might remember another recipe she wanted to try out. In the course of a day's preparations, a "simple" menu consisting of two salads, roast duck, baked apples and one kind of special bread could have inflated easily to five salads, roast duck, baked apples, plates filled with halvah and cookies, *placinta* (filled pies), and two kinds of special bread. It was a rare village cook who could keep the cost of even a small feast (for about ten people) much below €100 in 2009. Thus the annual cycle of birthday parties, namedays, religious holidays, and national days of rest required a substantial outlay of cash for even the most frugal households (see Cash 2011). Still, women were compelled to cook, not because they lacked the ability or will to economize further, but because through the preparation of feasts they performed substantial care work within the family, demonstrated their skills (and commitment) to the community, and satisfied their own creative energies (cf Williams 1996 [1984]).

Even when the actual food offered is simple and inexpensive, presentation bespeaks a lavish spread. Simple foods include bean pâtés, baked apples, raw fruits and vegetables, and various breads. The two photographs are of such simple feasts. Figure 12.1 is of a Hram celebration in the church courtyard at Răscaieți in 2009, and Figure 12.2 is of a household Hram in a village of the central region in 2005.

Every time I attended a wedding or baptism, my close associates would debrief me (just as they asked others) over the next several days about the numbers and kinds of dishes that were offered, as well as the music played, gifts offered, toasts made, and speeches given. It was clear that they too were trying to rank the event in terms of its overall cost and in the ways that costs were distributed; they were interested in the display of both wealth and modesty, but unless they were already privy to information about the costs (e.g., if the family had traveled to the port-city of Odessa in nearby Ukraine to buy the raw ingredients), it was hard for anyone to decipher the real costs of an event. Friends and neighbors might have donated food (e.g., flour, bread, oil, wine) as well as their cooking labor; discounts or further donations may have been arranged with respect to meat, or music, or decorations. The display of abundance at feasts is therefore often successful, regardless of the actual food that is served or its cost.

Even households that are chronically short on cash are rarely perceived as lacking food. Everyday consumption is not quite so spectacular as feasts, but even normal meals consisting of the most "basic" foods (like soup with bread and tomato salad) are prepared, presented, and consumed to convey a sense of abundance, satiety, and pleasure. Ubiquitous practices of hospitality also mean that even casual visitors rarely find a house with an empty table. Shortly after the arrival of an unannounced guest, food and drink is offered with one of several dramatic flourishes—of elegance if it is the leftovers from a feast; of speed if it is quickly scrambled or fried eggs (perhaps

Figure 12.1 Hram table at church, 2009 (©Jennifer Cash).

Figure 12.2 Hram table at home, 2005 (© Jennifer Cash).

borrowed from a neighbor), bread, and wine; of childish glee if is something even more frugal and impromptu, like a bag of unshelled walnuts fetched from the attic.

All this is to say that even if food is sometimes borrowed or improvised, food in rural areas is accessible. This is because, on the one hand, per capita land holdings are sufficient for providing adequate food. The main problem faced by smallholders is a lack of cash—for inputs like fertilizer (Petrick 2000). On the other hand, gifting, sharing, and feasting ensure the redistribution of food. The redistribution of food is also coupled with "work" in a broad moral, as well as economic, sense (see Cash 2015c). People who "work" are fed. Even those who do not or cannot "work" still receive some sustenance if they show up at certain church rituals, such as funerals and memorial services (see also Popa 2016). And, as a last resort, a request for bread is never denied. Beyond these local practices, villagers have recourse to resources from the state and other organizations, especially non-Orthodox religious organizations. It is easy to see how, from an emic perspective, it is true that "no one starves." There is "enough" food in rural areas, and it is available to all who participate in village life (Cash 2015b).

Memories of starvation, images of poverty and plenty

The emic perspective of bounty, described above, is at once an empirical observation and a moral claim. It can be contested in turn by various research, including sociological analysis. Of these, the most powerful source is probably that produced by two anthropologists in a report commissioned by the World Bank (De Soto and Dudwick 2003). Their study describes drastic poverty among individuals and families in the first five years of independence (1991–96). The story is dramatic and harrowing, describing families that strategically underfed according to age and gender; of nutritionally inadequate food substitutions; of children kept out of school to help their parent(s) secure fuel and food. As a study of the "poor" or poverty, the work is methodologically problematic: interviewees were selected on the basis of their own or others' ascription of them as poor without further empirical parameters, and it provides no way to distinguish descent into poverty rather than a continued status. Nevertheless, the report is important to address here because it provides evidence that counters my informants' own objections that the availability of food is not a problem.

I, too, have recorded stories of the lack of food. In urban areas, I was often told that people (mostly single elderly) had to choose between electricity and heat or food. Yet no informant directly told me that he or she had faced such a situation. One woman told me of an acquaintance who was in such a situation and managed, at least for some time, with a diet of cabbage and watery soup.

Even in rural areas, some families are known to have less food than others. But, when other villagers acknowledge the presence of such families, they usually also criticize them for moral faults and social lacks. Other families, with (many) children and few resources are identified as "needy" rather than poor. The emic perspective, after all, emphasizes the critical role of social status and relations: people in good moral standing in the community who maintain basic social ties (with neighbors, if not with kin) should have adequate food. Thus beyond reports and analysis, the claims and counter-claims about the availability of food form an important debate about the moral fabric of Moldova's rural communities. Denying the existence of food-based "poverty" draws attention to the values and accomplishments of the moral community; it also includes the recognition that many people fail to support kin and neighbors as they should.

Another reason Moldovans protest so strongly against associations of poverty and hunger is that mass starvation is within living memory. In comparison to the past, there really is enough food. Before World War II, Moldova's rural areas experienced regular famine from crop failures and drought (Hitchins 1994; Kaba 1919). The war, like others before it, brought famine, as did the early years of Soviet collectivization. Those who experienced famine as children remain literally haunted by the memory (Ivanova 2014). Even those who did not experience famine know the stories from their elder siblings, neighbors, and other relatives. At nearly every gathering of one extended family, the eldest brother recounted how he and his siblings gathered mussels and river grasses for food during the war years. It was never a tale of heroic survival, but one that ended in tears for a beloved younger sister who had not survived with such meagre fare.

After the initial hardships of collectivization, real progress was made during the Soviet period to overcome the impediments of prewar agriculture. Coupled with the extension of universal healthcare, improved water quality, and education in basic hygiene measures, the worst manifestations of Moldova's poverty—famine, malnutrition, disease, and maternal and infant mortality—were eradicated. Soviet agronomists spurred specialization, Moldova was integrated into the Soviet market, and the fruit and wine industries developed. Within the union, Moldova became renowned for its rich soil, good climate, abundant food, and quality wine. It was "a little piece of heaven," a desirable place to live for those in the Soviet Union (like retired military officers) who could choose a new home.

This reputation for abundance was tied into Soviet narratives of progress. Reading the local history compiled for Răscaieți and kept in its village museum, for example, one learns nothing of the early horrors of collectivization, now being documented by national historians to recover social memory (Cojocaru 2016). One learns only of the successes in the Soviet (re)building of agriculture and rural economies. Widespread depictions of the abundant harvests of grain, apples, grapes and other crops had a propagandistic function, but people in rural areas also felt their reality. For people who knew hunger, Soviet Moldova—in terms of available food—was, indeed, "heaven."

The combined memories of actual starvation and real progress, along with the still-lingering Soviet-made image of Moldova's abundance, are present in the rejection of post-Soviet calculations of poverty. Villagers "see" little evidence of starvation in the post-socialist period, but if they accept the country's statistical calculations of poverty, it means—in local terms—that the country has returned to its prewar, pre-Soviet reputation. In terms of international discourse about development, Moldova is no longer a success story. Instead, it appears as a region of perpetual impoverishment, which experienced only fleeting improvement in Soviet hands.

When people in Moldova reject an identification as "poor," they are therefore rejecting much more than a statistical measurement. At stake is not the state's basic concept of poverty nor the measurement of income. People agree that they are cash-poor; they accept the basic premise that "real" poverty entails an absolute lack of food (and starvation). The problem comes from equating food and income. At stake is a sense of pride linked to people's participation in moral economies, past and present, that are not constrained fully by the logic of the market. In a way that resonates with Martha Lampland's (1991) study of a rural community in Hungary during the 1980s, protestations against widespread ascriptions of Moldova's national poverty insist that good people work and will not starve, regardless of their lack of money. It is work—not money—that produces food. If extended, these protestations turn to critique the state for its failures. People work, but the state does not: it does not provide the necessary conditions for life and work in terms of infrastructure, agricultural investment, employment (money), and effective markets.

Missing the value of food in the calculation of poverty

Other commentators have found it paradoxical that anthropologists, working traditionally in the world's "poorest" societies, have tended to avoid theorizing poverty (Lewis 1975 [1959]; Hahn 2016; cf Kaneff and Pine 2011). Indeed, even the popular debate on the "culture of poverty" (Lewis 1975[1959]) was left primarily to other disciplines. In recent years, this has begun to change with anthropologists criticizing poverty measurements. For example, Akhil Gupta points to the lack of concern shown by statistical measures for "the aspiration for rich, rewarding life":

> Statistics function as a transnational disciplinary mechanism at the same time they
> function as an end that states aspire to achieve. The goal of development is not
> necessarily to have a populace whose lives are rewarding, meaningful, rich, and
> varied but have certain rates of growth, to decrease the unemployment rate, or to
> achieve a GNP per capita that crosses a certain threshold. The aspiration for rich,
> rewarding life would be dismissed as impractical or without content in most state
> bureaucracies and among development practitioners because it is hard to measure.
> (Gupta 2012: 158)

Similarly, Michael Jackson (2011) finds even quality-of-life measurements problematic. Though such measurements are meant to be a refinement for studying levels of development beyond the concerns of "poverty," they still seem inadequate when gauged against the knowledge produced by long-term fieldwork. As Jackson notes, "When the factors include such things as school enrollments, literacy rates, GNP, civil rights, child immunization, life expectancy, and public debt . . . [many in Sierra Leone] might agree that his or her country was relatively impoverished" but also "object to the conclusion that his or her life was thereby bereft of quality" (183).

Both Gupta and Jackson point to a double weakness in the ability of poverty measurements to report accurately on the quality of life in local communities. First, the measurements report on indicators that are important for states and other institutional bodies that are—at best—only proxies for quality of life. Secondly, as Jackson makes explicit, many factors are simply not included: "Family, friendship and community ties, or attachment to home" (183) being among the most critical, but also the taste of food, clemency of the weather, or mental health indices. It may be that poverty measurements can never be adjusted to truly resonate with the lifeways and perceptions of local communities—at least not for long. After all, poverty measurements are not static, and they are repeatedly adjusted to respond to both social change and intellectual critique. As Geremek (1994) has demonstrated, "poverty" always refers to what appears to be a social problem in the time that it is being used. With reference to Moldova's poverty measurements, we must then ask, in whose vision is food the social problem that needs to be solved?

Food has been of diminishing value in discussions of poverty in Europe over several decades. While many European countries (like Moldova) maintain a "basket" calculation for domestic use, absolute methods have been discouraged for official calculations of data that are placed into international use. The support for relative approaches to measuring poverty have been strong enough that it can be claimed that, since 1975, poverty in "Europe" has been calculated on a relative scale (Betti et al. 2012). As the number of countries included in "Europe" has increased quickly since 2000, so too has the use of relative scales. Most former socialist countries now use relative scales, whether or not they are EU members, as a sign of their commitment to a broader European project. Using relative scales, "European countries" acknowledge the existence of "extreme" poverty, but not of "absolute" poverty.

To some degree, the objections of my informants in Moldova might seem to indicate a concurrence with this line of European thinking and policy-making. The most recent round of European policy-making, which re-defines poverty as a problem of access to existing administrative and legal protections (Council of Europe 2012), might also seem in line with the objections I have recounted: that the problems in Moldova are related to lack of income (and jobs), but that food is widely available.

Yet it would be wise to expect, at best, a mixed reception to such "European" views on poverty as they reach Moldova through the activities of various international and European agencies, NGOs, and legal reforms. Most other efforts to "Europeanize" Moldova's legal and administrative apparatuses receive a mixed reception. In the case of poverty measurements, a redefinition in relative terms, with concern for social inclusivity, legal access, and human rights, threatens to silence the extant social and political critique embodied in my informants' objections that "no one is starving."

This objection insists that people, especially in rural communities, are already exercising significant effort not only to "not starve," but also to "live well." People object to ascriptions of poverty because they are not attempting to just "get by" nor to "eke out" a living; they are attempting to live in a state of abundance. The "basics" of life, in their view, should be prepared, presented, and enjoyed richly. As they see it, they are already doing their part; it is the state that has not provided the necessary conditions for life and work (or blocks access to them). How (and why) should they further prevail on the state? If food is removed entirely from the discussion of poverty, people lose the chance to explain why and how food is critical to the quality of their lives. They also lose the chance to critique the failings of the post-socialist state to provide the rural development and social welfare that they valued from the Soviet state.

Conclusion

In Moldova, food and poverty are not interrelated through a simple calculation. Poverty figures are thus misleading if one assumes that income and access to nutritionally adequate food are directly related. The additional statistics that seem to bear out poverty—namely migration, high levels of remittance, and the use of remittances to purchase food (National Bureau of Statistics 2010)—point to other social dynamics. These have to do with a desire for cash, and more precisely for the flexibility and status that comes with it. It is, after all, neither the poorest nor the richest households that engage in migration, but those in the middle (Goerlich and Luecke 2011). The problem that the poverty figures do adequately reflect is lack of cash. While it seems that everyone already knows this, no policy organization seems prepared to acknowledge it.

The statistics on poverty show the state's initial transformation from a socialist one to a "capitalist" one with the shift to tracking "minimal" consumption instead of "normal" consumption. The social priority is no longer to achieve an adequate level of nutrition for all, but to make sure that no one actually starves. As informants point out, there is something amiss in the calculations: while the statistics are not wrong, their underlying framework misses the real availability of food in rural Moldova. Food is not scarce in quantity or variety, and most people can access it—one needs only to work one's own private plots and/or maintain good social relations with kin and neighbors who work their plots. Blind to the real availability of food—in its production, distribution, and consumption through myriad social relations—the statistics also misconstrue the value of food in rural communities. In its production, distribution, and consumption, food mediates social values and relations in work, kinship, and the household. Food is entangled with gender and status; but it also serves as a medium for experiencing and expressing creativity, skill, care, pleasure, pride, and memory. Just as these things matter, so food matters well beyond its nutritional value or market cost.

Notes

1 The group's work is described by Gudeman and Hann (2010, 2012); main comparative results appear in Gudeman and Hann (2015a, b). This chapter benefited directly from comments by Detelina Tocheva and Bettina Mann.
2 Cash (2015a) contains a more detailed consideration of Moldova's status as Europe's "poorest country."

References

Betti, G., F. Gagliardi, A. Lemmi, and V. Verma (2012). "Subnational Indicators of Poverty and Deprivation in Europe: Methodology and Applications." *Cambridge Journal of Regions, Economy and Society*, 5: 129–47.

Bradshaw, J., and E. Mayhew (2011). "The Measurement of Extreme Poverty in the European Union." Report for the European Commission, Directorate-General for Employment, Social Affairs and Inclusion.

Cash, J. (2011). "Capitalism, Nationalism, and Religious Revival: Transformations of the Ritual Cycle in Moldova." *Anthropology of East Europe Review*, 29 (2): 181–203.

Cash, J. (2015a). "Between Starvation and Security: Poverty and Food in Rural Moldova." In I. Harboe Knudson and M. Demant Frederikson (eds.), *Ethnographies of Grey Zones in Eastern Europe: Relations, Borders and Invisibilities*, 41–56. London: Anthem.

Cash, J. (2015b). "How Much Is Enough? Household Provisioning, Self-Sufficiency and Social Status in Rural Moldova." In S. Gudeman and C. Hann (eds.), *Oikos and Market: Explorations in Self-Sufficiency after Socialism*, 47–76. New York and Oxford: Berghahn.

Cash, J. (2015c). "Economy as Ritual: The Problems of Paying in Wine." In S. Gudeman and C. Hann (eds.), *Economy and Ritual: Studies of Postsocialist Transformations*, 31–51. New York and Oxford: Berghahn.

Cojocaru, L., ed. (2016). *Arhivele Memoriei: Recuperarea și valorificarea istorică a memoriei victimelor regimului totalitar-comunist din Republica Sovietică Socialistă Moldovenească, vol. I*. Chișinău: Academy of Sciences.

Council of Europe (2012). *Redefining and Combating Poverty: Human Rights, Democracy and Common Goods in Today's Europe*. Strasbourg: Council of Europe Publishing.

De Soto, H., and N. Dudwick (2003). "Eating from One Pot: Survival Strategies in Moldova's Collapsing Rural Economy." In N. Dudwick, E. Gomart, and A. Marc (eds.), *When Things Fall Apart: Qualitative Studies of Poverty in the Former Soviet Union*, 333–77. Washington, DC: The World Bank.

Geremek, B. (1994). *Poverty: A History*. Oxford: Blackwell.

Goerlich, D., and M. Luecke (2011). "International Labour Migration, Remittances and Economic Development in Moldova." In D. Kaneff and F. Pine (eds.), *Global Connections and Emerging Inequalities in Europe: Perspectives on Poverty and Transnational Migration*, 57–78. London: Anthem.

Gorton, M., and J. White (2003). "The Politics of Agrarian Collapse: Decollectivisation in Moldova." *East European Politics and Societies*, 17 (2): 305–31.

Gudeman, S., and C. Hann (2010). "Economy and Ritual: Max Planck Institute for Social Anthropology." Report 2008–09, vol. I: 58–61. Halle/Saale.

Gudeman, S., and C. Hann (2012). "Max Planck Institute for Social Anthropology." Report 2010-11, vol. I: 55–60. Halle/Saale.

Gudeman, S., and C. Hann (2015a). *Economy and Ritual: Studies of Postsocialist Transformations*. New York: Berghahn.

Gudeman, S., and C. Hann (2015b). *Oikos and Market: Explorations in Self-Sufficiency after Socialism*. New York: Berghahn.

Gupta, A. (2012). *Red Tape: Bureaucracy, Structural Violence, and Poverty in India*. Durham, NC: Duke University Press.

Hahn P. H. (2016). "Auf der Suche nach den Armen. Warum Armut in den Kulturwissenschaften so oft unsichtbar bleibt." In H. Meller, H. P. Hahn, R. Jung, and R. Risch (eds.), *Arm und Reich - Zur Ressourcenverteilung in prähistorischen Gesellschaften* (Proceedings of the 8th Mitteldeutscher Archäologentag vom 22. bis 24. Oktober 2015). Halle: Landesmuseum für Vorgeschichte.

Hitchins, K. (1994). *Rumania 1866–1947*. Oxford: Clarendon Press.

Hutton, S., and G. Redmond (2000). *Poverty in Transition Economies*. London: Routledge.

International Bank for Reconstruction and Development (1999). *Moldova: Poverty Assessment*. Washington, DC: The World Bank.

Ivanova, M. D. (2014). "'The Black Famine': Life Histories of Bulgarians and Gagauz who Survived the 1947–1948 Famine in Bessarabia." Paper presented at 2014 Congress of InASEA, September 18–21, 2014, Istanbul, Turkey.

Jackson, M. (2011). *Life within Limits*. Durham, NC: Duke University Press.

Kaba, J. (1919). *Politico-Economic Review of Basarabia*. Hoover Commission for Roumania. https://www.wdl.org/en/item/7313/view/1/9/.

Kaneff, D., and F. Pine, eds. (2011). *Global Connections and Emerging Inequalities in Europe: Perspectives on Poverty and Transnational Migration*. London: Anthem.

Klugman, J., and J. Braithwaite (1997). "Introduction and Overview." In J. Klugman (ed.), *Poverty in Russia: Public Policy and Private Responses*, 1–28. Washington, DC: The World Bank.

Lampland, M. (1991). "Pigs, Party Secretaries, and Private Lives in Hungary." *American Ethnologist*, 18 (3): 459–79.

Laur, E. (2005). "The Brief Characteristic of Creating and Developing the Poverty Monitoring and Analysis System in the Republic of Moldova." Paper prepared for the International Seminar on Poverty Measurement, National Institute of Statistics and Economic Studies, Paris, November 30–December 2. Online: http://www.insee.fr/en/insee-statistique-publique/default.asp?page=colloques/pauvrete/pauvrete.htm (accessed October 11, 2012).

Lewis, O. (1975 [1959]). *Five Families: Mexican Case Studies in the Culture of Poverty*. New York: Basic Books.

Lokshin, M. (2008). "Does Poverty Research in Russia Follow the Scientific Method?" Policy Research Working Paper 4528. The World Bank Development Research Group, Poverty Team.

Luetchford, P., and J. Pratt (2011). "Values and Markets: An Analysis of Organic Farming Initiatives in Andalusia." *Journal of Agrarian Change*, 11 (1): 87–103.

March, L. (2004). "Socialism with Unclear Characteristics: The Moldovan Communists in Government." *Demokratizatsiya*, 12 (4): 507–26.

McAuley, A. (1979). *Economic Welfare in the Soviet Union: Poverty, Living Standards, and Inequality*. Madison: University of Wisconsin Press.

National Bureau of Statistics of the Republic of Moldova (2010). "Household Budget Survey." http://www.statistica.md/pageview.php?l=en&idc=263&id=2206 (accessed February 28, 2013).

National Bureau of Statistics of the Republic of Moldova (2011). "Minimul de existență în anul 2010." Press release, April 6. http://www.statistica.md/newsview.php?l=ro&idc=168&id=3367 (accessed October 11, 2012).

Orshansky, M. (1965). "Counting the Poor: Another Look at the Poverty Profile." *Social Security Bulletin*, 28: 3–29.

Petrick, M. (2000). "Land Reform in Moldova: How Viable Are Emerging Peasant Farms?" Discussion Paper no. 28. Institute of Agricultural Development in Central and Eastern Europe (IAMO). http://www.iamo.de/dok/dp28.pdf (accessed February 28, 2013).

Popa, M. (2016). *Between Institutions and Hearts: Dynamics of Need, Redistribution and Social Security in a Village from Northern Dobruja*. Ph.D. Thesis, Martin Luther University.

Pratt, J. (2007). "Food Values: The Local and the Authentic." *Critique of Anthropology*, 27 (3): 285–300.

Roosa, M. W., S. Deng, R. L. Nair, and G. Lockhart Burrell (2005). "Measures for Studying Poverty in Family and Child Research." *Journal of Marriage and Family*, 67 (November): 971–88.

Strader, E., and J. Misra (2018). "Poverty and Income Inequality: A Cross-National Perspective on Social Citizenship." In A. Javier Trevino (ed.), *The Cambridge Handbook of Social Problems*, vol. 1, 385–408. Cambridge: Cambridge University Press.

United Nations (2012). *Rapid Food Security and Vulnerability Assessment – Moldova*. http://www.un.md/drought/2012/RapidAssessmentMoldova2012Final.pdf (accessed February 28, 2013).

World Bank (2011). *Migration and Remittances Factbook 2011*. Washington, DC: The International Bank for Reconstruction and Development/World Bank.

Williams, Brett (1996 [1984]). "Why Migrant Women Feed their Husbands Tamales: Foodways as a Basis for a Revisionist View of Tejano Family Life." In W. A. Haviland and R. J. Gordon (eds.), *Talking about People: Readings in Contemporary Cultural Anthropology* (2nd ed.), 130–36. Mountain View, CA: Mayfield Publishing Company.

Zenker, O., and M. Hoehne (2018). "Processing the Paradox: When the State Has to Deal with Customary Law." In O. Zenker and M. Hoehne (eds.), *The State and the Paradox of Customary Law in Africa*. London: Routledge.

13

Food Values among African Caribbean Migrants in England

Dana Conzo

Introduction

"I used to love to be outside at home," said Patricia, a middle-aged Caribbean woman who moved to England when she was a teenager. We were sitting at a table during a lunch put on by a community organization where I volunteered during fieldwork. At the start, our conversation was about gardening, since spring was around the corner, but it quickly turned to a discussion of the challenges of living a Caribbean life in such a culturally and environmentally different place as England. "Now, I hardly ever garden because I don't like to be outside as often here. But my daughter has three allotments in [the neighboring town]. My grandfather was a farmer at home, and I taught my daughter when she was little. It's in our DNA." Patricia's daughter is able to grow food for her family and sometimes even enough to share with her extended family. Additionally, the practice of growing food connects her to her Caribbean heritage. Sherry, a younger woman at the table next to us leaned into our conversation to add that she has a plot in her backyard that she uses to grow fruits and vegetables, but of course only seasonally, and they still have to buy Caribbean produce they cannot grow in the UK. Because of her upbringing in the Caribbean, Sherry said she is used to having fresh produce around, but a Caribbean diet doesn't mean you are limited to tropical produce. Part of following a Caribbean diet is working the land when possible to cultivate fresh produce. Patricia and Sherry's stories show that moving to England requires some modification of Caribbean culture in order to maintain social values. Still, they are able to maintain the core of their values such as source sharing and social networking and maintaining cultural heritage through food. This chapter explores how these social values are reconfigured and maintained in the diaspora through a focus on food production and consumption.

Racism, exclusion, and the importance of Caribbean food values

The maintenance of social values of a migrant group is particularly important when that group experiences generations of racism, social exclusion, and cultural disconnection, as in the case of African Caribbeans in England. The neighborhood where this research took place was home to Jewish migrants until the 1950s (Hylton 1999: xvii), when Great Britain recruited Caribbean people to replenish a depleted workforce after the Second World War. The well-established Jewish population began to move out of this neighborhood and into middle and upper middle-class neighborhoods as new African Caribbean migrants began to take their place in the lower-cost housing.

Housing was especially difficult for new migrants, with many landlords explicitly refusing to rent to Black tenants (Høgsbjerg 2014; Phillips and Phillips 1998). Migrants were restricted to the designated periphery of the city in what David Sibley calls spatial purification (2002: 49, 77), the explicit segregation of society's "undesirables" away from city centers. Because of this racial segregation, many people from St. Kitts, Nevis, Barbados, Dominica, and Jamaica settled in this neighborhood in the postwar years. Residential segregation "has serious implications for the present and future mobility opportunities of those who are excluded from desirable areas" (Charles 2003: 168). Referencing Jargowsky (1996) and Wilson (1987), Charles asserts that "where we live affects our proximity to good job opportunities, educational quality, and safety from crime (both as victim and as perpetrator), as well as the quality of our social networks." New migrants were banned from public spaces, through what was called "The Colour Bar." Andy, a British-born man in his forties, in reference to his father's experience as an African Caribbean migrant in the 1960s said, "It's terrible what they went through. Public places had signs in the window that say 'No Coloured. No Irish. No Dogs.' Terrible." An elderly man from Nevis and respected man in the community, said

> Many people who came over in my time, if they had the opportunity, they would have gone straight back home because England was not welcoming. It was a very hostile and a racist place. The Englishman think, "These Black guys come from the jungle, they're not educated" and you had this kind of nonsense. People used to tell you "why don't you go back to the jungle?"

Today, the challenges facing migrants and their families have shifted since the 1950s and 1960s, from interpersonal and overt discrimination to structural racism specifically understood through social exclusion. While explaining the politics an upcoming election in which UKIP and Conservatives were gaining ground in neighboring communities, an employee of a community organization explained that "England is a very class-structured society and very racist. The sad thing is that now, it's institutionalized." Exposure to racism has caused many to feel unwelcome in Britain, even if they were born there. The growing anti-immigrant, racist rhetoric of the political right has exacerbated these feelings. Abby, a 24-year-old British-born woman of Jamaican heritage, says she does not feel British because of Britain's colonial past and destruction of her familial homeland. She said, "Racism is getting worse because of anti-immigrant propaganda, but Britain is quick to forget their history of colonialism." Several other participants pushed against the idea of identifying as English stating that was an identity reserved for the White citizens. Jacqueline Nassy Brown echoed this sentiment in her analysis of Black identity in Liverpool, UK. She states being "'Black English' is nearly impossible. Being "just" British—without the Black signifier—is unheard of" (2005: ix).

While Black residents in the United Kingdom often are excluded from or uncomfortable in predominantly White areas in the public sphere, this neighborhood has become a safe zone through the creation of what Carole Boyce-Davies would describe as Caribbean spaces, the "essential ingredients" being "a sizable demographic shift in the population to this given location and the development of Caribbean business communities" (Boyce-Davies 2013: 2). African Caribbean churches, beauty salons, barbershops, funeral homes, community organizations, a West Indian cricket club, and two African Caribbean nightclubs line the main road. Once a year, this space hosts carnival, a multiday festival celebrating Caribbean culture.

Food is often central to these Caribbean spaces. Tookes (2015: 65) calls food a "portable medium" in which migrants can demonstrate their shared cultural identity and separate themselves from people within the larger host country society that do not share their cultural identity. In a conversation about her research on African Caribbean mothers and the importance of feeding their children a Caribbean diet, local scholar Bertha Ochieng said "Sometimes diets are the only thing people, especially marginalized people, can control in their lives." Dr. Ochieng's comment highlights the symbolic and practical importance of food in the lives of Black people in the United Kingdom. Food sharing and communal eating, home meals, and food activism within this community demonstrate the ways in which food is used to strengthen Caribbean cultural values such as strong social networks, autonomy, and cultural heritage knowledge transmission. Maintaining and strengthening these food values create a strong base from which migrants can navigate racism and structural oppression.

Cooking and eating at home: Enculturating Caribbean food values in Chapeltown

The home is arguably the most important space for maintaining and strengthening Caribbean cultural values. Tolia-Kelly (2004: 315) describes the home of postcolonial migrants as "a site where a history linked with past landscapes is refracted through the material artefacts in the domestic sphere." Family members, friends, and neighbors often fill the kitchens in this neighborhood. Subtle displays of Caribbean culture pepper the kitchen. Traditional cooking vessels, such as Jamaican "Dutch pots," Kittitian doving pots, or Barbadian buck pots are prominent features in many African Caribbean households. They usually live on the stovetop, only being rinsed after use and placed right back where it belongs. Tolia-Kelly (2004) highlights the importance of material culture for memory and re-memory of "geographies of lived environments" of people in transnational contexts. She states that material culture invokes memories. These memories and re-memories link people with their past, and interactions with memories and re-memories through material culture create and reshape a shared social identity within a group in the transnational community.

Family matriarchs are typically the center of the kitchen. Abby and her best friend Rodina discuss that while they love to cook and feel a connection with Caribbean food, the kitchen is their grandmothers' territory:

> I could cook real food like my grandma as well. It makes you feel a part of something. But my grandma never lets me into the kitchen! I feel like I need an initiation. My grandma, as far as she knows, I don't know how to cook. I feel like you have to be some type of older woman. I feel like you have to be someone's mom or older to be in the circle, like to cook rice and peas. She would never let me cook rice and peas! NO! It's almost like it's her kitchen, like its *hers*.

Rodina agreed, saying, "This Christmas, I helped my grandma cook for the first time and it's like 'Oh Rodina made that?!' and it's like wow." Laughing, Abby said, "You have to be initiated into the club. It's actually real, you know?" Williams-Forson (2006: 105) notes "the intersection of gender, race, class, and food converge to make the home a culinary battleground and a site of female empowerment." Abby and Rodina note that only women in a certain family position are able to assert their agency and power in the kitchen space, demonstrating and reaffirming the cultural values of the matriarchal family structure but also showing how they are still able to see food as a way to form social networks within their family through cooking and learning to cook.

Diana, a middle-aged Caribbean woman, describes her mother as a fiery, bossy woman right up to the end. Her mother maintained her and her family's connection to the Caribbean after moving to England through regular visits to St. Kitts returning with foodstuffs. Diana reminisced about a time her mother brought back a pear. "My mom said 'come! I want you to taste our pear' [imitating her mother's Caribbean accent] and I was running because our pear's sweet, innit. She brings it, shaped like a pear. Green hard skin and I was like 'oh I can't wait for this!' She go 'You put it on bread' And she put this on the bread—the most disgusting thing I ever tasted!" Diana said making a sour face, "I will never eat that again!" As it turns out, Caribbean pears are what they call avocados in England. Despite Diana's disconnection with island life (and vernacular), it was important to her mother to cultivate her and her sibling's connection with the culture through foodways. Caribbean pears were not a hit with Diana and her siblings, but she remembers fondly other Caribbean goods her mother would bring back, namely sugarcane, which has a long and tumultuous history in the Caribbean and is almost impossible to find in England, except during Carnival.

Diana's place in the home changed when her mother was diagnosed with and eventually passed away from cancer. Before her mother passed away, she taught Diana the family recipe for Saltfish fritters. "Well, my mom's dead now. Cancer killed her. And I loved her Saltfish fritters. Now she taught me that before she died. Well she had cancer. She had the cancer already. She taught me when she had cancer. Handed that to me and that was the last thing she taught me" said Diana. Being able to make this dish turns the recipe into an inalienable possession. Cooking her mother's recipes has become a status symbol within her family and community. "I am the queen of Saltfish fritters. So everybody comes to me to make their fritters," she said proudly. "I think it's because I am the only one that *can* do it. You know, she died and left me that so that makes me feel good." This moment gave Diana the power to provide her family with traditional recipes and a connection with their culture. She was catapulted from daughter to matriarch and maker of the family recipes, a social place she is proud and happy to hold.

Diana only makes saltfish fritters for special occasions such as Christmas, Easter, and birthdays, due to the time it takes to make a sufficient amount and the extremely high price of saltfish. For Williams (1984: 136), "to prepare their own foods when possible is to reaffirm the dignity of Tejano identity in an Anglo world which offers it little respect, as well as to root the celebrants in a long and great tradition mediated—made present—by the family." Likewise, Diana's ability to make her family saltfish fritters strengthens their connection to Caribbean cultural values in an often racist and hostile environment. Diana's ability and willingness to make her family saltfish fritters reinforces her position as matriarch as well as allows her to create and strengthen family networks and link her family with their Caribbean roots through eating together.

Similarly, Gladys, or "Nana G" to her grandchildren, including Rodina, usually occupies the space around the stove while her grandkids and their friends, all in their twenties, sit around the kitchen table, eating, talking, and laughing. Occasionally, they peek over her shoulder or steal a fried dumpling fresh from the pan before retreating back to the kitchen table. While it is a fairly large house, with a comfortable living room, they never leave the small eat-in kitchen. Despite not being allowed to cook, Abby and Rodina spend most of their social time in Gladys's kitchen where they are able to connect with their family and cultural heritage.

Williams (1984: 134) states that "just as tamales ritually underscore women's domestic commitments, the everyday preparation and sharing of food routinely reaffirms family ties and allows families to work as efficiently and profitably as possible." Similarly, the matriarchs' commitment to cooking Caribbean meals for their families demonstrate their commitment to their family and cultural values of family networks, commensality, and cultural connection to Caribbean foodways. Gladys and Diana's connection to their cultural heritage manifests each time they provide their family with traditional dishes and a connection with their heritage they cannot get anywhere else. For migrants, this connection to cultural foodways is especially important. The maintenance of foodways often alleviates some cultural mourning and the stress of living in a new environment by connecting them with the home they left behind. For the younger generation, often born and raised in England, eating at home connects them to their Caribbean identity, which is made even more important by their feelings of marginalization from the larger British society.

Shared community meals as a source of resilience and memory

Community and cultural centers' affordable food programs are important events within this neighborhood. In low-income communities, access to and the ability to afford food are always a concern. This became an increasingly pressing issue during the 2008 welfare reforms that dramatically altered the already fragile economic situation in this neighborhood. In addition, there is a large elderly population in this neighborhood who have limited physical access to grocery stores.

The function of these centers and weekly lunches in this community goes beyond providing respite from economic hardships experienced by Caribbean migrants. Although my research focus was food security and activism, I realized the social and cultural value of these events during my first time volunteering at one. Walking up to the lunch being held in the recreation room of the church, I could hear laughing and talking from the street. Despite the cold weather, the door to the rec room where lunch was being served was propped opened, allowing some of the warmth and the smell of pumpkin soup and fried fish to hit me before I even entered. As I entered, I was struck by how warm, cozy, and busy it was. There were eight tables, in two rows of four on each side of the room. The tables had four to eight people sitting at them chatting and drinking tea while they waited for lunch. The volunteer wait staff buzzed around getting tea and cookies for the service users, joking and laughing with them and among each other while they worked.

Across the room from the entrance is the door to the kitchen, which is closed off from the dining room. In the kitchen, the chef worked to fulfil orders and members of the wait staff periodically filtered in to chat with each other or the chef. The energy was slightly frenzied. The manager of the lunch pulled me aside to welcome me to the job. She told me that they can sometimes integrate English food into the meals but for the most part, they try to stick with African Caribbean staples, like rice and soup. "Soup is such a Caribbean thing and so popular at events because it is easy and makes you warm inside," she elaborated. After our talk about how things run and why they serve the food they do, I was promptly put to work taking drink and food orders. I was just as quickly part of the jokes. My American accent and white skin made me stand out but also perfectly placed me in a prime position to be the butt of some innocent teasing. After a few awkward conversations, I was in the flow of laughing and joking, delivering food, and making tea.

Giacoman (2016) notes that communal eating, commensality, is a "practice that fulfills the role of strengthening cohesion among the members of a group, both in serving as an interactive space and in symbolizing a sense of belonging and respect for shared norms." In this way, these shared meals promote the social values of cultural identity, group cohesion, and social networks held close by this community. They provide a sense of community and a gathering place within the neighborhood. Luncheons are also spaces of community education or organizational outreach for things like where to go for health care screenings, upcoming community events and parties, and even police outreach. Particularly for the older generation, these luncheons provide more than just a meal they can afford. These luncheons provide socialization for the community's most isolated people. For the younger generation, who are rarely service users but instead are usually the volunteers and organizers, these events provide a connection to their Caribbean heritage despite the generations of disconnection through their cooking and serving Caribbean food to and interacting with the older generation.

The food events in the centers serve as a social glue, binding people together by creating a space for them to discuss and make sense of their position as Caribbean people in England. They are places for the volunteers, employees, and patrons of the organizations to connect with each other while eating a Caribbean meal. As mentioned above, the kitchens and dining rooms are bustling with neighborhood residents, laughing, joking, fighting, and gossiping. Conversations about family in the Caribbean, reminiscing about what the neighborhood used to be like, what store was finally selling fresh breadfruit, who has the cheapest and best goat, or what time of year could you expect to find fresh sugarcane, often filled the rooms during lunches and other food events. These lunches create spaces "where immigrants can begin to negotiate their adaptation to the new environment but also surround themselves for a moment with memories of 'back home'" (Ainslie 1998 *in* Plaza 2014).

The economic and social benefits these communal meals provide are not mutually exclusive. Julier (2013: 3) notes that "people with greater access to resources that accrue from gender, race, and class privilege have access to more variety and more nutritionally rich food and can focus on the meal as a social accomplishment rather than a necessity." While this is true, these communal meals mitigate the effects of high food prices and limited economic and physical resources of many residents, allowing space for commensality, socialization, and knowledge transmission valued by this community. Additionally, much like Williams' (1984) ethnography on migrant women's devotion to investing time and money into making tamales, these communal meals create and strengthen social networks in which migrants rely on during hard times.

"Food values" in health and food justice work in Chapeltown

While direct interpersonal racism in formal institutions is less prevalent than a few decades ago, people of African Caribbean descent in England often still feel that "professionals and other statutory agencies marginalize black interests in society and do little to address the concerns that black people have" (Reynolds 2003: 15). Dr. Bertha Ochieng said, "Not only are people marginalized but their foodways are as well. The health sector does not appear to support culturally appropriate foods because they don't understand the factors that influence the diet patterns of Black families." My host, Roy, noted that while there is an African Caribbean menu available in the hospital, most people do not even know it exists. John, a 24-year-old resident of the neighborhood and part-time employee of the hospital in the city center, noted that employees are not encouraged to promote the African Caribbean menu although patients should know that they have options that are more "familiar with home." "We have to tell patients about the Kosher and Halal menus. I don't know if it's because there is no religious aspect, or if they don't want to promote Black culture," he stated. This leads many to describe health care facilities as spaces of exclusion (see David Sibley 2002), despite the UK having a universal health care system. As a result, many African Caribbeans neglect their health out of fear or distrust of the medical system.

The racism toward and negative reputation of the neighborhood and the people that live there prompted early intervention by community activists. Activists established community and cultural centers to create a sense of safety and community around a shared Caribbean heritage. Specifically, they created programs related to food and diet to mitigate the lack of institutional support. Black Health Initiative's weekly lunch incorporates a pre-meal exercise routine and workshops on a variety of health-related topics, such as how to maintain healthy diets or the importance of getting regular cancer screenings. The centers also run or host food and health-related programs and events. Black Health Initiative runs several events a month at the West Indian Centre promoting general health and education or focusing on a specific issue such as blood pressure and hypertension or prostate cancer. They also have a monthly wellness check with stations set up around the room including a heart disease informational session, joint check, diabetes check, dental check, and vision test. Participants of this event are rewarded with homemade Caribbean soup when they visit all the stations. These functions not only disseminate general nutritional information, they ensure this information is culturally appropriate for this community. Centered on building a healthy community in ways culturally appropriate for Caribbean migrants and descendants, these functions are social events that strengthen community cohesion, cultural identity, and group autonomy, despite overall feelings of exclusions from the broader British community.

A major disconnection between the formal medical community and Caribbean migrants is the structure of a healthy diet. The Caribbean diet includes foods such as rice and peas, yams, pumpkins, green bananas, and animal protein such as saltfish and goat, that are not used widely outside of Caribbean or other migrant groups. Understanding how to maintain the healthy aspects of their Caribbean diet such as the fresh fruits and vegetables while moderating some of the salty and starchy products for their lifestyle in England can be a challenge to some Caribbean migrants. A younger British-born Nevisian feels that "the culture we live in makes it hard to eat good, organic, healthy, homemade foods." Further, an older Jamaican-born employee of the West Indian Centre feels that "[Caribbean Migrants] are unhealthy because they do not take into consideration the change in climate and change in activity level." As such, nutritional education is key. "With the healthy eating, often in this area it's not so much about teaching people how to cook because most of the time people know how to cook. It's about it being healthier," stated an employee of a community wellness organization. Referencing her research on African Caribbean mothers' experiences raising children in the United Kingdom, Dr. Ochieng noted that there is no widely published food pyramid with African Caribbean or African foods that has been widely accepted by the formal medical community and doctors do not consider cultural foods when giving nutritional information. In Dr. Ochieng's research, this often means that new mothers do not follow the nutritional advice given to them by the doctors.

Additionally, as local scholar Dr. Hylton (1999), noted racism makes it "difficult to know who can be trusted" and to "remain loving and open to others." A white woman working in the community highlights the importance of community health educators by saying "If I was going to the South Asian women's group and teaching them about healthy curry making, they wouldn't really listen to me because I haven't grown up making Pakistani curry, but they have."

To mitigate this mistrust of outsiders and the lack of cultural understanding by the medical community, the centers have published and circulated cookbooks that demonstrate how to create healthy versions of Caribbean dishes on a budget. Two community wellness organizations in the neighborhood offer programs that teach people how to cook healthy foods on a limited budget. These community cookbooks and nutritional education programs teach people how to eat healthy while emphasizing their cultural connection, something that mainstream health care initiatives miss. Initiatives like these allow people in this neighborhood to learn healthy eating habits without giving up cultural heritage. Moreover, these initiatives promote the cultural values of cultural identity, autonomy, group cohesion and bonding, and cultural knowledge transmission.

Community and cultural centers have also established a small number of food production initiatives by way of community gardens in the neighborhood. Community gardens provide a space for community empowerment, address some social needs, and create community cohesion (Cumbers et al. 2018). Many residents have gardens in their yards or rent allotments in the neighboring community. Additionally, there are garden initiatives that have been employed by grassroots organizations that continue to do quite well. An employee of one community wellness organization explained that volunteers come once a week to tend the gardens kept on the property. "They grow their own fruit and vegetables. Even during the winter when they can't do anything in the garden, they will come in and make soups with what they have grown. It's really good. We've got herbs growing around. We've got all sorts of fruit and veg, flowers, and we have little children come in as well." This organization draws service users in from other groups such as South Asians and a new African migrant group beginning to filter into the primarily African Caribbean community. This space for community bonding across ethnic lines provides what Cumbers et al. borrowing Massey (2005) calls a form of "throwntogetherness." In this case, community gardens provide "an outward and relational sense of community, rather than a parochial and exclusionary sense of place that leads to social and individual empowerment among disadvantaged and economically marginalized groups" (Cumbers et al. 2018: 147).

The West Indian Centre has also put together a gardening project. The project is aimed at young adults, aged eighteen to twenty-five, who are interested in starting a gardening business. The goal of this project is to provide young people of color skills in business and a trade while providing them with a sense of pride that comes from working hard toward a tangible goal. These organizations were able to implement initiatives that stuck with the community for several reasons. Primarily, the initiatives were proposed by people of that community working within trusted organizations. Further, they proposed initiatives that people of the community actually needed and wanted in cultural appropriate ways. Much like communal eating, communal procurement of foodstuffs in the gardens and the preparation of food in the cooking classes create a strong social network, a sense of autonomy, and cultural knowledge transmission, which is strongly valued by this community as part of their Caribbean cultural heritage and creation of a healthy life in the harsh political and social environment of England.

Outside organizations have not been able to replicate those successes. During my 2015 fieldwork, I met with the then-secretary of a food justice organization based in the city center. She is a white human geographer from Western Europe who was working as a professor at the university in the city center at the time of our interview. She told me about the community garden projects her organization runs. One program is designed to teach people how to grow their own food and make practical use of public spaces while one teaches people how to grow food on their limited property. While these projects have been successful in many other neighborhoods in the city, including low-income white and South Asian neighborhoods, the projects were unsuccessful in the African Caribbean neighborhood. She explained that there was little to no interest and some active resistance by the African Caribbean community. She speculated that people do not want others to think they need to grow food.

While this may be true, many Caribbean people feel that cultivating the land is a valued part of their cultural heritage. As such, I offer several other reasons for this disconnection. First, this African Caribbean community is an insular community. The neighborhood has everything you need, grocery stores, restaurants, community and cultural centers, a funeral home, schools, and a library. Most businesses are owned by African Caribbeans or other migrant groups. The West Indian Centre even publishes a list of approved home repair, legal, and health care services. Other than some business with the City Council, community and cultural centers and community service organizations interact little with other organizations outside of the migrant community. This extends to food justice programs. Organizations in neighboring communities do little to no outreach in this African Caribbean neighborhood. As seen by the Food Justice program's failed attempt at constructing a community garden, even when external groups attempt to work in this community, they are met with distrust, resistance, or indifference. Dr. Hylton noted that the "mistrust of outsiders in the African Caribbean Community owes something to the specific history of African Caribbean residents in the city after the second world war. Its history of isolation and fight for spatial identity against Patriotism and informers. The fight against these events caused some community individuals to adopt insular values" (Hylton 1999: 21).

Melissa Checker's concept of environmental gentrification highlights another way in which the neighborhood's marginalized space within the broader British society would contribute to discord between community groups and external groups looking to deploy community garden projects in the neighborhood. Environmental gentrification is the process of improving neighborhoods under the "discourse of sustainability which simultaneously describes a vision of ecologically and socially responsible urban planning, a 'green' lifestyle which appeals to affluent, eco-conscious residents, and a technocratic, politically neutral approach to solving environmental problems" (Checker 2011: 212). Similarly, Lubitow and Miller (2013: 125) note that environmental development projects that are promoted as a public good or actions for community safety often displace marginalized people and signify gentrification. They add that these projects demonstrate that "as cities gravitate toward narrow apolitical notions of sustainability, more nuanced considerations of environmental justice, race, and health become marginalized" (Lubitow and Miller 2013: 125). Like other forms of gentrification, the seemingly beneficial environmental projects potentially alienate long-time residents of the neighborhood who do not have the economic or social capital to compete with affluent newcomers, while simultaneously ignoring other social problems of the neighborhoods.

In addition to general skepticism of outsiders and fears regarding gentrification of the community, these externally organized community garden projects often fail to adhere to community values. External groups often superimpose their ideals and goals onto the neighborhood without taking into consideration the cultural ideals and values of the neighborhood. The outside Food Justice organizations which attempted to deploy their Guerilla Gardening and Public Food Growing programs along the neighborhood's main road, would have turned lots left vacant by closed businesses into spaces to grow food during the warmer months. This idea, while ideal from the "apolitical," sustainability perspective (Checker 2011; Lubitow and Miller 2013), does not align with the culturally held value of entrepreneurialism (Freeman 2014) and does not address other problems in this neighborhood, such as rising rent and low incomes which caused businesses to abandon these lots in the first place. Externally organized community garden projects, including these, often focus on food and nutrition security as their primary objective. This often comes in the form of "affluent White activists trying to teach low-income minorities how to eat properly" (Guthman, 2008; Slocum, 2006, 2007 *in* Drake 2014: 180). Alkon and Mares (2012: 351) state that projects like these are "often geared toward transforming the lives of marginalized people rather than explicitly challenging the systemic conditions that produce marginalization." Still, external organizations can be potentially important partners for community garden projects but these projects are unsuccessful without the support and participation of community members at all levels, including management of the gardens (Mees and Stone, 2012 *in* Drake 2014: 179). Unsurprisingly, the projects implemented by the outside organizations in this neighborhood failed without community support.

Yosso (2005: 82) notes that "the main goals of identifying and documenting cultural wealth are to transform education and empower People of Color to utilize assets already abundant in their communities." Unfortunately, outside organizations are not always willing or able to identify the cultural wealth of a community. Grassroots organizations within the community are able to deploy more useful or accepted forms of activism with their already deep knowledge of the community's cultural wealth as well as their needs. Taking these points into consideration, we begin to understand the trouble that well-intentioned and potentially helpful organizations have working in neighborhoods like these as a combination of distrust of outsiders caused by generations of racism and a cultural disconnection between the organization's services and the needs and values of potential service users.

Drake (2014: 190) quotes a participant's comments on community gardens stating that "[Organizers] think it's a global thing, [meaning] if you get people coming from all over the place . . . working together, then that makes it a community garden. No. The community is the neighborhood." Indeed, this neighborhood is a community with their own ideas of what the community needs, what it means to be healthy, how to improve community conditions, and how to build community among residents.

Conclusion

Scholars have noted that Caribbean people within the region and in the diaspora hold close social values such as group cohesion and social networks (Reynolds 2007), cultural identity (Bauer 2018), and autonomy (Farley 1964; Mintz 1974; Trouillot 1988; Mintz and Price 1992; Besson 2002). This chapter asks how Caribbean migrants use food to reconfigure these social values to help navigate racism and marginalization in the diaspora.

Communal eating practices in the home and in public spaces create social networks where people come together around a shared meal. In the home, preparing and eating Caribbean food allows the older generation to pass down family recipes which are vehicles for Caribbean heritage. This bonds family members to each other as well as to the broader Caribbean cultural identity. Eating together in public spaces allows for knowledge transmission and social networking beyond the family. Sharing Caribbean meals together opens a space for migrants to discuss their lives and work through problems they face as migrants, creating a sense of group cohesion and cultural identity.

Healthy food programs and cookbooks that cater directly to Caribbean migrants allow them to maintain their cultural identity while remaining healthy. These programs directly address the marginalization migrants feel by the general formal medical community. In many ways, grassroots food activism functions in this community because of the shared and cultivated community values of social networks and group cohesion. This is demonstrated by the inability of outside organizations to successfully carry out projects in this neighborhood.

Food is a medium for people to assert agency and control of their place in the English society while maintaining their connection to cultural heritage. To return to Dr. Ochieng's observation, "Sometimes diets are the only thing people, especially marginalized people, can control in their lives."

References

Ainslie, R. (1998). "Cultural Mourning, Immigration, and Engagement: Vignettes from the Mexican Experience." In M. Suarez-Orozco (ed.), *Crossings: Mexican Immigration in Interdisciplinary Perspectives*, 355–70. Cambridge, MA: Harvard University Press.

Alkon, A. H., and T. M. Mares (2012). "Food Sovereignty in US Food Movements: Radical Visions and Neoliberal Constraints." *Agriculture and Human Values*, 29 (3): 347–59.

Bauer, E. (2018). "Racialized Citizenship, Respectability and Mothering among Caribbean Mothers in Britain." *Ethnic and Racial Studies*, 41 (1): 151–69.

Besson, J. (2002). *Martha Brae's Two Histories: European Expansion and Caribbean Culture-Building in Jamaica*. Chapel Hill: University of North Carolina Press.

Boyce-Davies, C. (2013). *Caribbean Spaces: Escapes from Twilight Zones*. Urbana: University of Illinois Press.

Brown, J. N. (2005). *Dropping Anchor, Setting Sail Geographies of Race in Black Liverpool*. Princeton, NJ: Princeton University Press.

Charles, C. Z. (2003). "The Dynamics of Residential Segregation." *Annual Review of Sociology*, 29: 167–20.

Checker, M. (2011). "Wiped Out by the 'Greenwave': Environmental Gentrification and the Paradoxical Politics of Urban Sustainability: Wiped Out by the 'Greenwave.'" *City & Society*, 23 (2): 210–29.

Cumbers, A., D. Shaw, J. Crossan, and R. McMaster (2018). "The Work of Community Gardens: Reclaiming Place for Community in the City." *Work, Employment and Society*, 32 (1): 133–49.

Drake, L. (2014). "Governmentality in Urban Food Production? Following 'Community' from Intentions to Outcomes." *Urban Geography*, 35 (2): 177–96.

Farley, R. (1964). "The Rise of Village Settlements in British Guiana." *Caribbean Quarterly*, 10 (1): 52–61.

Freeman, C. (2014). *Entrepreneurial Selves: Neoliberal Respectability and the Making of a Caribbean Middle Class*. Next Wave: New Directions in Women's Studies. Durham, NC: Duke University Press.

Giacoman, C. (2016). "The Dimensions and Role of Commensality: A Theoretical Model Drawn from the Significance of Communal Eating among Adults in Santiago, Chile." *Appetite*, 107: 460–70.

Guthman, J. (2008). "Bringing Good Good to Others: Investigating the subjects of Alternative Food Practice." *Cultural Geographies*, 15: 431–47.

Høgsbjerg, C. (2014). *C. L. R. James in Imperial Britain*. Durham, NC: Duke University Press.

Hylton, C. (1999). *African-Caribbean Community Organisations: The Search for Individual and Group Identity*. Stoke-on-Trent: Trentham.

Jargowsky, P. (1996). *Poverty and Place: Ghettos, Barrios, and the American City*. New York: Russell Sage.

Julier, A. P. (2013). *Eating Together: Food, Friendship and Inequality*. Champaign Urbana: University of Illinois Press.

Lubitow, A., and T. R. Miller (2013). "Contesting Sustainability: Bikes, Race, and Politics in Portlandia." *Environmental Justice*, 6 (4): 121–26.

Massey, D. (2005). *For Space*. London: SAGE.

Mees, C., and E. Stone (2012). "Zoned Out: The Potential of Urban Agriculture Planning to Turn against Its Roots." *Cities and the Environment*, 5(1). Retrieved from http://dig italcommons.lmu.edu/cate/vol5/iss1/7.

Mintz, S. W. (1974). *Caribbean Transformations*. (Morningside ed.). New York: Columbia University Press.

Mintz, S. W., and R. Price (1992). *The Birth of African-American Culture: An Anthropological Perspective*. Boston, MA: Beacon Press.

Phillips, M., and T. Phillips (1998). *Windrush: The Irresistible Rise of Multi-Racial Britain*. London: HarperCollins.

Plaza, D. (2014). "Roti and Doubles as Comfort Foods for the Trinidadian Diaspora in Canada, the United States and Britain." *Social Research: An International Quarterly*, 81 (2): 463–88.

Reynolds, T. (2003). "Black to the Community: An Analysis of 'Black' Community Parenting in Britain." *Community Work & Family*, 6 (1): 1–19.

Reynolds, T. (2007). "Friendship Networks, Social Capital and Ethnic Identity: Researching the Perspectives of Caribbean Young People in Britain." *Journal of Youth Studies*, 10 (4): 383–98.

Slocum, R. (2006). "Anti-racist Practice and the Work of Community Food Organizations." *Antipode*, 38: 327–49.

Slocum, R. (2007). "Whiteness, Space and Alternative Food Practice." *Geoforum*, 38: 520–33.

Sibley, D. (2002). *Geographies of Exclusion: Society and Difference in the West*. New York: Routledge.

Tookes, J. S. (2015). "'The Food Represents': Barbadian Foodways in the Diaspora." *Appetite*, 90: 65–73.

Tolia-Kelly, D. (2004). "Locating Processes of Identification: Studying the Precipitates of Re-Memory through Artefacts in the British Asian Home." *Transactions of the Institute of British Geographers*, 29 (3): 314–29. http://www.jstor.org/stable/3804494.

Trouillot, M. R. (1988). *Peasants and Capital: Dominica in the World Economy*. Johns Hopkins Studies in Atlantic History and Culture. Baltimore, MD: Johns Hopkins University Press.

Williams, B. (1984). "Why Migrant Women Feed Their Husbands Tamales: Foodways as a Basis for a Revisionist View of Tejano Family Life." In L. K. Brown and K. Mussell (eds.), *Ethnic and Regional Foodways in the United States: The Performance of Group Identity*, 113–26. Knoxville: University of Tennessee Press.

Williams-Forson, P. A. (2006). *Building Houses out of Chicken Legs: Black Women, Food, and Power*. Chapel Hill: University of North Carolina Press.

Wilson W. J. (1987). *The Truly Disadvantaged: The Inner City, the Underclass, and Public Policy*. Chicago, IL: University of Chicago Press.

Yosso, T. J. (2005). "Whose Culture Has Capital? A Critical Race Theory Discussion of Community Cultural Wealth." *Race Ethnicity and Education*, 8 (1): 69–91.

14

Debating Halal in Contemporary Denmark

Johan Fischer

Introduction

Over the last two decades, the global markets for halal food, particularly meat, have grown rapidly. Muslim scholars base their halal food rulings on statements from selected verses from the Qur'an. According to these passages, halal is that which is beneficial and not detrimental to Muslims. A number of conditions and prohibitions must be observed. Muslims are expressly forbidden from consuming carrion, spurting blood, pork, and foods that have been consecrated to any being other than God himself: these substances are called haram (unlawful or forbidden). The lawfulness of meat depends on how it is obtained. During ritual slaughter, *dhabh*, animals should be killed in God's name by making a fatal incision across the throat, with the blood being drained as fully as possible. Consuming halal food is a form of Muslim religious observance in daily life. In 2014, a ban on halal slaughter without prior stunning of animals came into effect in Denmark. Among Muslim groups and individuals, the question of the stunning of animals prior to slaughter is highly contested. While some Muslims only consider meat from non-stunned animals to be halal, others consider it lawful to consume meat prepared by all People of the Book (Jews and Christians as well as Muslims), and they thus accept that stunning is part of modern and ethical food production. The halal slaughter policy debate revealed how different groups in Danish society attribute moral, ethical, and quality values to food.

In Denmark, the ban came into existence in the wake of ongoing debates in Denmark about halal slaughter and the marking of halal-slaughtered meat, and it stirred controversy among Jewish and Muslim groups both within the country and beyond. The Danish minister for food, agriculture, and fisheries referred to a Danish animal protection law that allows the minister to make a unilateral decision without first taking it to the national parliament. He once served as president of the Animal Welfare Intergroup, which advocates animal welfare and conservation issues, and argued that the imperative to legally protect animal welfare trumps religious liberty. However, the ban raises a number of issues beyond this one. First, food consumption is an important way of expressing religious identity and rights at the personal and organizational level. Second, the heated controversy over the ban largely overlooked an essential question: Why are some Muslim groups adamant about consuming only un-stunned meat? I argue that halal is not well understood in contemporary Denmark and that the above question is underexplored. Muslim groups' carefulness about everyday halal consumption has led to rigorously enforced regulations on global production and trade. The ban is a clear move in the opposite direction, flying in the face of various transnational attempts to bridge the gap between animal rights advocates and religious interest groups. For example, an EU-supported research project, DIALREL, aims to improve public knowledge on religious slaughter through dialogue on issues of welfare, legislation, and socioeconomic concerns. That project explicitly focuses on religious slaughter as a controversial and emotive subject, caught between animal welfare considerations and cultural/human rights issues. The Danish ban seems to consider the conversation closed.

I explore ongoing debates over what halal is or ought to be in contemporary Denmark with specific reference to stunned versus un-stunned slaughter. The increasing visibility of halal (meat) products in non-Muslim countries such as Denmark in recent decades has been accompanied by controversy about the religious slaughter of animals. These debates are reinforced in a Danish national context in which it is a widely held and strongly embedded popular perception that the public sphere is strictly secular. Most scholarship on halal explores this issue in the context of Muslim majority groups and/or in larger countries where halal is a major market. I argue that halal is not well understood in contemporary Denmark and that a particular aspect of halal is underexplored: the relationship between the everyday consumption of halal among Muslim groups in Denmark and the country's secular outlook. This chapter is based on ethnographic material from fieldwork among Muslim consumers and organizations in Copenhagen, Denmark, namely participant observation and interviewing. Specifically, I explore why and how Muslim organizations and consumers are focused on un-stunned meat, rather than other facets of halal certification and consumption explored elsewhere (Fischer 2008, 2011, 2015; Bergeaud-Blackler et al. 2015). This chapter forms part of a larger research project (Lever and Fischer 2018) that explores kosher and halal comparatively in the UK and Denmark. The 2014 ban also included a ban on kosher (a Hebrew term that means fit or proper) slaughter without stunning, and I have explored this issue elsewhere (Lever and Fischer 2018; Fischer 2018).

What is halal meat?

Halal meat emerge from specific passages in the Qur'an (Campbell et al. 2011). Carrion, blood and pork are *haram*—"unlawful" or "forbidden." In all instances, the lawfulness of meat also depends on how it is obtained. Animals that have suffered injury, death, or illness are strictly prohibited as haram. Prior to *dhabh*, animals for slaughter must be clean, healthy, fed and watered, and treated gently; at the time of slaughter they should be calm. A healthy Muslim must conduct the act of slaughter with a cut to the throat that severs the carotid arteries, jugular veins, the esophagus, and the trachea. The knife used must be clean, sharp, free from nicks, regularly inspected, and the slaughterer must recite the *Tasmiyah—Bismillah Allahu Akbar* (God is Great)—over every animal or bird being slaughtered. All blood must be allowed to drain from the body of the animal post-slaughter and death must be caused by exsanguination (bleeding); the slaughtered animal must not be disturbed until it is dead (Mukherjee 2014).

For Muslims the question of stunning is highly contested, and what *dhabh* actually means in practice is under constant negotiation by scholars, imams and consumers, particularly in non-Muslim countries. These disputes originate in debates about the origins of Islam, which Muslims believe are derived from two sources—the Qur'an and *sunnah* (the life, actions and teachings of the Prophet Muhammad). While the Qur'an provides a detailed and for some an infallible source of information about the origins of Islam, the *sunnah* provides an account based on the application of the principles established in the Qur'an through the lived experience of the Prophet Muhammad—as recorded in the *hadiths* (traditions concerning the life and works of the Prophet Muhammad). Two prescriptive sets of guidelines for halal slaughter follow from these sources and it is the underlying discourses as they are now interpreted on which current controversy about the authenticity of halal meat stands (Lever and Miele 2012). The first position is based on an understanding that all People of the Book share common slaughter practices and that Muslims can consume meat from animals reared and slaughtered by Jews and Christians as well as by Muslims. This position is aligned with EU legislation that requires all animals to be made unconscious by stunning prior to slaughter. The second position, which emerges from derogation of the above legislation, allows EU member states to grant slaughterhouses an exception from the requirement to stun animals before slaughter in line with human rights legislation that provides minorities with the freedom to practice their religion. More specifically, while some European countries—Norway, Iceland and Switzerland—banned religious slaughter without stunning in the 1930s or earlier, EU legislation now grants a derogation from stunning that respects religious freedom in line with Article 10 of the Charter of Fundamental Rights of the European Union. In countries with large Muslim populations where the derogation is legal and applied—for example, in the Netherlands, Germany, Italy and France—there are now halal markets for meat from *both* stunned and non-stunned animals (Lever and Miele 2012). Apart from Germany, where there are controls on the number of animals that can be slaughtered without stunning in line with consumer demand, a number of European countries also use the derogation from stunning to supply export markets (Miele 2016).

While all Muslims agree that halal meat must emerge from the act of slaughter, adherents of this position argue that the status of halal meat is linked more directly to Islam through traditional halal practices. On this account, Muslims are permitted to consume the meat of an animal only if the method of stunning is reversible (i.e., animals are unconscious but still alive at the time of slaughter), the animal has been blessed by a Muslim reciting the *Tasmiyah* prior to slaughter, and all blood is allowed to drain from the body completely post-slaughter. The main area of concern for those adhering to this position is with the perceived risk that instead of being made unconscious by stunning animals will suffer or be killed. If this occurs, the meat produced is rendered haram rather than halal. As we shall see, these debates are central to the way in which non-stunning activists and consumers argue and practice their halal consumption in contemporary Denmark.

Halal activist practices

Conceptually, I draw on food activism and practice theory as tools for the analysis of stunning and non-stunning. Counihan and Siniscalchi (2014) show how diverse groups of activists across the globe challenge the agro-industrial food system and its exploitation of people and resources, reduction of local food varieties, and negative health consequences. However, in the case of halal activism in Denmark, it is not so much the agro-industrial food system that is targeted, but rather what is seen as excessive "secular" dominance and regulation within the Danish political system (Fischer 2009). In a similar vein, Pratt and Luetchford (2014) have shown that concerns about food systems are growing and that alternative food movements respond to concerns by trying to create more closed economic circuits. Wilk (2006) examines how food systems are changing around the globe building on a cultural perspective to explore markets, industrial production, and food economies. Most importantly, perhaps, for my study of halal in Denmark, Wilk argues that food economies incorporate moral values as well as utilitarian motives related to industrial food systems and the complex politics of food.

Warde (2016) observes that agribusiness, sustained economic growth, multinational companies, and ever greater international trade has not only transformed the economic foundations of Western diets but also created possibilities of eating in much more varied ways. In short, food systems experience the effects of globalization, which is essential in understanding contemporary halal practices. Drawing on practice-theoretical approaches, Warde sees eating as a type of cultural consumption inseparable from aesthetics and everyday life. Most importantly, perhaps, I am inspired by the term "compound practice" that captures the complexity of eating in the intersections between different levels of the social scale. Compound practices are shaped by the sharing of practices among family members, for example, and are subject to "pressures" from other areas—for example, "health" and "spirituality." Moreover, food practices condition and are themselves conditioned by the learning of new tastes, handbooks and manuals on eating, cultural intermediaries as well as controversies in popular judgments and justification. In contemporary secular Europe, significant religious observance coexists with a proliferation of well-advertised specialized diets, that is, it is a feature of the modern world that many options associated with religious conviction, health concerns, political commitment, and aesthetic consideration coexist and overlap.

In this sense, halal consumption encompasses values such as "nutrition" and "spirituality" (Coveney 2000). For modern consumers, "nutrition" functions as both a scientific and a spiritual/ethical discipline. It serves this dual function by providing a range of scientific knowledge about food and the body as "spiritual" disciplines: spiritual here not only refers to theological but also refers to the means by which individuals are required to construct themselves with a "correct" concern for the "proper" way of behaving in relation to eating. Food practices are subject to direction, coordination, and regulation by different (secular/religious) activists and contemporary and historical social environments, institutions, and organizations thus condition compound eating practices in Denmark.

Islam and halal in Denmark

With an estimated 207,000 Muslims in Denmark (Statistics Denmark 2016), Muslims make up the country's second-largest religious community, comprising an estimated 4 percent of the total population (Jacobsen 2012). Muslims in Denmark come from many countries, with Turks, Iraqis, Lebanese, Pakistanis, Somalis, and Afghans comprising the largest groups; there is also a small number of Danish converts (Jensen and Østergaard 2007: 30). There are fifty-six Islamic congregations in the country. Halal food is widely available in Denmark, and the country is a major exporter to the Muslim world. Almost all of the chicken sold in Danish shops is halal-slaughtered, and there are many halal butcher shops in Copenhagen alone. Studies on halal among Muslims in Denmark mostly focus on halal in institutional settings such as schools (Jensen 2016; Karrebæk 2014). However, even studies that explore Muslim immigrants in particular neighborhoods such as Nørrebro in Copenhagen (Schmidt 2011a) with regard to space, relationships, neighborhood, and identity politics do not, or only in passing, examine halal (Schmidt 2011b).

Both right-wing and left-wing political parties have tried to prohibit ritual slaughter without stunning since the mid-1990s (Jacobsen 2009: 106). The production of un-stunned meat was banned in 2014, accentuating debates among both Jewish and Muslim groups over discrimination and the right to practice one's religion. This led several Muslim organizations to argue that established food regulations in Denmark did not represent the requirements of observant Muslims. The ban on un-stunned slaughter in 2014 lessened sensitivities among non-Muslim Danes about halal slaughter in Denmark, but in 2017 a right-wing party reopened the debate by arguing that money from halal certification supported Islamic extremists and terrorism. In public discourses, the sentiment now seems to be that even if certain groups are not comfortable with Islamic slaughter the issue is unrelated to animal welfare now that stunning is mandatory and a large percentage of the chicken produced in Denmark is aimed at exports important for the country's economy (Bradley et al. 2015).

Approximately 99 percent of chickens in Denmark are slaughtered at abattoirs approved for halal slaughter by the Islamic Cultural Center of Scandinavia (ICCOS[1]) and/or Muslim World League's office in Copenhagen. ICCOS, a privately run organization founded in 1976, houses a mosque, a Qur'an school, and courses on halal understanding and practice for local Danish Muslims, who for the most part are of Arab and Pakistani origin. ICCOS is the largest halal certifier of meat as well as non-meat products in Denmark. Denmark is a major exporter of food products, and thus halal is an important question for the state and companies. Danish embassies in Malaysia and other Muslim markets try to help Danish companies manufacturing products to meet halal requirements for export. The ICCOS imam is the organization's "halal supervisor," and he is also involved in halal certification for companies in Germany, Sweden, Poland, and the UK. The imam receives delegations from countries where halal is important, and his function is also important, as meat and poultry following Danish law is now stunned before slaughter. In the eyes of many Muslims and Islamic organizations that prefer non-stunned meat, this is a controversial question that reinforces the need for proper Islamic oversight of such products. ICCOS is responsible for ensuring that slaughtering follows proper Islamic procedures and record-keeping, including the appointment of the Muslim slaughterer. In Denmark it is mandatory that a state veterinarian and a Muslim abattoir employee control the ritual slaughter process. ICCOS must approve the Muslim abattoir employee. He pronounces the phrase *Allahu Akbar* (God is Great) at the start of the slaughter process and after each break.

While the main halal certifier is ICCOS, many Muslims from other organizations argue that ICCOS supervision and control is inadequate and unclear. These organizations formed the Danish Halal Fund, a halal activist organization. Benyones has a Moroccan background and represents the Danish Halal Fund and is a board member of Det Islamiske Trossamfund (DIT[2]) (literally, Islamic Faith Community). He works as a paramedic and also does volunteer work in DIT with a specific focus on youth work. Benyones argues that the Muslim community in Denmark needs an independent organization to control the market for halal meat. This call emerged in 2011 when DIT realized that penetrating captive bolt pistols were used to stun animals. As chairman of the Danish Halal Fund, Benyones bases his argument on visits to abattoirs supervised by ICCOS. It is of particular concern that there is no constant supervision in the abattoirs and that stunning with a captive bolt pistol is being used. When I discuss halal certification with Benyones, he explains that halal has to be based on supervision, control, and transparency. Thus, modern halal has to move beyond the traditional relationship of trust between seller and buyer, as has happened in the organic market, for instance. Moreover, in many cases, it is still the company itself that is responsible for the halal process, in that they have one or several Muslim employees that make sure halal logos are put on the packaging of products. He explains that more and more companies are approaching DIT to enquire about halal certification because their customers in the Middle East and Southeast Asia are asking about reliable and independent halal certification by third parties. As many producers in Denmark are unsure about halal certification processes, he points out that they thus miss out on lucrative business opportunities. Benyones believes that draining the blood in connection with ritual slaughter without stunning as well as pork avoidance, including pork gelatin, makes halal consumption healthier. He wonders why halal meat is not more expensive than non-halal meat since proper certification practices and processes should drive the price up.

While the Halal Fund has challenged the halal establishment in Denmark, it is by no means clear that being strict and fastidious about halal is the mainstream position among Muslims in Denmark. The ban on halal slaughter without stunning spurred halal activist groups' focus on this specific type of meat consumption and opened up discussion in Muslim communities on halal food practices. The question I will now turn to is how consumers understand halal consumption as a "compound practice."

Halal consumers: Contested values between stunned and un-stunned meat

I now discuss meat in relation to stunning and un-stunning in the bigger picture of food activism in Denmark. More specifically, I explore how Muslim consumers understand halal slaughter and everyday observance and the wider implications for food activism in such a "secular" and highly regulated national context. This section presents the perspectives of a spectrum of Muslim consumers, ranging from those who observe a strict interpretation of halal with respect to un-stunned meat to those consumers with a less observant or more relaxed approach to halal.

Tahir is in his mid-thirties and single with four children. Of Pakistani heritage and background, he grew up in the UK before moving to Denmark with his family; he has a degree in IT. Tahir is engaged in work with the Islamic Faith Community and he manages the organization's shop, which sells a wide range of Islamic texts, paraphernalia, food products such as olive oil and halal-certified sweets. In his own words, Tahir is "extreme" when it comes to halal: with regard to meat he will ask the seller where the meat is from and if the seller is unconvincing Tahir will not eat it. More broadly, Tahir sees food as a sign of spirituality and of proper religious practice. He clearly prefers un-stunned meat, and he found a butcher in Nørrebro that sells this kind of imported meat that is hard to come by in Denmark. Unfortunately, this butcher had to close, and he then found another butcher selling un-stunned lamb from Ireland among other kinds of un-stunned meats. What is more, this butcher guarantees that Muslims are involved in the production of the meat in Ireland: the shop also sells meat from Lithuania and Spain. Tahir hasn't noticed any halal logos on the meat, but there is a logo on the façade of the shop and he basically trusts the butcher. Tahir tries to avoid Danish un-stunned meat because of the risk that the animal is dead before slaughter and because he also feels that un-stunned meat signifies resistance to the fundamentally anti-Muslim political agenda in Denmark. He recalls that his father used to slaughter animals at a farm in order to make sure that ritual slaughter was properly carried out. Tahir's main concern regarding halal is to ensure that meat is un-stunned and he would like greater availability of such meat in Denmark. The relationship of trust between seller and buyer is better in halal butcher shops than it is in major supermarkets, he argues, which in the eyes of Tahir are not trustworthy and sell only halal meat from stunned sources. The high cost and limited availability of un-stunned meat in Denmark is one reason why Tahir and his family limit their meat consumption to one or two days a week, when lamb is on the menu. Tahir rarely eats out at restaurants in Denmark—especially after what he calls the "halal crisis," when an abattoir claimed to be producing un-stunned meat that was actually stunned. Moreover, the law against stunning made him more aware that all or most of the meat produced in Denmark is stunned. He opposes and challenges the position of Islamic scholars who argue that specific types of stunning are acceptable.

Hassan is in his sixties and he moved to Denmark from Zanzibar in the early 1970s. He is married with three children and works as a constructing architect. He describes himself as "very observant" with regard to halal, which he sees as a central part of the belief of any practicing Muslim. Conversely, a person who does not follow the halal/ haram binary is not a Muslim, and so, Hassan and his family are careful about the food they buy and eat. To Hassan, the Qur'an and the *sunnah* are clear guidelines not only for consumption but also for life more generally to avoid "transgressing boundaries": marriage and the legality of one's source of income, for example. During our discussions, Hassan reads several verses of the Qur'an and passages from the *sunnah* that refer to halal/doubtful/haram. Hassan became more fastidious about halal after leaving Zanzibar for Europe. When going to a halal butchers' shop, for example, he naturally expects the meat to be properly slaughtered according to Islamic ritual principles. If he can't find halal food or if the food at hand is doubtful, he will find something "neutral" such as fish or vegetables. Halal meat is important in Hassan's everyday life, and he values halal meat for its health and wholesomeness as well as for its ritual adherence. Draining the blood makes meat healthier and pork avoidance is also healthier as pork contains cholesterol and "bacteria that cannot be eradicated." In general, Hassan does not trust supermarkets to respect Muslim sentiment and will only buy meat from a supermarket if a halal logo with a recognizable certifier is visible on the packaging like the logo issued by the ICCOS on Danpo chicken. Hassan's wife has actually called Danpo to make sure products were halal. Some shops import un-stunned meat from England and elsewhere and Hassan agrees with the viewpoint that only un-stunned meat can truly be considered halal. Quite simply, stunned meat is not allowed in Islam, as the animal must be conscious when slaughtered: a stunned animal will also contain blood, which cannot be consumed by Muslims. Thus, Hassan assumes that meat in supermarkets that does not appear to contain any blood is un-stunned. However, since the 2014 ban, Hassan now makes greater effort to find meat from a butcher that can guarantee the meat is un-stunned.

Hanan is in her thirties and she moved to Denmark from Somalia in the 1990s. She is married with three children and completed her academic education in Denmark and the UK. Hanan currently works for an NGO. She makes it clear that halal has always been a "major priority" for her: since childhood, Hanan has been aware of the dietary laws of Islam and because of improved availability in Denmark she has a "normal halal lifestyle." However, compared to the UK, where Hanan studied, the convenience and availability of halal are limited. She goes to the local halal butcher and sometimes asks whether the meat is stunned or not to ensure that the meat is "as halal as possible," and her preference is clearly for un-stunned meat; but she notes that meat with these qualities is not easy to come by in Denmark. She notes that this issue was particularly topical in 2014, when stunning was made mandatory. Un-stunned chicken from the supermarket is therefore a good option and acceptable. Shopping and cooking in the family are shared between Hanan and her husband. While her husband makes enquires about meat before he buys it in halal butcher shops and also discusses the pros and cons of stunning versus un-stunning with a local imam, Hanan believes that halal is healthier in that halal slaughter and the draining of blood can be considered as a way of "purifying" meat. Her main concerns are assuring halal observance in meat, rennet-based cheese, and gelatin, as well as in everyday convenience in her family.

Basra was born in Somalia and came to Denmark when she was three years old. She's now a student in her twenties, living with her Somali flatmate in Copenhagen. When Basra left home to live on her own she had to figure out how to manage shopping and cooking in a market where food is expensive, and halal is not always easy to come by. At the start of each month, Basra and her flatmate go to a halal butchers in Nørrebro to buy meat in bulk: they normally go to the same butcher every month and they frequent this shop because they heard by word of mouth that the quality and price of the meat is very good; they typically buy chicken in a supermarket because they know that almost all of the chicken produced in Denmark is certified by the ICCOS. Basra notes that meat is essential to Somali cuisine: "Somalis prefer beef or chicken, and we eat a lot of meat—food is not really food if it doesn't contain meat. Serving non-meat dishes to guests would be considered disrespectful." When it comes to stunning, Basra is undecided. One the one hand, she is well aware that religious texts state that meat should be ritually slaughtered without stunning, and she notes that the 2014 public debate made more Muslims aware of the underlying debates. On the other hand, she's not convinced about the arguments that stunning is necessary to ensure animal welfare. She sums her feelings up by stating that "Halal can mean a lot of things, and I don't think stunning is the major issue."

Fatima is of Palestinian background. In her mid-forties, she grew up in Denmark, trained and worked as a teacher and is married with two children. She maintains that she tries to be as "observant as possible" with regard to halal, but admits that this is often difficult in contemporary Denmark. If halal observance is compromised in the everyday life of the family, it's because "we don't have the necessary knowledge." Fatima and her family do try their best to remain updated on what they can do to meet halal observance in everyday life. For example, when her kids are at a birthday celebration or playgroup, Fatima and her husband tell the kids what to look out for and sometimes they call ahead to talk with parents or organizers about dietary requirements just to make sure everything is fine. Fatima basically trusts Muslim halal butchers, but if she has doubts about their meat she will ask them about it; Fatima's husband normally buys the family's beef and lamb from their local halal butcher. As the chicken sold in supermarkets displays halal logos this is where the family buys most of their chicken. The family eats meat a couple of times a week and generally they are happy with the availability of halal in Denmark; Fatima argues that the law against stunning in Denmark is politically motivated. She's aware that a limited number of halal butchers sell or specialize in un-stunned meat, but she doesn't really know whether the meat the family buys is stunned or un-stunned, even if she stresses that in principle animals must be conscious when slaughtered. When eating out the family will only go to outlets that are clearly marked as halal.

Asena is in her forties and is married with two children; she came to Denmark from Turkey when she was five years old. She's worked in different professions, and in her spare time, she is part of a sewing and cooking network for migrant women. The network is also a forum for discussing halal understanding and practice among

Muslims in Denmark. Asena, along with many of the women in the network, is fastidious about halal, especially meat (which is eaten on a daily basis), pork avoidance, and gelatin. She also argues that the availability of halal in Denmark has improved and that chicken certified by ICCOS is now widely available in supermarkets: "When we see the logo on chicken in supermarkets we buy it." Conversely, halal beef and lamb are not offered in supermarkets and consequently this is bought at a local halal butcher. Asena acknowledges that going to the halal butcher is simply based on a question of trust: "We have to trust him." She believes that the butcher can provide documentation about the halalness of meat upon request, but normally she doesn't take that opportunity. Butchers are mainly selected from discussions about the quality and price of the meat sold in a specific place among friends and family and the same can be said about halal butchers to be avoided: a friend of Asena's, for example, observed that a "secular" supplier delivered meat to a particular butcher and the word quickly spread that this butcher was not halal. The ethnicity of the butcher does not really play a role. Comparing prices between supermarkets and reliable halal butchers showed prices in the latter are higher, but the quality is also better, Asena argues. Asena states that in principle only un-stunned meat can be considered halal, but she's aware of the law against un-stunned slaughter in Denmark and contends that Muslim consumers must be pragmatic when they go about their everyday shopping for halal meat in Denmark. One of the halal butchers Asena frequents suggested that the meat sold in the shop was imported from un-stunned sources, but Asena explains that questions about the origins of meat are generally not discussed with butchers, as it can potentially undermine the authority and expertise of the butcher and the trust consumers have in them. As Asena states: "If you're really focused on halal, you should not live in Denmark."

Atilla is a man in his twenties of Turkish background. He was born in Denmark and is studying at university. He states that halal is very important in his everyday life: "What I eat is important for my body and you are what you eat. For example, when I buy sweets, I'm always careful to avoid pork gelatin." Atilla's family share this attitude and he's thus been brought up with the notion that halal is important both religiously and physically. Atilla and his family consume meat on a daily basis. At the university he will eat the chicken that he knows is produced in Denmark and thus halal-certified, but not other kinds of meat, and sometimes he will ask about the halalness of the meat served. Similarly, he buys chicken with halal logos in supermarkets, but not meat such as beef or lamb. Instead, he will go to halal butcher and for cold meat products he will typically go to Muslim shops in Nørrebro. Atilla believes that slaughter without stunning is quicker and more humane to animals compared to slaughter with stunning: "You might as well get it over with without stunning—I can't see it's necessary to spend money and time on stunning that only complicates the whole process. For religious reasons, I prefer un-stunned meat, and I oppose the law in Denmark that prohibits slaughter without stunning—this law results in conflicts and misunderstandings." Atilla believes that halal is healthier physically and spiritually. Arguably, this is the case because un-stunned slaughter is so quick that it does not stress the animals and thus no "stress chemicals" are transferred to humans through consumption. Moreover, draining the blood and blood cells makes for a "purer animal," more suitable for human consumption.

Ehab is in his sixties. He grew up in Egypt and came to Denmark in the 1980s to study. He married in Denmark and the couple had one child. Before leaving for Denmark, Ehab recalls that halal was not a big issue in Egypt. When he first arrived in Denmark, he ate pork and sausages because this was widely available/affordable; he also consumed alcohol. However, little by little he was reminded, especially at celebrations and events by local Muslims, that "You're Muslim—you can't eat pork," and after a while, Ehab thus started to become more conscious of food in Denmark. The main issue for Ehab and his friends is pork avoidance and over the last ten to fifteen years, he has also stopped drinking alcohol as he became more observant. Even so, Ehab does not think it appropriate to ask his mother-in-law for halal meat when he visits her in rural Denmark, where halal meat is hard to come by. More generally, he accepts non-halal meat at the homes of friends and family. He argues that in Denmark he has to be pragmatic as a Muslim consumer, although he will choose halal if it's available. Ehab argues that it's hard to find a halal butcher who sells halal meat of good quality in Denmark and that when he finds one he buys in bulk and shares the meat with a Muslim neighbor. Quality is important, as is a butcher's expertise, and when a butcher says that meat is halal he trusts them. Ehab's family eats meat every day, and they are not overly concerned about whether the meat is stunned or not just as long as the meat is said to be halal.

Danial is a single man in his thirties of Pakistani background who trained as an academic. He is third-generation Ahmadiyya (an Islamic reform movement founded in India in the 1860s) and his family came to Denmark when he was a child. Danial thinks that generally Ahmadiyya may not be as focused on halal as other Muslim groups. He argues that South Asian Islam is different from Southeast Asian Islam and Muslims from the region are less fastidiousness when it comes to halal. If halal meat is available Danial will buy it, but if not he's flexible and pragmatic as long as pork can be avoided. His family was even more flexible when he was a child because there were fewer halal butchers in Denmark than there are today. As availability improved, his family's views on halal meat transformed. Danial follows the position of the founder of Ahmadiyya and its present caliph, who stresses the linkages between the material and practical, on the one hand, and the spiritual, on the other. "Basically, I trust a person who states products are halal, and it's his problem if they're not." Danial usually buys meat at local halal butchers and chicken in supermarkets. Typically, he eats meat two or three times a week. He follows the position of the Ahmadiyya caliph on stunning, who argues that it's acceptable to stun animals before slaughter if it makes them suffer less. As in the *hadith* traditions, a sharp knife must be used, and animals shouldn't be slaughtered in front of each other. To Danial, ritual slaughter is basically about animal welfare, draining the blood, and remembrance and gratitude to God on whose authority we take life.

Discussion

Halal meat consumption in Denmark qualifies as a compound practice, that is, a practice that sits uneasily between nutrition, spirituality, halal activism, and everyday pragmatism at different levels of the social scale. Many consumers find halal to signify "health" and "spirituality" simultaneously, but the question of stunning remain highly contested. The Muslim population in Denmark is small, but halal availability in urban areas such as Copenhagen has vastly expanded over the last decade or so. Almost all of the chicken produced in Denmark is halal-certified by the ICCOS, and thus Muslim consumers can have a wide range of shopping choices. However, some Muslim consumers are faced with the challenge that all meat produced in Denmark is stunned according to Danish law. The ban on slaughter without stunning in 2014 drew attention to the fact that most of the halal meat in Denmark was already stunned in the first place. It is still meat most of all that is subjected to religious requirements. In the eyes of observant informants such as Hassan and Tahir, it is paradoxical that state secularism prohibits un-stunned meat when this is allowed in a number of other countries. Tahir is the only informant who actively searches for and buys un-stunned meat. Conversely, Danial, who was an active Ahmadiyya, argued that the issue of stunning animals before slaughter is not a major concern. Other informants find that stunning is not an important issue, and as I could only find one halal butcher specializing in un-stunned meat, this seems to be a shared sentiment among Muslims in Copenhagen. If more consumers were focused on un-stunned meat, there would be a larger market for this specific product. Thus, rhetorically many of my informants prefer un-stunned meat, but they mostly buy stunned—lamb and beef from butcher shops. Even though slaughter without stunning was prohibited in 2014, an informant pointed out that only a few butcher's shops were in fact selling un-stunned meat imported from the UK, France, and Poland prior to this. However, the ban on un-stunned meat made more Muslims aware of the underlying issues surrounding stunning/un-stunning and this generated halal activism among organizations and consumers. In general, the market for un-stunned imported meat is unregulated, and distributors and sellers have a hard time checking what qualities the meat they sell has acquired before they receive it. In this chapter I have shown how halal activists or organizations advocate for un-stunned meat in Denmark. While many Muslims are not deeply concerned about this issue, halal activists constantly call on the state to repeal halal regulation. The efforts of animals' rights activists have proven to be more forceful and politically successful.

Last, but not least, my discussion shows how food values are linked and contested at different levels of the social scale. All informants are acutely aware that they live in a world where halal markets, regulation, and food values are globalizing. Even the most "secular" of these consumers must relate to and negotiate larger issues such as halal as formative of distinctions between individuals and groups in everyday life as well as the specific global, European, national, and local contexts that frame their lives. In short, this analysis shows that food values are conditioned by and themselves condition a divergent range of understandings and practices at different levels on the social scale.

Notes

1   www.islamiccc.com/index.php/en/
2   www.wakf.com/index. php/da/

References

Bradley, D., J. Nganga, A. Marechal, and M. Garrone (2015). *Study on Information to Consumers on the Stunning of Animals*. Brussels: European Commission, DG Heath and Food Safety.

Campbell, H., A. Murcott, and A. MacKenzie (2011). "Kosher in New York City, Halal in Aquitaine: Challenging the Relationship between Neoliberalism and Food Auditing." *Agriculture and Human Values*, 28 (1): 67–79.

Coveney, J. (2000). *Food, Morals and Meaning: The Pleasure and Anxiety of Eating*. London; New York: Routledge.

Counihan, C., and V. Siniscalchi, eds. (2014). *Food Activism: Agency, Democracy and Economy*. London and New York: Bloomsbury.

Bergeaud-Blackler, F., J. Fischer, and J. Lever, eds. (2015). *Halal Matters: Islam, Politics and Markets in Global Perspective*. London and New York: Routledge.

Fischer, J. (2008). *Proper Islamic Consumption: Shopping among the Malays in Modern Malaysia*. Copenhagen: Nordic Institute of Asian Studies Press.

Fischer, J. (2009). "Feeding Secularism: Consuming Halal among the Malays in London." *Diaspora*, 18 (1): 275–97.

Fischer, J. (2011). *The Halal Frontier: A Global Religious Market in London*. New York: Palgrave Macmillan.

Fischer, J. (2015). *Islam, Standards and Technoscience: In Global Halal Zones*. London and New York: Routledge.

Fischer, J. (2018). "Kosher Biotech: Between Religion, Regulation and Globalization." *Religion and Society*, 9 (1): 1–16.

Jacobsen, B. A. (2009). "Denmark." In J. S. Nielsen, S. Akgönül, A. Alibašić, B. Maréchal, and C. Moe (eds.), Yearbook of Muslims in Europe, vol. 1, 97–109. Leiden and Boston, MA: Brill.

Jacobsen, B. A. (2012). "Islam i Danmark." In M. Nielsen (ed.), *Religion i Danmark: En E-årbog fra Center for Samtidsreligion*, 111–15. Aarhus: Aarhus University.

Jensen, Sidsel V. (2016). "Institutional Governance of Minority Religious Practices: Insights from a Study of Muslim Practice in Danish Schools." *Journal of Ethnic and Migration Studies*, 42 (3): 418–36.

Jensen, T., and K. Østergaard (2007). *Nye Muslimer i Danmark: Møder og Omvendelser*. Højbjerg: Univers.

Lever, J., and M. Miele (2012). "The Growth of Halal Meat Markets in Europe: An Exploration of the Supply Side Theory of Religion." *Journal of Rural Studies*, 28 (4): 528–37.

Lever, J., and J. Fischer (2018). *Religion, Regulation, Consumption: Globalising Kosher and Halal Markets*. Manchester: Manchester University Press.

Karrebæk, S. M. (2014). "Rye Bread and Halal: Enregisterment of Food Practices in the Primary Classroom." *Language & Communication*, 34: 17–34.

Miele, M. (2016). "Killing Animals for Food: How Science, Religion and Technologies Affect the Public Debate about Religious Slaughter." *Food Ethics*, 1 (1): 47–60.

Mukherjee, S. R. (2014). "Global Halal: Meat, Money, and Religion." *Religions*, 5 (1): 22–75.

Pratt, J., and P. Luetchford (2014). *Food for Change: The Politics and Values of Social Movements*. London, Sterling, and Virginia: Pluto Press.

Schmidt, G. (2011a). "Understanding and Approaching Muslim Visibilities: Lessons Learned from a Fieldwork-Based Study of Muslims in Copenhagen." *Ethnic and Racial Studies*, 34 (7): 1216–29.

Schmidt, G. (2011b). "'Grounded' Politics: Manifesting Muslim Identity as a Political Factor and Localized Identity in Copenhagen." *Ethnicities*, 12 (5): 603–22.

Statistics Denmark (2016). Denmark in Figures 2016. www.dst.dk/en/Statistik/Publikationer/VisPub?cid=21500 (accessed March 25, 2017).

Warde, A. (2016). *The Practice of Eating*. Cambridge and Malden, MA: Polity Press.

Wilk, Richard, ed. (2006). *Fast Food/Slow Food: The Cultural Economy of the Global Food System*. Lanham, MD: Altamira Press.

15

Concluding Comments: The Essential Ambiguity of the Value of Food

Richard Wilk

This volume boasts an unusually well-focused collection of chapters which use concepts of value to explore the boundary between food as a mass-market commodity and food as a meaningful and essential part of human social life. Each chapter reflects on the active responses of different communities to the pressures of neoliberal "reforms" which have eroded the welfare state while consolidating the position of large corporate actors in food production and trade. What sort of general lessons emerge from these ethnographic case studies?

Types of resistance

There has always been some level of resistance to the commodification of food in the marketplace. After all, sharing food between parents and children instantiates the most basic human social bonds and in every culture food is therefore laden with meanings that go well beyond its cost. Large-scale social and political processes are often reflected, symbolized, or actualized through food and cuisine. At the same time the meaningful content of food depends on each particular historical and cultural context.

Reading through these chapters, I find different combinations of three consistent sets of values at the core of resistance movements. The first can be generalized under the rubric of "human rights and social justice," including fair prices for producers and consumers, adequate food for the poor, working conditions in the food system, and the freedom to produce and consume food following established cultural values. Some people extend the concept of human rights to include food animals and contest their treatment. Second, we have the category of "health and food safety," which includes knowing how and where foods are produced, how that production is regulated and monitored, and the ability to maintain a healthy diet. Finally, resistance often forms around issues of "sustainability and environmental impact" focusing on such issues as land stewardship, factory farming, the impact of food production and trade on global climate change. All of the chapters deal with some combination of these three, depending on their setting and in doing so they make it clear that local politics and history (language, events) are a foundation on which these more abstract categories of values are erected. So on one hand, all of these cases are similar and connected, but on the other hand, they are each quite distinct. Each chapter reflects upon the altruistic, idealistic, and utopian visions that give substance to resistance, and connect them to historical events in a chain going back through the struggles of peasants and workers as they resisted mercantile and industrial capitalism (e.g., Linebaugh and Redicker 2013).

These utopian visions have a common ground in social norms granting a general human right to food, mandating that certain categories of people should be fed by individuals and communities; the young, the aged, the disabled, and the unfortunate. As dramatized by Colin Turnbull in his book about the starving Ik people in Ethiopia, people neglect these fundamental social obligations only in the most extreme conditions (Turnbull 1972).[1] There is nothing more fundamental to social life than sharing food. Every major world religion teaches that the social collective—above and beyond the level of the family—is responsible for feeding the hungry and needy.[2] Public feasts with shared food have been a staple of civic life since the very invention of the town and city, and even the very earliest states and temples held large stores of grain and other foods for feasts and as insurance against shortage and poor harvests (Steel 2013). The social contract of early cities, as well as modern states, required state and/or religious institutions to feed the destitute, and open their stores in times of general hunger, in exchange for the loyalty, public service, taxes, and tribute of their citizens. Therefore, since the beginning of the Bronze Age, the responsibility for providing food has never settled exclusively on the individual, family, state, institution, business, class, or temple. In something like the game of hot potato, the parties have often juggled responsibilities and tried to pass them on, so famine and starvation have been far too common. Food as a general category therefore always raises the question of who is ultimately responsible for providing it when people cannot feed themselves. It often occupies the gap between how things are and how they should be. Even in times of abundance, this moral issue does not go away, for there are always dependents.

Gift and commodity

Because food carries moral weight, it also occupies and dramatizes the gap between monetary exchange and other kinds of economic activities. One of the enduring contributions of economic anthropology is the recognition that the economy does not begin and end in the marketplace, and that the purchase of commodities in the marketplace is only one form of exchange. Unfortunately, many economic anthropologists in the twentieth century, following Polanyi, used this distinction to develop ideal types centered on a basic opposition between gifts and commodities (e.g. Gregory 1982). They defined the commodity as fungible and anonymous, while the gift is culturally meaningful and embedded in social relationships. Empirical work by economic anthropologists has rarely found such a neat division. Instead, markets, anonymous commodities, and monetary exchange usually exist alongside gift economies, or are even enmeshed with them in mutual dependence. As many have pointed out, material goods and services often move back and forth, acquiring commodity-like attributes at one point in their history, and then changing and becoming objects with transcendent values based on their meaning, history, and associations with people and events and places.

In this regard, the anti-WTO activism of the 1990s, movements toward fair trade and political environmentalism are particularly important. They represent the escape of social science discourse into popular discourse, into public life and politics. Public intellectuals like Noam Chomsky, Naomi Klein, and Carlo Petrini (and more recently David Graeber) have translated the academic discourse of gift versus commodity, of culture and values as the counterweight to money and wealth, and the danger of consumer capitalism into terms that pervade popular movements like freeganism, slow money, food localism, the sharing economy, and fair trade. *The Gift* by Lewis Hyde is an influential early work that used the anthropological concept to argue that culture provides alternatives to market-based capitalism (1983). The very analytical terms that anthropologists used to define the difference between traditional and modern have now become part of the phenomena that we are studying; the idea of the "moral economy" has gone from being an object of academic debate to a central concept in the way people envision new kinds of economic relations. The irony is that at the same time anthropologists were moving away from dividing transactions into the categories of gift versus commodity, it became a regular part of public discourse, particularly among those seeking alternatives to corporate dominance

For this reason I find it more useful to think of goods as labile and full of the "affordances" and the quasi-agency attributed to them in actor network theory. As Latour says in *We Have Never Been Modern*, the world is full of messy hybrids, in this case strange mixtures of objective and subjective qualities, market values, and powerful meanings (1993). Objects can be more than just hybrids, mixtures of commodity-like and gift-like qualities: they can be like Schrödinger's cat, existing in two states at the same time. Until an item is sold or given a price, it hangs in a peculiar quantum-like state where it has the potential to be one or the other. In the UK/US versions of the television program "Antiques Roadshow" the appraiser tries to turn the gift, the meaningful object, the vase inherited from a grandmother or the grandfather's railroad watch, into a commodity by giving it a price, a monetary value in the marketplace. But this does not determine the object's fate. Instead the owner can resist, by saying they would never sell it, that it has emotional significance and family history which makes it invaluable. But the audience can also see how the object has been changed in the owner's eyes at the moment when it became a potential commodity, when the owner is forced to compare its market value with its cultural and social values. And in a further ambiguity, the market value itself is often a product of the object's history and associations with famous people, the invaluable shirt worn in a particular game by a famous baseball player, for example.

Despite the timeless and universal social embeddedness of food, most of the chapters in this volume describe systems undergoing rapid change in very different places. Modern consumer capitalism has demonstrated an ability to commodify almost anything, even resistance to capitalism itself (as in greenwashing) and this requires that people constantly invent new forms of resistance.[3] It is easy to portray this as a simple challenge and response, the dynamic of Polanyi's "double movement" as described in the introduction to this volume. But at a larger scale we could also portray them as two parts of the same system, a long-term European cultural theme which opposes the sacred, religious, and spiritual values of home and nation with the mundane heartless greed of the marketplace. In many ways the two extremes require one another, and force public discourse into an either/or position when options actually exist along many other dimensions. We can trace this back to early states and empires in which traders and merchants were excluded from nobility and higher social ranks on the grounds that they really produced nothing and profited from others' work.

We can also see this dichotomy as an extended political argument, which began in the revolutionary days of the mid-nineteenth century, about the emergence of national economic policies, open markets, and unbound labor, and the decay of the traditional patriarchal state. How far should money enter into everyday life? Should the rich get better medical care than the poor? Is the state responsible for monitoring and improving public health, or providing public utilities? Should the government set the prices of basic staples? Though this debate is presented as an opposition with utilitarianism on one side and social welfare systems on the other, between modernity and tradition, rationality versus religion, neither of these two is actually objective and value free (Wilk and Cliggett 2007); in many ways utilitarianism is just as laden with value judgments and cultural assumptions as its putative opposition.

Even the most vociferous proponents of free trade and open markets would allow aid to cities devastated by floods or hurricanes. Those in favor of radical privatization and marketization of all goods and services, that the least government is the best government, do so in the name of "efficiency" and "growth," and many sincerely believe that open markets and free trade will lead to a fairer distribution of wealth. They believe in a model of fairness where wealth goes to those who are willing to work hard and use their entrepreneurial skills. If there is a shortage of food, people will pay more for it, and this will spur greater production bringing prices down once again. In the mind of a neoclassical economist, the market system rewards those deserving, and punishes those who are lazy, spendthrift, or corrupt. If this is not a system of moral values, what is it? It is too easy to just dismiss this ideology as a rationalization or self-serving smokescreen by the rich, or a veneer that capitalism hides behind, but these values and ideals are in fact widely shared by those who are not rich. Lakoff argues instead that utilitarianism is based on a strong and coherent set of values rooted in ideas about gender and family (1997). For the utilitarian, the commodification of food and other social practices is not just efficient; it is fairer, more transparent, and promotes democratic values.

In the United States religion has consistently been the strongest force in anti-market resistance (see for example Shprintzen 2013). Even in secular Europe religious proscriptions and prohibitions still slow down the commodification and circulation of food, though even halal and kosher prescriptions have turned out to be negotiable and sometimes ambiguous labels. Craft, and complex notions of flavor, and systems of connoisseurship have also moderated some of the effects of neoliberal reforms and policies, but, at the same time, in the form of terroir they have become effective marketing tools. In contemporary secular Europe, the only secure transcendent values are grounded in health, the boundaries of the human body, ideals of personal freedom, and sometimes nationalism.[4] Environmental sustainability and global climate change, while motivating many in opposition to the marketplace, are still in contention, with a neoliberal establishment that still wants to make environmental decisions on the basis of cost-benefit analysis. Ecological economists argue that the only way to save the natural world is to put a monetary value on it in the form of "ecosystem services," while environmental activists argue instead that biodiversity is essentially sacred, that even plants and natural landforms deserve protection regardless of whether or not they give a monetary benefit to humans. As Lakoff says, these are contending value systems, not a contest between emotion and reason, or a fundamental conflict between social values and impersonal logic.

Values

I want to strike another challenging note here when it comes to the anthropological definition of value as presented by Graeber and more indirectly by Munn. While food sharing and commensality may be acts that create value, we should not jump to the conclusion that these values are always positive, nor should we expect them to be completely or even widely shared by participants or observers. Sharing and exchange can also be part of a destructive act which alienate the participants from one another. The feast at the "Red Wedding" in the television series *Game of Thrones* with its bloody massacre during a festive meal is modeled on the real Black Dinner in 1440 and the Massacre of 1692, both in Scotland, and "treacherous feasts" are attested in ethnography, history, and legend (Conradt 2013). In research on the public policy in the United States that promotes family dinners, I found that while most of my informants believed that shared family dining is valuable and important, they also cited personal experiences of family dinners that were painful and even traumatic. The anthropological literature is replete with examples of feasts that fail, meals intended to insult or emphasize rank, of ambiguous generosity, or in which the participants disagree fundamentally on the meaning and value of the event.

The positive value people place on an event inevitably raises the possibility of its opposite. The criteria that make an event valuable always cast a shadow, the specter of social failure, the risk of anger or even violence. Remember that food can be punishment—the US Navy did not do away with the "bread and water" punishment until 2018. Ruth Reichl recalls her mother's home-cooked meals as traumatic and even dangerous; creating associations that took a lifetime to escape (1998).

Food sharing, gifting, and hospitality may be deceitful or even poisonous, an attack on value rather than its promotion. The circle that builds solidarity among members may also exclude, be a critique of or attack upon the things that others eat, or the way they eat it. Elsewhere, I have discussed culinary racism and the role of food in nationalism in xenophobia. If we accept that food sharing and new forms of commensality, trade, and solidarity have the potential to advance positive social and economic values, we should also recognize the potential for "alternatives" to be seen by others as dangerous and destructive, or for events that are positive for one group to be negative for others, especially those at the distant end of the food chain. Eating local, as many have pointed out, may lower the demand for the broccoli grown by poor peasants in Guatemala (Fisher and Benson 2006) or beans imported from Zambia (Freidberg 2004).

In the last two decades, as neoliberal governments have increasingly shirked the responsibility for ensuring that citizens are fed, the food system itself has become increasingly globalized and dominated by large multinational corporations. As it becomes delocalized, food has also become more highly processed, manipulated, and anonymous, in ways that many people find threatening and dangerous. At the same time people have become more cynical about the transformative potential of other kinds of political action and participation in democracy, as political and economic structures appear to have become more resistant to change. In this setting, it makes perfect sense that food would become a focus for resistance to free-market fundamentalism and neoliberalism, bringing together high-level politics and embodied personal life. It also makes sense that social scientists would be drawn to the theme of food as resistance, given their long engagement with popular movements, their interest in the role of culture and religion in everyday life, and theories of value in economic life, as the economy itself becomes more abstracted from tangible money.

Though I am writing from the standpoint of the Americas, I see many similarities with the European movements studied in these chapters. Often seen as the global leaders of the movement toward the modern, and the neoliberal commodification of everyday life, Europe and North America today may actually be exceptional for their resistance to modernity. In contrast, in many developing countries, particularly those that emerged from state socialism, neoliberalism has not faced serious opposition, while the power of neoliberalism is backed by weighty global institutions like the World Bank and the global flow of investment capital through stock markets. In Belize I witnessed the complete transformation of the economy to open markets and private enterprise, the destruction of safety nets, and the ending of government price supports for farmers and food producers in the 1980s and early 1990s. There was virtually no opposition, just minor compromises with labor unions and environmental organizations which did nothing to actually slow down the pace of neoliberal reform. In contrast, farmers in the European Union have demonstrated their opposition in many conspicuous ways and have forced the adoption of protections of many kinds, not just price and wage supports and trademark protection for artisans but also Protected Designation of Origins (PDOs) and popular opposition to GMO technology along with strict precautionary controls on food quality.

This level of activism has not emerged in the United States. The US government continues to subsidize extensive ranching on public lands in the West and Southwest, generally and sparsely settled areas where rural voters are extremely powerful, with an official rationale of preserving an important and threatened way of life. But elsewhere public policy has consistently undermined small and diversified farmers and supported large-scale industrial production largely under the control of large integrated agribusinesses. Lacking a history rooted in peasants and artisanal food production, the United States is a latecomer to many movements that have a long history, more legitimacy, and more public support in Europe. So far there has been very little high-level political support in the United States for changes in food policy that would substantially support alternative forms of food production. While we can point to many creative initiatives for food cooperatives, farmers markets, farmland trusts, slow money, urban farming, school gardens, large-scale composting, community orchards, and food hubs for artisans, this whole enterprise still provides less than 4 percent of the total diet in the United States, just a small fraction of that sold by the abundant fast food chains that dot the American landscape.

Do the case studies in this volume present viable alternatives for the future which may have influence outside of Europe? One of the greatest strengths of the collection is its emphasis on the close connections between production and consumption in food resistance movements. Previous work has tended to concentrate on one or the other, and even commodity chain work has emphasized the distance between consumers and producers rather than the way they can articulate with one another in productive ways. Several chapters point out the potential for coalitions of producers and consumers to force changes in local or even national food systems under the banner of food sovereignty. This may be an important way forward for food reform in other parts of the world as well.

As Marx would lead us to expect, these coalitions can be fraught with conflict based on contradictory goals in the marketplace (producers want higher prices, while consumers want lower prices and increased quality). Several studies herein demonstrate that shared ideas, particularly related to sustainability and public health, can bridge differences, and keep coalitions and networks and alliances alive. Only time will tell if they are capable of producing lasting change, or if they become just more "bumps in the road" under the wheels of corporate capitalism.

Notes

1 Many anthropologists challenged the extent of social breakdown in Turnbull's dystopian account (Wilson et al. 1975).

2 For a quick summary of the positions of world religions see https://hds.harvard.edu/n ews/2013/12/13/why-give-religious-roots-charity#.

3 Frank and Welland (1997) detail the process through which market culture "commodifies dissent."

4 For example, we still recognize a right to emergency healthcare for those who cannot pay, we ban the purchase of many drugs on the grounds of public health, and the trade in blood or human organs is not fully monetized and subject to the market.

References

Conradt, S. (2013). "The Real-Life Events That Inspired Game of Thrones' Red Wedding." https://theweek.com/articles/463588/reallife-events-that-inspired-game-thrones-r ed-wedding (accessed January 16, 2019).

Frank, T., and M. Weiland, eds. (1997). *Commodify Your Dissent: Salvos from the Baffler*. New York: W. W. Norton & Company.

Freidberg, S. (2004). *French Beans and Food Scares: Culture and Commerce in an Anxious Age*. New York: Oxford University Press.

Gregory, C. A. (1982). *Gifts and Commodities*. London: Academic Press.

Hyde, L. (1983). *The Gift: Imagination and the Erotic Life of Property*. New York: Vintage.

Lakoff, G. (1997). *Moral Politics: What Conservatives Know That Liberals Don't*. Chicago, IL: University of Chicago Press.

Latour, B. (1993). *We Have Never Been Modern*. Cambridge, MA: Harvard University Press.

Linebaugh, P., and M. Rediker (2013). *The Many-Headed Hydra: Sailors, Slaves, Commoners, and the Hidden History of the Revolutionary Atlantic*. Reprint edition. Boston, MA: Beacon Press.

Reichl, R. (1998). *Tender at the Bone: Growing Up at the Table*. New York: Random House.

Shprintzen, A. D. (2013). *The Vegetarian Crusade: The Rise of an American Reform Movement, 1817–1921*. Chapel Hill: The University of North Carolina Press.

Steel, C. (2013). *Hungry City: How Food Shapes Our Lives*. London: Random House UK.

Turnbull, C. M. (1972). *The Mountain People*. New York: Simon and Schuster.

Wilk, R.R., and L. Cliggett (2007). *Economies and Cultures: Foundations of Economic Anthropology* (2nd ed.). Boulder, CO: Westview Press.

Wilson, P. J., G. McCall, W. R. Geddes, A. K. Mark, J. E. Pfeiffer, J. B. Boskey, and C. M. Turnbull (1975). "More Thoughts on the Ik and Anthropology [and Reply]." *Current Anthropology*, 16 (3): 343–58.

Contributors

Ana Isabel Afonso is Professor in the Department of Anthropology at NOVA FCSH, New University of Lisbon, Integrated researcher at CICS.NOVA (Interdisciplinary Centre of Social Sciences), and Fulbright-Schuman Visiting Scholar at Umass-Amherst, Anthropology Department (Fall 2013). Her research focuses social change and development, visual anthropology, renewable energy and environment, food systems and applied anthropology. An ethnographer who has worked in Portugal and the United States, she is co-editor of *Working Images* (Routledge, 2003), editor of *Etnografias com Ciganos: Diferenciação e Resistência Cultural* (Colibri, 2012) and co-editor of Participatory approaches to Visual Ethnography, from the Digital to the Handmade (*Visual Ethnography*, Special Issue, 2016).

Guntra Aistara is Associate Professor in the Department of Environmental Sciences and Policy at the Central European University in Budapest, Hungary. She is an environmental anthropologist whose research lies at the intersection of political ecology, food sovereignty, and environmental justice. She is author of *Organic Sovereignties: Struggles over Farming in an Age of Free Trade* (University of Washington Press, 2018) and co-editor of *Lessons from the Eco-Laboratory: Negotiating Environment and Development in Costa Rica* (University of Arizona Press, forthcoming). Her research interests include organic agriculture and alternative food movements, agrobiodiversity, seed sovereignty, agroecology, permaculture, culinary heritage revivals, multi-species ethnography, and socioecological resilience of local food systems.

Jennifer Cash is an Associate of the Max Planck Institute for Social Anthropology, independent researcher, and freelance editor. Her major research interests in national and ethnic identity, social and economic transformation, and ritual life in the Republic of Moldova and Southeast Europe have drawn her attention, unavoidably, to food and its symbolism, the production and consumption of wine, and poverty measurements from a variety of perspectives. She is the author of *Villages on Stage: Folklore and Nationalism in the Republic of Moldova* (Lit Verlag, 2011), and is completing a second book, *Bread and Wine: Labor, Respect and Poverty in Rural Moldova*.

Dana Conzo is a PhD candidate in Anthropology at the University of Massachusetts Amherst. Her dissertation research project, "The Cultural and Economic Logic of Small-Scale Farming," is a political economic study of local food production within a primarily tourism-driven economy in St Kitts, WI. Her contribution to this book is based on her ongoing research in an African Caribbean neighborhood in England. This research focuses various aspects of migrant foodways through ethnography and spatial analysis. Conzo has also conducted research with African Caribbean migrants in the Bronx, New York, focusing on traditional herbal medicine use following migration. Her research interests include food consumption, agricultural development, race and space, and migration, and transnationalism.

Carole Counihan is Professor Emerita of Anthropology at Millersville University and has been studying food, gender, and culture in Italy and the United States for forty years. She is author of *Italian Food Activism in Urban Sardinia* (2019), *A Tortilla Is Like Life: Food and Culture in the San Luis Valley of Colorado* (2009), *Around the Tuscan Table: Food, Family and Gender in Twentieth Century Florence* (2004), and *The Anthropology of Food and Body* (1999). She is co-editor of *Food and Culture: A Reader* (1997, 2008, 2013, 2018), *Food Activism* (2014), and *Making Taste Public: Ethnographies of Food and the Senses* (2018) and editor-in-chief of the scholarly journal *Food and Foodways*.

Johan Fischer is Associate Professor in the Department of Social Sciences and Business, Roskilde University, Denmark. His work focuses on modern religion and consumer culture. More specifically, Johan explores the interfaces between class, consumption, market relations, religion, and the state in a globalized world. A central focus in this research is the theoretical and empirical focus on the proliferation of religious commodities and services on a global scale. He is the author of *Proper Islamic Consumption: Shopping among the Malays in Modern Malaysia* (NIAS Press 2008), *The Halal Frontier: Muslim Consumers in a Globalized Market* (Palgrave Macmillan 2011), *Islam, Standards, and Technoscience: In Global Halal Zones* (Routledge 2015), *Halal Matters: Islam, Politics and Markets in Global Perspective* (Routledge 2015), *Religion, Regulation, Consumption: Globalising Kosher and Halal Markets* (Manchester University Press 2018) and *Kosher and Halal Business Compliance* (Routledge 2018), as well as articles in journals and edited volumes.

Krista Harper is Professor in the Department of Anthropology and the School of Public Policy at the University of Massachusetts Amherst. Her research focuses on social movements and mobilizations related to the environment, food systems, and urban public space. An ethnographer who has worked in Hungary, Portugal, and the United States, she is author of *Wild Capitalism: Environmental Activists and Post-socialist Political Ecology in Hungary* (Columbia University Press 2006), coauthor of *Participatory Visual and Digital Methods* (Left Coast Press 2013), and co-editor of *Participatory Visual and Digital Research in Action* (Left Coast Press 2015).

Patricia Homs is Adjunct Professor at the Department of Social Anthropology at the University of Barcelona, Spain. She has been a member of the research team in the Grassroots Economics ERC project. Her research interests include cooperatives, social, and solidarity economy and entrepreneurship, especially as these relate to agrofood systems. She is member of L'Aresta Agroecological Cooperative.

Elisabeth Kosnik is Research and Teaching Fellow (Postdoc) at the Department of European Ethnology and Cultural Anthropology at the University of Graz, Austria. She has also taught at the University of Innsbruck, Austria. She has been studying rural households, non-conventional agriculture, environmentalism, and human-nature relationships in contemporary Europe and New Zealand since 2008. Her PhD research investigated the international volunteer organization WWOOF (World Wide Opportunities on Organic Farms). Her current research interests in economic anthropology, environmental anthropology, and food studies focus on livelihood, (self-) provisioning, and (alternative) foodways. She is currently involved in an interdisciplinary research project on small-scale organic family farmers in Austria, investigating historic and contemporary practices of food production and distribution before and beyond capitalism.

Susana Narotzky is Professor of Social Anthropology, University of Barcelona, Spain. She was awarded a European Research Council Advanced Grant to study the effects of austerity on Southern European livelihoods (*Grassroots Economics* [GRECO]). Her work is inspired by theories of critical political economy, moral economies, feminist economics, and valuation regimes. Her interest in food production and consumption practices is longstanding. Recent writing addresses the themes of making a living in futures without employment, political mobilization, social reproduction, and class. Recent publications include "Rethinking the concept of labour," *JRAI*, 2018, and "Where Have All the Peasants Gone?" *Annual Review of Anthropology*, 2016. She is past president of the European Association of Social Anthropology (EASA) and has served as secretary of the American Anthropological Association (2015–18).

Bibiana Martínez is visiting researcher at the Institute of Heritage Sciences in the Spanish National Research Council and member of the GER (*Grup d'Estudis sobre Reciprocitat*) research group in the Department of Social Anthropology, University of Barcelona, Spain. She has recently finished her thesis titled: "Tensions between different aspects of social, economic and environmental sustainability: the case of dairy farms in Galicia" (*Tensiones entre los distintos aspectos de la sostenibilidad económica, social y mediomabiental: el caso de las explotaciones agropecuarias en Galicia*). Her thesis analyzed concepts such us "the just price" through the lens of moral economy, with a focus on dairy family farms in the northwest of Spain. Her main research interests are political economy, economic anthropology, peasant studies, food sovereignty, and moral economies.

Marco Pitzalis is Professor of Sociology in the Department of Political and Social Sciences, University of Cagliari (Italy). His main research fields are policies and micropolitics of education and "Sardinian shepherds and neoliberal policies: social movement, cultural change, economic conditions and political struggles in the pastoral world in Sardinia." Among his recent publications with F. Zerilli are "*Pastore Sardu non t'arrendas como! Il Movimento pastori sardi: alterità, resistenza, complicità (The Sardinian shepherds movement: Otherness, resistance, complicity)*" and "They Cannot

Teach Me How To Be a Shepherd: Sheepherding, Neoliberalism, and Animal Welfare in Post-Peasant Sardinia" in *Utopia and Neoliberalism: Ethnographies of Rural Spaces* edited by H. Horáková, A. Boscoboinik, and R. Smith.

Theodoros Rakopoulos is Associate Professor in the Department of Social Anthropology at the University of Oslo. He is the author of *From Clans to Co-ops: Confiscated Mafia Land in Sicily* and the editor of *The Global Life of Austerity* (both from Berghahn Books, 2018) as well as co-editor (with Knut Rio) of *Towards an Anthropology of Wealth* (Routledge, 2019). He has worked in Sicily and Greece on solidarity, mafia, cooperatives, and food. More recently, his work focused on austerity (e.g., special section in *Focaal* 83), conspiracy theory (e.g., "Show me the money," History and Anthropology), silence and personhood (e.g., "The social life of mafia confession," Current Anthropology). He is currently working in Cyprus on an ethnographic project "purchasing citizenship."

Valeria Siniscalchi is Professor at the EHESS (Centre Norbert Elias). Her teaching activities focus on "anthropology of economic spaces." Her research subjects include the politics of nature, industrial work and districts, food activism and the relationship between food, social movements, and politics. She has done extensive research in the north and south of Italy, in the French Alps, and inside the Slow Food movement. Valeria Siniscalchi publications include *Antropologia culturale: Un'introduzione* (Roma, 2001, 2009) and the edited volumes *Frammenti di economie: Ricerche di antropologia economica in Italia* (Cosenza, 2002) and (with Carole Counihan) *Food Activism: Agency, Democracy and Economy* (2014, Bloomsbury). She is publishing a monograph for Bloomsbury, *Slow Food: The Economy and Politics of a Global Movement.*

Cary Speck is a PhD student with an MA in Anthropology at the University of Massachusetts Amherst. His current research focuses on gender, immigration, and urban food systems in the Czech Republic.

Delphine Thivet is Associate Professor in the Department of Sociology at Bordeaux University, France. Her current research interests focus on farmers' movements, agroecology, organic farming, food and seed sovereignty, right to food, urban farming, both at the national and the international level. Her PhD in sociology (EHESS, 2015) examined transnational peasant activism through the construction of La Vía Campesina as a casestudy. She is coeditor of *Dynamiques des agricultures biologiques: Effets de contexte et appropriations* (Quae/Educagri, 2014) and author of "Peasants' Transnational Mobilization for Food Sovereignty in La Vía Campesina"(Bloomsbury Academic, 2014), "Une appropriation oblique de l'advocacy. La défense et la promotion des 'droits paysans' auprès des Nations Unies par La Vía Campesina" (*Critique Internationale*, 2015), "De la confrontation à la participation: La Vía Campesina à l'Organisation Mondiale du Commerce et à l'Organisation des Nations Unies pour l'agriculture et l'alimentation" (Presses Universitaires de Rennes, forthcoming),

"La participation de La Via Campesina à la construction d'un internationalisme du commun" (Editions Hermann, forthcoming).

Richard Wilk is Distinguished Professor and Provost's Professor Emeritus at Indiana University and is director of the Open Anthropology Institute. He has also taught at the University of California (Berkeley and Santa Cruz), New Mexico State University, and has held visiting professorships at University College London, Gothenburg University, the University of Gastronomic Sciences, and Birkbeck College. He has lived and worked in Belize for more than forty years but has recently begun fieldwork in Singapore with a Fulbright teaching and research fellowship. Trained as an economic and ecological anthropologist, his many publications has covered different aspects of global consumer culture. Much of his recent work has turned toward the global history of food and the prospects for sustainable consumption as a means to minimize climate change. His most recent books are a textbook on the anthropology of everyday life, coauthored with Orvar Lofgren and Billy Ehn, a co-edited collection with Candice Lowe Swift, *Teaching Food and Culture*, and *Seafood: Ocean to Plate*, coauthored with Shingo Hamada.

Filippo M. Zerilli is Associate Professor of Anthropology in the Department of Political and Social Sciences at the University of Cagliari. He has carried out fieldwork in Romania on property restitution disputes and processes, exploring the intersection between law, morality, religion, il/legality, and rights. Since 2011, he is conducting a research on sheep farmers in Sardinia focusing on their political mobilizations and environmental concerns. Among his publications are *Il lato oscuro dell'etnologia* (CISU, 1998), *La ricerca antropologica in Romania* (co-editor, ESI, 2003), and "Non-binding coercions: Ethnographic perspectives on Soft law" (guest editor, *Focaal* n. 56, 2010). He serves as editor-in-chief of *Anuac*, journal of the Italian Society of Cultural Anthropology (SIAC).

Index